HEINEMANN PHYSICS 11

SKILLS AND ASSESSMENT

Doug Bail

VCE Units 1 and 2
Written for the VCE Physics Study Design 2023–2027

Pearson Australia
(a division of Pearson Australia Group Pty Ltd)
459–471 Church Street
Level 1, Building B
Richmond, Victoria 3121
www.pearson.com.au

First published 2023 by Pearson Australia
2026 2025 2024 2023
10 9 8 7 6 5 4 3 2 1

VCE Heinemann Project Leads: Bryonie Scott, Misal Belvedere, Malcolm Parsons
Content and Learning Specialists: Sam Trafford, Zoe Hamilton
Senior Development Editor: Fiona Cooke
Development Editor: Lucy Bates
Schools Programme Manager: Michelle Thomas
Senior Production Editor: Laura Pietrobon
Production Manager: Aisling Coughlan
Editor: Kath Kovac
Series Designer: Anne Donald
Rights & Permissions Editor: Amirah Fatin Mohamed Sapi'ee
Production Services Design Analyst: Jennifer Johnston
Desktop Operator: Jit Pin Chong
Illustrators: DiacriTech and QBS
Proofreader: Marcia Bascombe
Printed in Australia by Pegasus Media & Logistics

ISBN 978 0 6557 0016 6

Pearson Australia Group Pty Ltd ABN 40 004 245 943

Indigenous Australians
We respectfully acknowledge the traditional custodians of the lands upon which the many schools throughout Australia are located. We acknowledge traditional Indigenous Knowledge systems are founded upon a logic that developed from Indigenous experience with the natural environment over thousands of years. This is in contrast to Western science, where the production of knowledge often takes place within specific disciplines. As a result, there are many cases where such disciplinary knowledge does not reflect Indigenous worldviews, and can be considered offensive to Indigenous peoples.

Some of the images used in *Heinemann Physics 11 Skills and Assessment* might have associations with deceased Indigenous Australians. Please be aware that these images might cause sadness or distress in Aboriginal or Torres Strait Islander communities.

Attributions
We thank the following for their contributions to our skills and assessment book.

The following abbreviations are used in this list: t = top, b = bottom, l = left, r = right, c = centre.

Front and back covers: Science Photo Library: NASA/ESA/STScI

Alamy Stock Photo: Science History Images, p. 1.

American Association of Physics Teachers: Extract from How I Misunderstood Newton's Third Law by Mark J. Hughes, *The Physics Teacher*, volume 40, number 6, pp. 382-82, p. 152.

ANSTO: pp. 78t, 78b.

Science Photo Library: Lawrence Berkeley Laboratory, pp. 48-9, 86-8; Lunau, Claus, p. 20; Trevor Clifford Photography, p. 91l; Victor Habbick Visions, pp. 127, 202, 209.

Shutterstock: AGorohov, p. 136; mimagephotography, p. 135l; ostill, p. 152t.

Victorian Curriculum and Assessment Authority (VCAA): Selected extracts from the VCE Physics Study Design (2023–2027) are copyright Victorian Curriculum and Assessment Authority (VCAA), reproduced by permission. VCE® is a registered trademark of the VCAA. The VCAA does not endorse this product and makes no warranties regarding the correctness or accuracy of its content. To the extent permitted by law, the VCAA excludes all liability for any loss or damage suffered or incurred as a result of accessing, using or relying on the content. Current VCE Study Designs and related content can be accessed directly at www.vcaa.vic.edu.au, pp. 1, 49, 87-8, 127, 202, 209.

Contents

Contents

Unit 2 How does physics help us to understand the world?

AREA OF STUDY 1

How is motion understood?

AREA OF STUDY 2

Options: How does physics inform contemporary issues and applications in society?

AREA OF STUDY 3

How do physicists investigate questions?

ISBN 978 0 6557 0016 6

How to use this book

The *Heinemann Physics 11 Skills and Assessment* book provides the opportunity to practise, apply and extend your learning through a range of supportive and challenging activities. These activities reinforce key concepts and skills, and enable a flexible approach to learning. There are also regular opportunities for reflection and self-evaluation in the final worksheet in each area of study.

This resource has been written to the VCE Physics Study Design 2023–2027 and is divided into six areas of study: three in Unit 1 and three in Unit 2. Areas of Study 1–3 in Unit 1 and Area of Study 1 in Unit 2 consist of four main sections:

- key knowledge
- worksheets
- practical activities
- exam-style questions.

PHYSICS TOOLKIT

The Physics toolkit supports development of the skills and techniques needed to undertake practical and secondary-sourced investigations, and covers examination techniques and study skills. It also includes checklists, models, exemplars and scaffolded steps. The toolkit can serve as a reference tool and be consulted as needed.

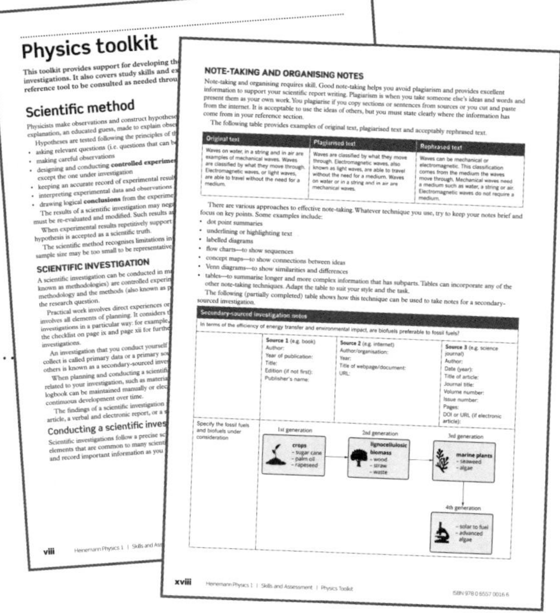
Physics toolkit

Scientific method

SCIENTIFIC INVESTIGATION

Conducting a scientific investigation

NOTE-TAKING AND ORGANISING NOTES

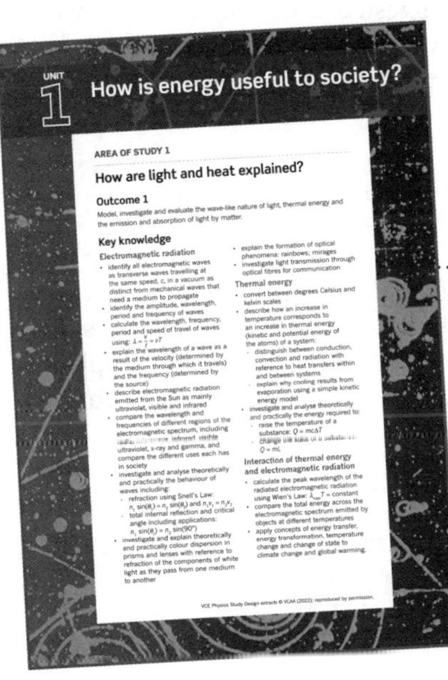
UNIT 1 How is energy useful to society?

AREA OF STUDY 1

How are light and heat explained?

Outcome 1

Key knowledge

Electromagnetic radiation

Thermal energy

Interaction of thermal energy and electromagnetic radiation

AREA OF STUDY OPENER

Heinemann Physics 11 Skills and Assessment is structured to follow the study design units and areas of study. The area of study opening page lists the study design key knowledge for easy reference to the activities that follow.

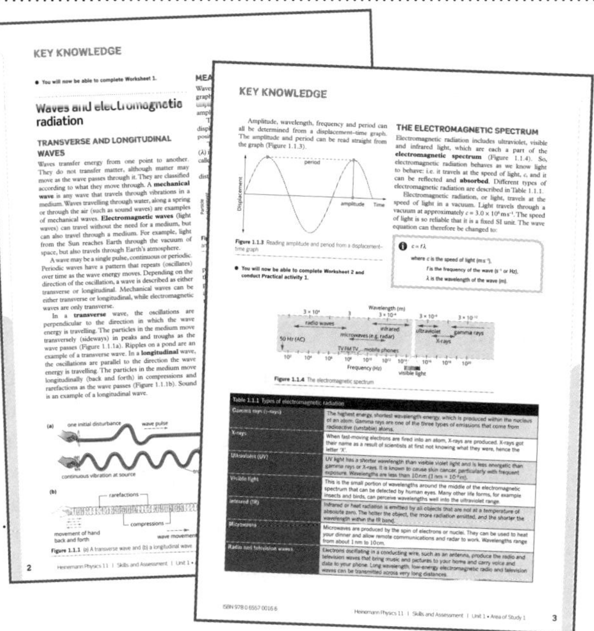
KEY KNOWLEDGE

Waves and electromagnetic radiation

TRANSVERSE AND LONGITUDINAL WAVES

THE ELECTROMAGNETIC SPECTRUM

KEY KNOWLEDGE

Each area of study begins with a key knowledge section. This consists of a set of summary notes that cover the key knowledge for that area of study. Key terms are in bold and are included in the glossary of the student book. The section also serves as a ready reference for completing the worksheets and practical activities.

WORKSHEETS

The worksheets feature questions that allow you to practise and apply your knowledge and skills. Each area of study includes a 'Knowledge review' worksheet to activate prior knowledge, a 'Literacy review' worksheet that provides opportunities for vocabulary and literacy support, and a 'Reflection' worksheet, which you can use for self-assessment. Other worksheets provide opportunities to revise, consolidate and further your understanding. All worksheets function as formative assessment and are clearly aligned with the study design. A range of questions building from foundation to challenging is included in each worksheet.

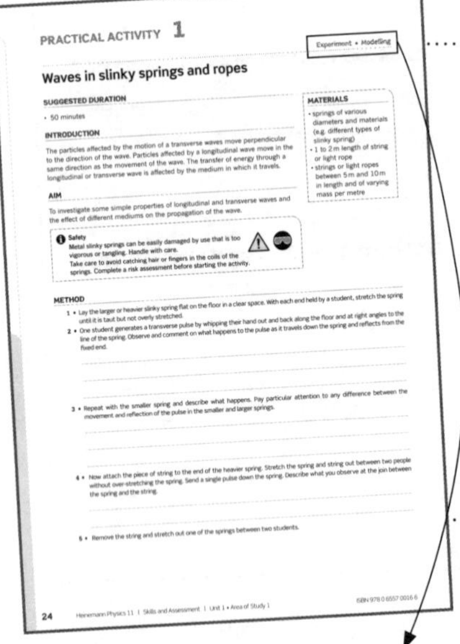
PRACTICAL ACTIVITY 1

Experiment • Modelling

Waves in slinky springs and ropes

SUGGESTED DURATION

• 50 minutes

INTRODUCTION

The particles affected by the motion of a transverse wave move perpendicular to the direction of the wave. Particles affected by a longitudinal wave move in the same direction as the movement of the wave. The transfer of energy through a longitudinal or transverse wave is affected by the medium in which it travels.

MATERIALS

• springs of various diameters and materials (e.g. different types of slinky spring)
• 1 to 2 m length of string or light rope
• strings or light ropes between 5 m and 10 m in length and of varying mass per metre

AIM

To investigate some simple properties of longitudinal and transverse waves and the effect of different mediums on the propagation of the wave.

Safety
Metal slinky springs can be easily damaged by use that is too vigorous or tangling. Handle with care.
Take care to avoid catching hair or fingers in the coils of the springs. Complete a risk assessment before starting the activity.

METHOD

1 • Lay the larger or heavier slinky spring flat on the floor in a clear space. With each end held by a student, stretch the spring until it is taut but not overly stretched. Ensure the spring is not stretched so far that it remains extended.

2 • One student generates a transverse pulse by whipping their hand out and back along the floor and at right angles to the line of the spring. Observe and comment on what happens to the pulse as it travels down the spring and reflects from the fixed end.

3 • Repeat with the smaller spring and describe what happens. Pay particular attention to any difference between the movement and reflection of the pulse in the smaller and larger springs.

4 • Now attach the piece of string to the end of the heavier spring. Stretch the spring and string out between two people without over-stretching the spring. Send a single pulse down the spring. Describe what you observe at the join between the spring and the string.

5 • Remove the string and stretch out one of the springs between two students.

24 Heinemann Physics 11 | Skills and Assessment | Unit 1 • Area of Study 1 ISBN 978 0 6557 0016 6

Experiment • Modelling

PRACTICAL ACTIVITIES

Practical activities offer you the chance to complete practical work related to the various themes covered in the study design. You have the opportunity to design and conduct scientific investigations; generate, evaluate and analyse data; appropriately record results; and prepare evidence-based conclusions. Where relevant, you will also need to conduct risk assessments to identify any potential hazards.

Each practical activity includes a suggested duration. Together with the Unit 2 Area of Study 3 scientific investigation, the practical activities meet the 32 hours of practical work mandated for Units 1 and 2 in the study design.

METHODOLOGIES

Each worksheet and practical activity is mapped to one or more of the scientific investigation methodologies outlined in the study design. Completing these activities gives you experience in applying the methodologies in a wide variety of contexts and prepares you for designing and conducting your own scientific investigation in Unit 2 Area of Study 3.

EXAM-STYLE QUESTIONS

Each area of study finishes with a selection of exam-style questions. These give you the opportunity to gain valuable experience applying your knowledge and understanding to exam-style questions.

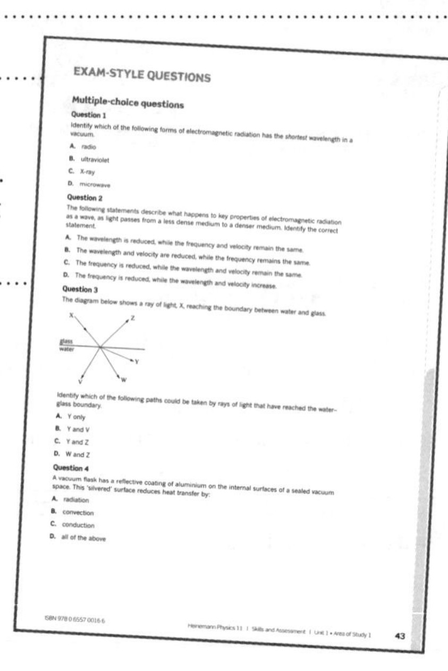
EXAM-STYLE QUESTIONS

Multiple-choice questions

Question 1

Identify which of the following forms of electromagnetic radiation has the shortest wavelength in a vacuum.

A. radio
B. ultraviolet
C. X-ray
D. microwave

Question 2

The following statements describe what happens to key properties of electromagnetic radiation as a wave, as light passes from a less dense medium to a denser medium. Identify the correct statement.

A. The wavelength is reduced, while the frequency and velocity remain the same.
B. The wavelength and velocity are reduced, while the frequency remains the same.
C. The frequency is reduced, while the wavelength and velocity remain the same.
D. The frequency is reduced, while the wavelength and velocity increase.

Question 3

The diagram below shows a ray of light, X, reaching the boundary between water and glass.

Identify which of the following paths could be taken by rays of light that have reached the water–glass boundary.

A. Y only
B. Y and V
C. Y and Z
D. W and Z

Question 4

A vacuum flask has a reflective coating of aluminium on the internal surfaces of a sealed vacuum space. This 'silvered' surface reduces heat transfer by:

A. radiation
B. convection
C. conduction
D. all of the above

ISBN 978 0 6557 0016 6 Heinemann Physics 11 | Skills and Assessment | Unit 1 • Area of Study 1 43

TEACHER SUPPORT

Comprehensive answers and fully worked solutions for all worksheets, practical activities and exam-style questions are provided via the *Heinemann Physics 11 eBook + Assessment* or Pearson Places. In-depth support for Unit 2 Area of Study 3 in the form of samples, templates and teacher notes is also included, along with an interactive SPARKlab for every practical activity.

 ISBN 978 0 6557 0016 6

Physics toolkit

This toolkit provides support for developing the skills required to undertake scientific investigations. It also covers study skills and examination preparation. The toolkit can serve as a reference tool to be consulted as needed throughout the year.

Scientific method

Physicists make observations and construct hypotheses to account for their observations. A **hypothesis** is a possible explanation, an educated guess, made to explain observations.

Hypotheses are tested following the principles of the **scientific method**. These include:

- asking relevant questions (i.e. questions that can be tested)
- making careful observations
- designing and conducting **controlled experiments**; in controlled experiments all **variables** are kept constant, except the one under investigation
- keeping an accurate record of experimental results
- interpreting experimental data and observations logically
- drawing logical **conclusions** from the experimental results.

The results of a scientific investigation may negate or refute the hypothesis being tested. In this case, the hypothesis must be re-evaluated and modified. Such results are useful in redirecting scientific investigation.

When experimental results repetitively support a hypothesis, it may become a **theory** or **principle**; that is, the hypothesis is accepted as a scientific truth.

The scientific method recognises limitations in investigations. For example, some factors cannot be measured; a sample size may be too small to be representative; or unknown factors may influence investigations.

SCIENTIFIC INVESTIGATION

A scientific investigation can be conducted in many ways. Examples of scientific investigation approaches (also known as methodologies) are controlled experiments, literature reviews and modelling. The scientific investigation methodology and the methods (also known as procedures) selected will depend on the aim of the investigation and the research question.

Practical work involves direct experiences or hands-on practical activities. Scientific investigation methodology involves all elements of planning. It considers the focus of the investigation and the rationale for approaching investigations in a particular way: for example, through controlled experiments, fieldwork or modelling. See the checklist on page ix and page xii for further information about methodology versus method in scientific investigations.

An investigation that you conduct yourself is known as a primary investigation, and the data and information you collect is called primary data or a primary source. An investigation that involves the analysis of data collected by others is known as a secondary-sourced investigation (see page xvii).

When planning and conducting a scientific investigation, you must maintain a logbook. This records information related to your investigation, such as materials and methods, raw data, data analysis, and sources of information. A logbook can be maintained manually or electronically. In either case, a record of dates of all work is needed to confirm continuous development over time.

The findings of a scientific investigation may be presented in a variety of formats, such as a scientific report, an article, a verbal and electronic report, or a scientific poster.

Conducting a scientific investigation

Scientific investigations follow a precise scientific method. The checklist on the following page summarises the elements that are common to many scientific investigation methodologies and scientific reports. Refer to the checklist and record important information as you conduct your scientific investigation.

 ISBN 978 0 6557 0016 6

Elements	Explanation	Tick ✔
date	• the date the scientific investigation was conducted and the report was written	
title/heading	• a statement of what is being investigated	
aim	• a statement that describes what the scientist wants to investigate, demonstrate or find out • can be written as 'to investigate the effect of *x* on *y*'	
hypothesis	• a tentative explanation for an observation that is based on evidence and prior knowledge • must be testable • written as a short statement • should include variables to be tested and a statement of the measurable, predicted outcome • can be written as 'If *x* happens, then *y* will happen'. The 'if' part relates to the independent variable. The 'then' part relates to the dependent variable.	
variables	• experiments measure relationships between variables • an independent variable is changed by the experimenter • a dependent variable responds to the change in the independent variable • controlled variables are kept constant throughout the experiment	
risk assessment/ safety	• an analysis of the potential risks of conducting the investigation • aims to maximise safety by managing and minimising risk (the risk assessment form on page xi guides you through the analysis of risk)	
materials	• a list of all equipment, chemicals and materials used, including specifications and resolutions of measuring equipment • includes quantity, volume, concentration and mass of materials used	
methodology	• a description of the overall approach undertaken in the scientific investigation and the reasons for taking this approach	
method	• a detailed, step-by-step list of exactly what is to be done. This doesn't need to be numbered, but must reflect a logical development that could be repeated exactly, without any other reference, by another student • includes details about the materials used at each step • may include scientific drawings or labelled diagrams • considers steps that can be taken to reduce errors	
results	• a record of all observations and measurements taken during the investigation, including reasonable estimates of the uncertainty for each measurement • a record of the variables involved, including independent, dependent and controlled variables • observations may be recorded as text, diagrams, photos or videos • data is commonly presented in tables and graphs and can include calculations • data should be reviewed for recording and omission errors	
discussion	• interpretation of data, linking results to physical concepts • includes analysis of the data, looking for trends and relationships through calculation, graphing and considering linearisation of data to more clearly establish a relationship between variables • identifies problems such as bias, inaccuracy, unreliable data and errors • evaluates the method used, including a discussion of limitations • comments on whether the results support or do not support the hypothesis • comments on the implications of the investigation and further investigations that may be undertaken	
conclusion	• a short statement based on evidence that summarises the findings of the investigation • provides a response to the research question or hypothesis • identifies the extent to which the investigation addressed the research question or hypothesis • does not introduce any new information	

RISK ASSESSMENT

Five levels of safety should be considered before carrying out a scientific investigation. The inverted pyramid below ranks these levels in order of importance. The school and your teacher are responsible for reducing most of these risks. As a student scientist, you can take measures to reduce the risks shown at the bottom of the hierarchy.

A risk assessment should be completed before conducting an investigation to determine the risks involved. Complete the risk assessment form on the following page to identify possible risks for which you can take responsibility, and to think of ways you can reduce risks to create a safe environment.

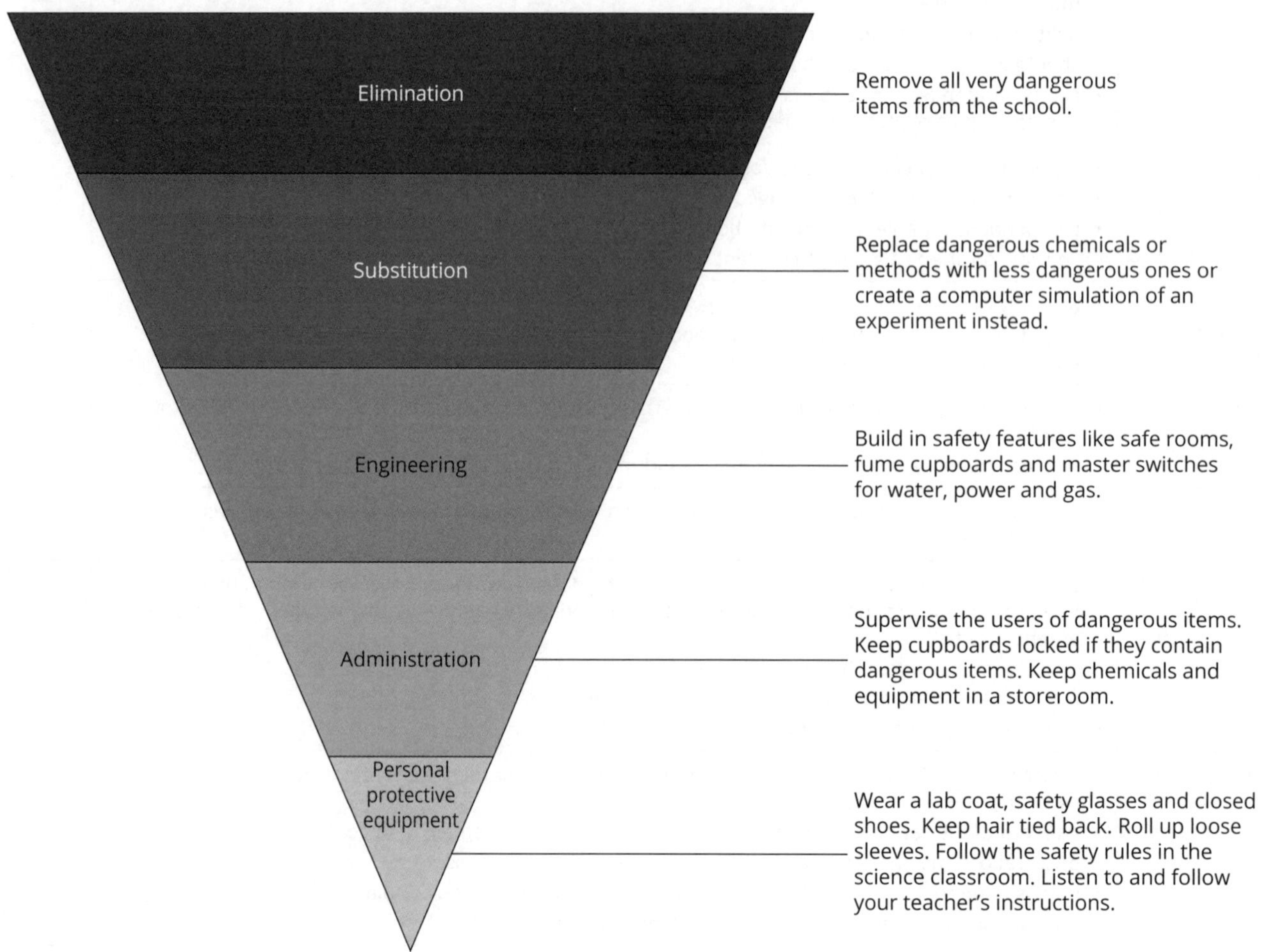

ISBN 978 0 6557 0016 6

Risk assessment form		
What activity are you doing?		
Title or description of the investigation:		
List ...	**Identify any risks**	**State how you will ...**
equipment you will be using:		use each piece:
chemicals you will be using:		carefully use each chemical: carefully dispose of each chemical:
ethical issues you need to consider:		ethically use animals in the laboratory: ethically use human participants in the investigation:
outdoor or fieldwork activities:		reduce these risks:
any other possible risks:		reduce these risks:

EXAMPLES OF SCIENTIFIC REPORTS

Two sample scientific reports are provided in the *Heinemann Physics 11 Skills and Assessment* book. They include annotations to draw your attention to key points to note on each scientific report. These points are also reflected in the checklist, so you are able to use this as a tool to evaluate whether all requirements of the scientific investigation are complete. As it can be hard to tell whether you have attained a high standard in your completed scientific report, looking at sample scientific reports can help you identify what is required.

High standard practical report

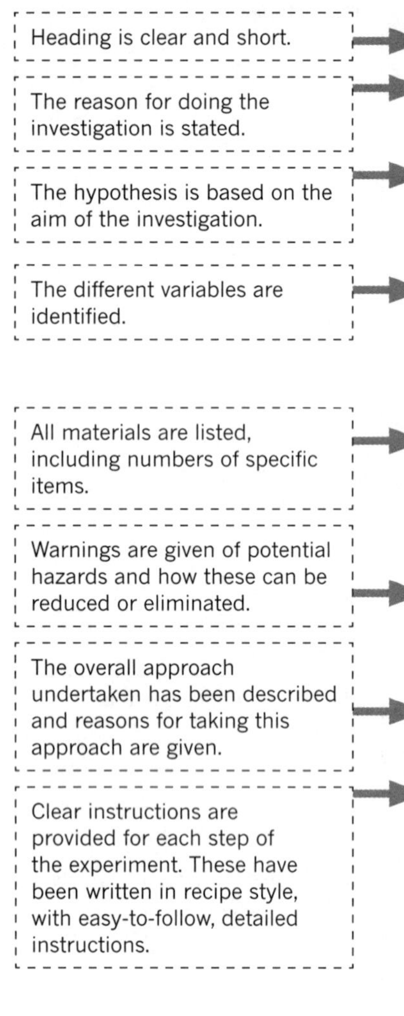

Investigation of motion using timed intervals

Aim

To investigate the motion of a student using timed intervals of measured distance.

Hypothesis

If the position of an object is known at regular timed intervals, the velocity can be calculated using the equations of motion.

Variables

Independent variable: Distance travelled

Dependent variable: Time

Controlled variables: Student running; students standing at 5-metre intervals

Materials

- plastic cones or other position markers
- 30-metre tape measure
- stopwatches

Risk assessment

Make sure the space is clear of trip hazards before running. If a student trips, report this to the teacher immediately.

Methodology

Controlled experiment measuring distance and time.

Method

1 In a large, clear space, stretch out the tape measure on the ground in a straight line. Mark out the beginning and end of the distance as well as every 5-metre interval.

2 Station a student with a stopwatch at each 5-metre marker. Zero each stopwatch and ensure that students are familiar with the basic operation of the stopwatch.

3 Select a student for testing and position them ready to run, walk, crawl or hop from the start of the 30 metres. On a call of 'GO', the student starts to move along the marked distance, and all student timers start their stopwatches.

4 As the moving student passes each 5-metre marker, have each student timer stop their stopwatch and note the time. Collate all times for the first trial.

5 Repeat the trial two or three times. Repeat any trials where times noted are incomplete or obviously wrong.

6 Average your results and use them to graph position versus time either manually or using a calculator or computer. Using the position–time graph, construct a graph of velocity versus time for a particular trial.

Results have been checked for consistency between trials. The number of significant figures shown indicates a good understanding of the limitations of the measuring technique.

If you take multiple measurements, calculating the mean (or average) gives a single representative value and can provide a clearer understanding of the data.

Results

Table 1 Results of trials

Distance travelled (m)	Trial 1 Time taken (s)	Trial 2 Time taken (s)	Trial 3 Time taken (s)	Trial 4 Time taken (s)	Average time taken (s)
0.0	0.0	0.0	0.0	0.0	0.0
5.0	2.3	2.2	2.3	2.4	2.3
10.0	4.2	4.1	4.2	4.3	4.2
15.0	6.5	6.6	6.4	6.5	6.5
20.0	8.4	8.4	8.3	8.4	8.4
25.0	10.3	10.2	10.4	10.3	10.3
30.0	14.2	14.1	14.3	14.2	14.2

ISBN 978 0 6557 0016 6

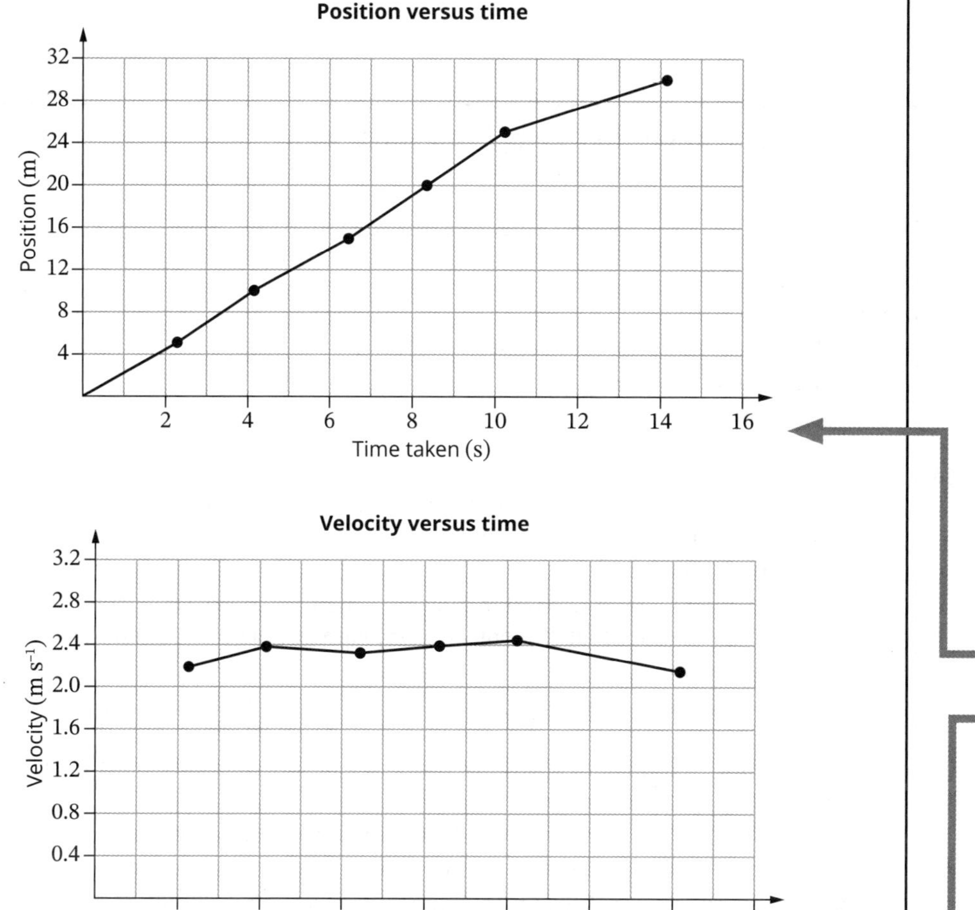

Axes have been labelled correctly and the graph includes a suitable descriptive title. An appropriate scale has been chosen to make best use of the space available.

Discussion

Discussion shows good understanding of the method and consideration of real sources of uncertainty or error. Avoid general comments unrelated to the specific investigation.

1 Describe the means by which you found velocity from the position versus time graph.

The gradient of a position–time graph can be used to calculate velocity because the change in position is displacement. Alternatively, the individual 5-metre intervals can be used to calculate the velocity for each interval, i.e. $v = \frac{\Delta s}{\Delta t} = \frac{5}{t}$.

2 Comment on the reliability of this means of measuring position, time and velocity.

The uncertainty in position can be expected to be small using a 30-metre tape measure to mark 5-metre intervals. Hand-held timing and watching students pass each marker introduces errors that can be significant if the student's velocity is large.

3 What is the major source of error in this activity?

Timing errors are the largest. A reaction time of 0.2 s is a large part of the time per interval.

4 Suggest an alternative that would improve the reliability of results.

Electronic timing methods such as a timing gate, as used in electronics, would eliminate errors associated with hand-held timing.

Continued over page

Continued from previous page

5 A ticker timer uses a constant time interval rather than a constant distance interval. Would this change the procedure by which you could calculate velocity? Which procedure would you expect to give the best results?

The ticker timer provides a more accurate timing method at the expense of errors due to friction between paper tape and timer.

Low standard practical report

The selected methodology is not outlined.

Risk assessment notes are absent.

No table number or title is given.

Check data carefully to be sure that it is entered in the appropriate row and column; data has clearly been entered incorrectly in trial 1.

The number of significant figures shown is greater than the precision the measuring technique allows.

Investigation of motion using timed intervals

Aim

To investigate the motion of a student using timed intervals of measured distance.

Materials

- plastic cones or other position markers
- 30-metre tape measure
- stopwatches

Method

1 In a large, clear space, stretch out the tape measure on the ground in a straight line. Mark out the beginning and end of the distance as well as every 5-metre interval.

2 Station a student with a stopwatch at each 5-metre marker. Zero each stopwatch and ensure that students are familiar with the basic operation of the stopwatch.

3 Select a student for testing and position them ready to run, walk, crawl or hop from the start of the 30 metres. On a call of 'GO', the student starts to move along the marked distance, and all student timers start their stopwatches.

4 As the moving student passes each 5-metre marker, have each student timer stop their stopwatch and note the time. Collate all times for the first trial.

5 Repeat the trial two or three times. Repeat any trials where times noted are incomplete or obviously wrong.

6 Average your results and use them to graph position versus time either manually or using a calculator or computer. Using the position–time graph, construct a graph of velocity versus time for a particular trial.

Distance travelled (m)	Trial 1 Time taken (s)	Trial 2 Time taken (s)	Trial 3 Time taken (s)	Trial 4 Time taken (s)
0	1.5	0	0	0.000
5	2.3	2.2	2.3	2.356
10	4.2	4.1	4.2	4.323
15	6.5	6.6	6.4	6.523
20	6.5	8.4	8.3	8.421
25	10.3	10.2	10.4	10.284
30	14.2	14.1	14.3	14.232

ISBN 978 0 6557 0016 6

Conclusion

This investigation demonstrated the connection between distance travelled and velocity of a moving object. The experimental evidence shows that the velocity is related to the distance travelled by the equation $v = \frac{\Delta s}{\Delta t}$.

The conclusion relates back to the purpose and states whether the hypothesis was supported or not supported. It also outlines the experimental evidence to support this.

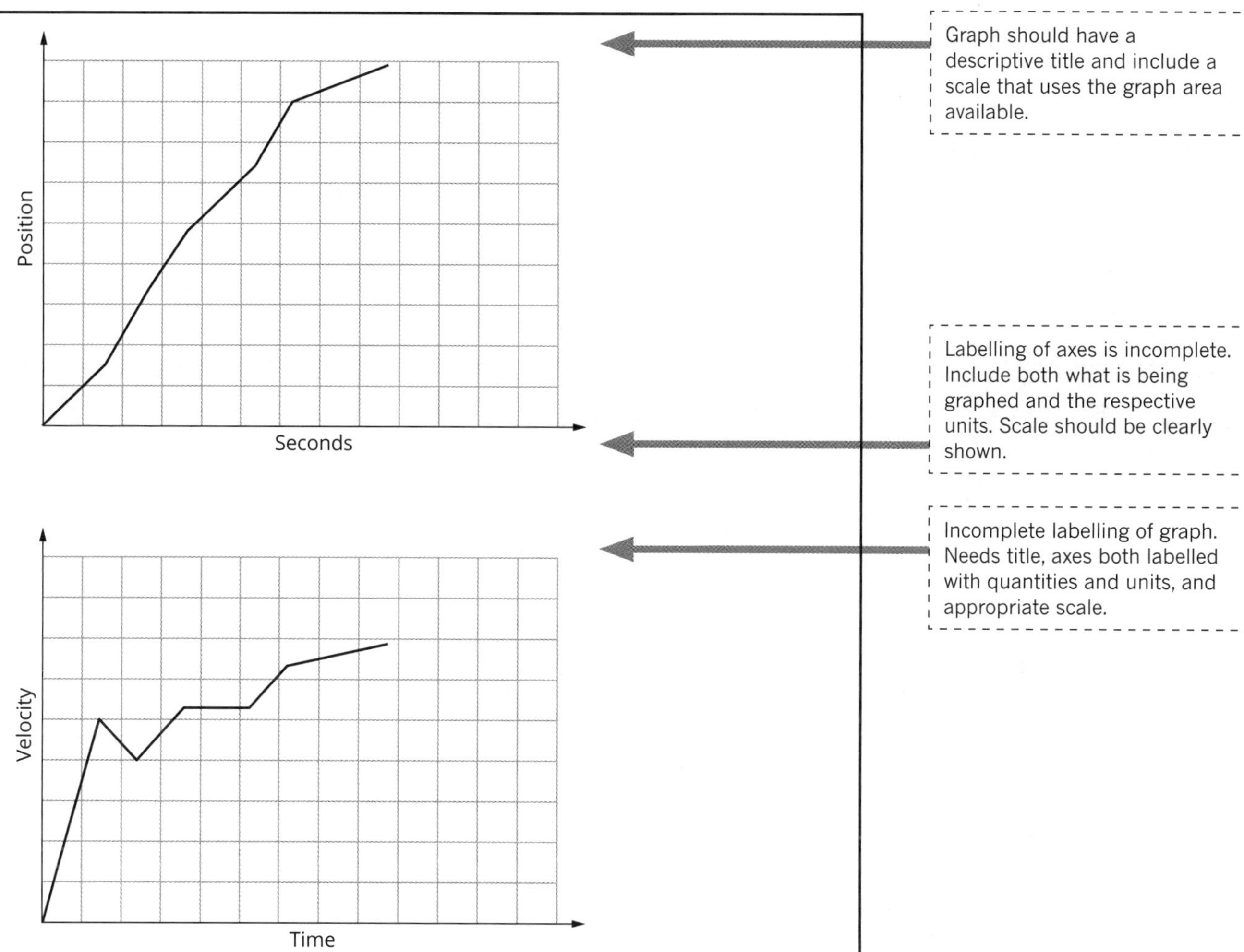

Discussion

1 Comment on the reliability of this means of measuring position, time and, hence, velocity.

There were some big errors because the answers didn't match. This meant the velocity was wrong.

2 What is the major source of error in this activity?

I think the biggest errors came from not reading the instructions. Also the timing was hard and not everybody tried.

3 Suggest alternatives that would improve the reliability of results.

You could try measuring it again or maybe try a different method.

4 A ticker timer uses a constant time interval rather than a constant distance interval. Would this change the procedure by which you could calculate velocity? Which procedure would you expect to give the best results?

The procedure that gives the best results is the ticker timer because it measures 50 times per second. If you measure distance it changes so it won't be the same.

Conclusion

We succeeded in completing this investigation.

This conclusion is vague—it doesn't respond specifically to the aim of the investigation, nor state whether the hypothesis was supported or not supported. It doesn't use the experimental results to support the conclusion.

STUDENT-DESIGNED INVESTIGATION

You will be required to design and conduct a scientific investigation based on the concepts you have learnt in Unit 2 in Areas of Study 1 and/or 2. This assessment task gives you the opportunity to apply key science skills and to pursue an area of interest to you, based on the key knowledge addressed during the course. You will be required to develop a question that drives your investigation, state an aim and hypothesis, select appropriate methodology and methods, and generate and collect primary quantitative data, recording important information in your logbook. You will then present your investigation as a scientific report. This could be in the form of a scientific poster, essay, report, oral presentation or article. It will be helpful to refer to page xii–xv to review what to include in a formal scientific report.

It will be important to carefully select the appropriate methodology and methods for your investigation. You will need to be clear about the difference between the two.

- Methodology: describes the overall approach undertaken in a scientific investigation. It considers the investigation more broadly, and includes the reasons for taking the chosen approach. For example, the methodology will identify and describe strategies, such as the methods used to obtain data, and the reasons why this is important to achieve the aim of your scientific investigation and address the question under investigation.
- Method: the specific procedure or steps taken to collect data during a scientific investigation.

DETERMINING YOUR RESEARCH QUESTION

As you develop a question for scientific investigation, be aware of the depth of thinking it will require. The table on the following page provides support in writing questions at different levels of thinking or complexity. It also provides some key words to help target these thinking levels and gives some examples of questions.

Be conscious of the level at which you are pitching your question when developing it for investigation, it. Questions for scientific investigation should generally be at the analysis level.

Level of question complexity	Type of thinking	Words that might be used		Examples of questions and commands
Simple	**Retrieval:** • remembering, producing information on demand	• who • where • list • show • describe • select • complete • define	• what • when • label • demonstrate • name • state • recognise • identify	**1** Define the term 'momentum'. **2** What factors affect inertia in a collision? **3** Identify the vector quantities in a straight-line motion. **4** What variables affect the movement of thermal energy between two objects?
↓	**Comprehension:** • the ability to understand information	• who • where • explain • represent • show how	• what • when • summarise • draw • describe	**1** Represent the process of energy transfer with a well-labelled diagram. **2** Why are houses wired as a parallel rather than serial circuit?
↓	**Application:** • using knowledge in new situations, including: - testing a hypothesis - experimenting and using data	• why • investigate • find out about • test • solve • develop • decide • construct	• how • research • experiment • predict • adapt • judge	**1** How does surface area affect melting rates? **2** Investigate the behaviour of a silicon diode in a simple circuit.
↓	**Analysis:** • scrutinising and breaking something into its smaller parts, including: - comparing - classifying - identifying errors - concluding - predicting	• why • categorise • contrast • sort • organise • generalise • evaluate • edit • assess • judge	• how • compare • distinguish • discriminate between • deduce • critique • identify misunderstandings	**1** Organise the following in order from the simplest measure to the highest level: velocity, acceleration, speed. **2** Compare a solenoid with an electromagnet. **3** Compare and contrast alpha and beta decay.
Complex (requires more thinking)	**Synthesis:** • combining knowledge and proposing new solutions, including: - problem solving - decision-making.	• justify • evaluate • design • create • investigate	• construct • simulate • how • why • what	**1** Some scientists believe that adopting nuclear energy in Australia is necessary to limit carbon emissions. Construct an argument for or against this statement. **2** Early scientists believed that heat energy was transferred by the spilling of 'caloric'. Construct an argument for or against this statement.

ISBN 978 0 6557 0016 6

SECONDARY-SOURCED INVESTIGATION

Some scientific investigations require the collation and analysis of data that others have collected. Data or information that was collected by someone else is known as secondary data or a secondary source. An investigation that uses secondary data is known as a secondary-sourced investigation. An example of a scientific investigation methodology that involves collating and analysing secondary sources is a literature review. This section guides you in conducting a secondary-sourced investigation.

Activities such as investigating an issue are likely to rely on secondary sources of information. Such investigations require you to think carefully about the topic; find, collect and organise information; analyse and synthesise findings; and present your ideas.

The process for undertaking a secondary-sourced investigation is summarised in the following flow chart. A secondary-sourced investigation is not necessarily a straightforward linear process, as shown in the flow chart. You can move back and forth between steps as needed.

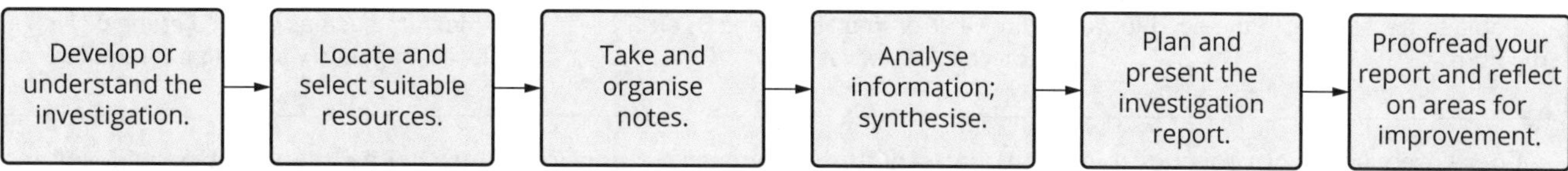

SOURCING INFORMATION

The resources you refer to in investigations may be primary or secondary.

Primary sources of information are created by a person directly involved in an investigation or study. Examples of primary sources are results from experiments (such as raw data or photographs), reports of scientific investigations, and peer-reviewed scientific articles reporting the results of an investigation.

Secondary sources of information are a synthesis, review or interpretation of primary sources. Secondary sources include textbooks, biographies, documentaries, newspaper articles and websites.

Refer to the following two checklists. The first shows features to look for when assessing and selecting the best sources of information. The second shows how to set out the information that is required for the references section of your report in American Psychological Association (APA) seventh edition style. This is only one of several referencing systems that you might be required to use throughout your career.

Selecting resources for the investigation	Tick ✔
The resource is:	
• **credible** and I can identify the author, author's expertise and publisher	
• **current** because the date of publication of the material is provided and is recent	
• **factual** and I know that it is objective material and not biased	
• **accurate** and all information is correct	
• **relevant** and covers the area I am investigating	
• **readable** and neither too simple nor too complex in its coverage of the material.	

Examples of information required for references and bibliographies (APA style)
Article in scientific magazine Author, initials. (year). Title of article. *Journal title*, volume number(issue number), page numbers. Digital object identifier (DOI) or URL Kensrud, J.R., Nathan A.M. and Smith L.V. (2017). Oblique collisions of baseballs and softballs with a bat. *American Journal of Physics*, *85*(8). 503–509, https://doi.org/10.1119/1.4982793
Book Author, initials. (year). Title of book (edition, if not first). Publisher. Black, L., Dommel, A., Dommel, N., Fischer, T., Jobson, K., Lewis, G., Madden, D., Moran, G., Trafford, S., White, G. (2023) *Heinemann Physics 11* (5th ed.). Pearson Australia. Include names of all authors or editors up to 20. Special rules apply for 21 or more authors. You can find information about the rules online.
Internet Author, initials/name of organisation. (year). Title of webpage or web document. <URL> American Institute of Physics. (2017). Periodic table. http://history.aip.org/history/exhibits/electron/

Always remember to record the above details for each resource you use. It is important to accurately cite resources in your reference section, as it can be time-consuming and difficult to find this information later.

NOTE-TAKING AND ORGANISING NOTES

Note-taking and organising requires skill. Good note-taking helps you avoid plagiarism and provides excellent information to support your scientific report writing. Plagiarism is when you take someone else's ideas and words and present them as your own work. You plagiarise if you copy sections or sentences from sources or you cut and paste from the internet. It is acceptable to use the ideas of others, but you must state clearly where the information has come from in your reference section.

The following table provides examples of original text, plagiarised text and acceptably rephrased text.

Original text	Plagiarised text	Rephrased text
Waves on water, in a string and in air are examples of mechanical waves. Waves are classified by what they move through. Electromagnetic waves, or light waves, are able to travel without the need for a medium.	Waves are classified by what they move through. Electromagnetic waves, also known as light waves, are able to travel without the need for a medium. Waves on water or in a string and in air are mechanical waves.	Waves can be mechanical or electromagnetic. This classification comes from the medium the waves move through. Mechanical waves need a medium such as water, a string or air. Electromagnetic waves do not require a medium.

There are various approaches to effective note-taking. Whatever technique you use, try to keep your notes brief and focus on key points. Some examples include:

- dot point summaries
- underlining or highlighting text
- labelled diagrams
- flow charts—to show sequences
- concept maps—to show connections between ideas
- Venn diagrams—to show similarities and differences
- tables—to summarise longer and more complex information that has subparts. Tables can incorporate any of the other note-taking techniques. Adapt the table to suit your style and the task.

The following (partially completed) table shows how this technique can be used to take notes for a secondary-sourced investigation.

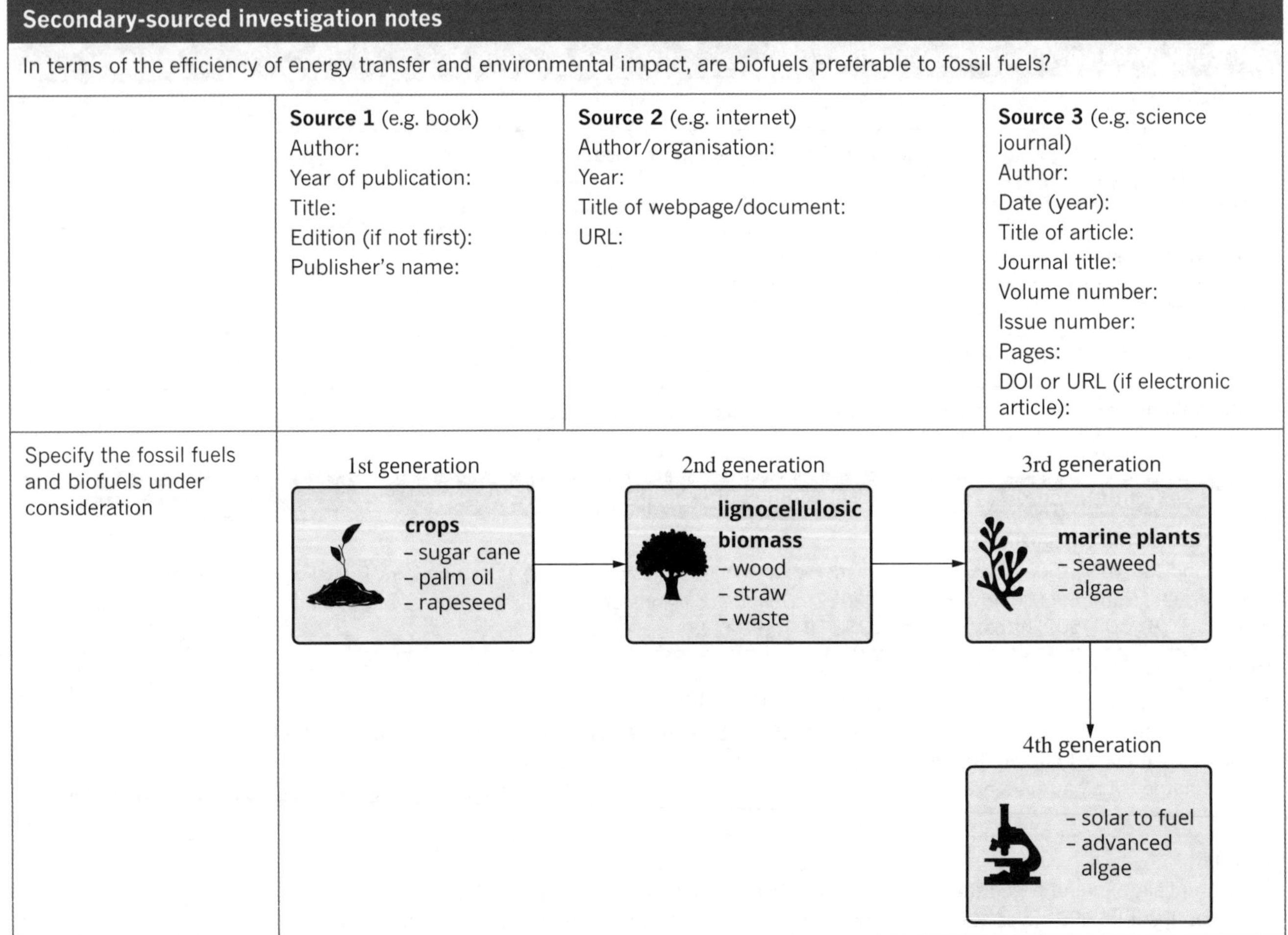

Secondary-sourced investigation notes			
In terms of the efficiency of energy transfer and environmental impact, are biofuels preferable to fossil fuels?			
	Source 1 (e.g. book) Author: Year of publication: Title: Edition (if not first): Publisher's name:	**Source 2** (e.g. internet) Author/organisation: Year: Title of webpage/document: URL:	**Source 3** (e.g. science journal) Author: Date (year): Title of article: Journal title: Volume number: Issue number: Pages: DOI or URL (if electronic article):
Specify the fossil fuels and biofuels under consideration	1st generation **crops** - sugar cane - palm oil - rapeseed	2nd generation **lignocellulosic biomass** - wood - straw - waste	3rd generation **marine plants** - seaweed - algae 4th generation - solar to fuel - advanced algae

ISBN 978 0 6557 0016 6

Secondary-sourced investigation notes			
Pros and cons of fossil fuels in terms of efficiency	• Biofuels can be replenished much faster than fossil fuels.		
Pros and cons of biofuels in terms of efficiency		• Global average efficiency is 36% for all fossil fuels.	
Pros and cons of fossil fuels in terms of environmental impact			Cons • air pollution • global warming
Pros and cons of biofuels in terms of environmental impact			

SCIENTIFIC WRITING

Scientists have a particular writing style. You should use this distinctive style to communicate your ideas. Scientific writing is:

- objective—it describes events rather than what people think or feel and is as free as possible of bias or personal opinion
- precise—it avoids exaggeration and uses qualified language
- formal—it uses scholarly language rather than colloquial or everyday language
- concise—it conveys information in short, clearly understandable sentences without unnecessary information
- simple—it uses short sentences where possible
- predominantly written in passive voice, although sometimes active voice can be used to avoid confusion: e.g. 'The counts per second were recorded' (passive voice) might be more difficult for a younger audience to understand than 'We recorded the number of counts per second' (active voice)
- structured to include headings, tables, diagrams and mathematical calculations.

Examples of unscientific and scientific writing are demonstrated in the following table.

Unscientific writing	Scientific writing
Subjective, biased writing: • The results were fantastic. • This produced a disgusting odour.	**Objective, unbiased writing:** • The results showed ... • This produced a pungent odour.
Exaggerated writing: • The object weighed a huge amount. • The magnesium burst into huge flames. • Safety crisis	**Accurate, precise writing:** • The mass of the object was 250 kg. • The magnesium burnt vigorously. • Safety issue ...
Everyday, informal language: • The experiment didn't work and we have no idea why. • The results don't ... • We guessed that ... • Previous researchers were slack and missed ...	**Formal language:** • Further research is needed to fully determine why the results of the experiment were not as expected. • The results do not ... • It was hypothesised that ... • Previous researchers have not found ...

ISBN 978 0 6557 0016 6

PRESENTING A REPORT ON A SCIENTIFIC INVESTIGATION

Scientific findings may be presented in a variety of ways. Common presentation formats are essays, reports, oral presentations and articles. At scientific conferences, posters are common, because they communicate ideas to a large audience in an organised, concise and creative way. Each presentation format has its own conventions, as summarised below.

Presentation format	Characteristics/inclusions	
poster	• balance of text and visuals • title, subheadings • balanced layout • captions for figures and tables	• references • hierarchy of font size according to subheading level • consistent font style—no more than three fonts
report/article	• structured with an introduction, paragraphs and conclusion • includes subheadings	• mainly text • can include diagrams, graphs and tables
essay	• structured with an introduction, paragraphs and conclusion • introduction states focus of essay • each paragraph makes a new point supported by evidence	• each paragraph links back to last paragraph • a text-style presentation format—visuals at end in appendix • conclusion draws all ideas together but does not include any new information
oral presentation	• needs to be engaging • refer to cue cards but do not read from them • watch audience as you speak	• stand still and avoid fidgeting • look at audience and appear confident

PROOFREADING

After you have completed the investigation and prepared your presentation, it is important to think about and check what you have done.

Proofread your work to minimise errors and maximise effective communication of the ideas from your investigation. Use the following questions as a proofreading checklist.

Proofreading checklist	Tick ✔
Have I:	
• investigated the question fully?	
• expressed myself clearly to communicate my ideas well?	
• used the scientific writing style?	
• included data analysis?	
• checked spelling, punctuation and grammar?	
• included references?	
• met the requirements of the presentation format?	

ISBN 978 0 6557 0016 6

Study skills

You can use a variety of techniques and strategies to help you study. You may find that you use different strategies in different situations. For example, you may prefer to highlight key phrases in your notebook throughout the year, but make summaries of topics before an examination. The strategies you choose will depend on personal preference and may not be the same as those used by your classmates.

Effective study skills involve more than the learning strategies you use. Equally important is when you use those skills. It is more effective to apply study skills throughout the year, revising and consolidating your knowledge as you progress through the course, rather than doing a rushed cram just before the examination. Revise your work regularly, and reduce stress by being organised and setting up a study plan.

GETTING ORGANISED

To get yourself organised, try the following steps.

- Use a diary to write down all homework and assessment tasks as soon as you get them. Note due dates and what is required.
- Be specific about the tasks you need to do. Rather than writing 'do physics', it is more effective to note things such as which questions to answer and which page to look at in your student book.
- Write a list of everything you need to do each day. Tick off or cross out items as you complete them.
- Break down larger tasks into smaller separate parts that are manageable.
- Make sure your lists and planners are realistic. Do not set yourself more than you can actually do.

STUDY TECHNIQUES

Studying requires concentration. Remove any distractions and factor in some breaks. Allow a 10-minute break every hour. Vary your study technique depending on the content to be learned and your personal preference. Although you may have already found a study technique that works for you, also consider the following options.

Study technique	Tips
Highlighting Radiation is a shortened form of <u>electromagnetic radiation</u>, which includes <u>visible, ultraviolet and infrared light</u>. Together with other forms of light, these make up the electromagnetic spectrum. The <u>transfer of heat</u> from one place to another <u>without the movement of particles</u> is by electromagnetic radiation. Electromagnetic radiation <u>travels at the speed of light.</u>	Highlight or underline key points as you read your notes or text.
Summary notes • Vector versus scalar quantities • Scalar quantities are fully defined by magnitude only • Vector quantities require a magnitude and direction • The direction can be in terms of a full circle or quadrant bearing • Vector quantities include displacement, velocity, force and acceleration • Equivalent scalar quantities are distance, speed, force and magnitude of acceleration	• Create a list of key headings and add some dot points about each heading. • Write your own summary of the key ideas in each chapter. • Use headings and subheadings. • Underline key words and key phrases. • Use simple diagrams. • The most effective chapter summaries are clear, concise and uncluttered.
Diagrams Lowest energy orbit where electron is normally found + Higher energy orbits	• Diagrams can be used as a summary of key concepts. • Diagrams are useful memory triggers. • Diagrams cover a lot of information in a visual way, with minimal text.

Study technique	Tips
Concept maps Graphs of straight line motion over time gradient ← position → area under curve (→ no meaning) gradient ← velocity → area under curve gradient ← acceleration → area under curve (gradient → no meaning)	• Concept maps are a great way of connecting key terms and ideas in a simple and ordered way. • Use the lines that connect ideas to note the relationships between the words and phrases. • They may include text and images. • They may be a simple or more complex summary tool. • Concept maps and other graphic organisers such as Venn diagrams and flow charts show how information is connected and help deepen understanding.
Tables *Subatomic particles* *Relative mass* / *Charge* / *Location* *1* / *neutral* / *nucleus* *1* / *positive* / *nucleus* $\frac{1}{1836}$ / *negative* / *orbiting nucleus*	• Tables are useful to show relationships between different factors. • Information is uncluttered.
Mnemonic devices *Work is fun, sir.* *...triggers your memory for... W = Fs*	• Mnemonic tools help you remember information. • To remember that work is a product of force and displacement, memorise the sentence shown on the left, which contains the initial letters of each variable.
Glossary *Electron: negatively charged particle in an atom* *Diode: a semiconductor*	• Compile your own glossary—writing the terms and definitions will make them easier to remember. • Add images to help you remember. • Write each term in a sentence. • Memorise these terms and definitions.
Trigger words **Origin of universe—two theories:** • *Big Bang* • *Steady state theory – Fred Hoyle*	• Write down the key words associated with a topic or theme. • Trigger words are useful in helping to remember other related words and ideas.
Repeating information aloud	This is a good way to remember information and helps you to slow down and absorb the information.
Practising	Complete as many review questions and past exams as possible.
Flash cards What is the Schrödinger model? Identify the states of matter and changes between them.	• Making flash cards helps your understanding. • Make your own cards. • Write a question on one side and the answer on the back. • Cards can include definitions, brief explanations, diagrams, equations and graphs.
Teaching someone	• Teach friends or family members. • Teaching a difficult concept to someone means you must first understand the concept yourself.

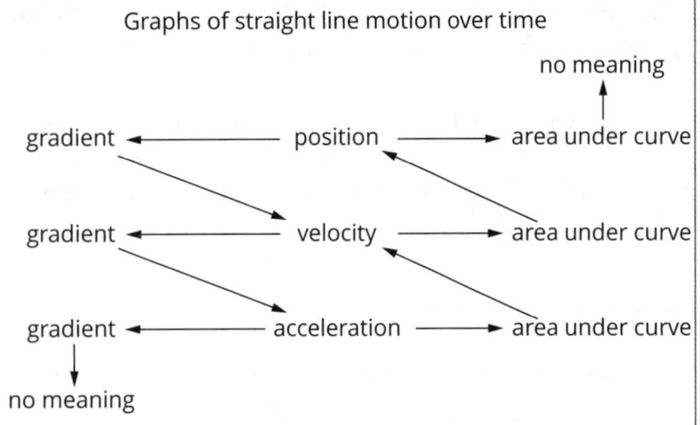

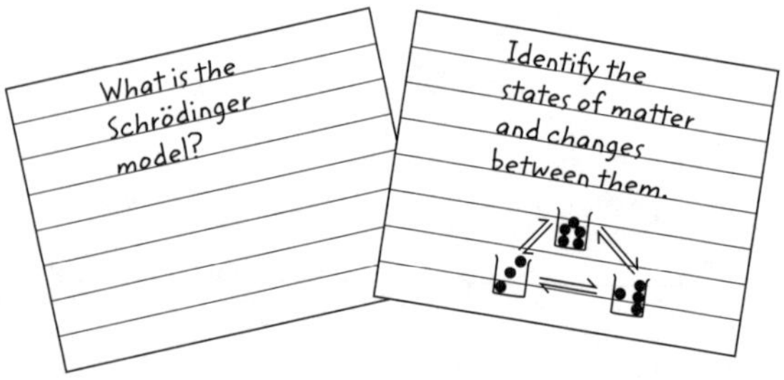

ISBN 978 0 6557 0016 6

Study technique	Tips
Handwriting notes	• Handwrite rather than type summary notes. • Remember, the examination requires you to write answers. • Practise writing for long stretches of time and make sure your writing is legible.
Responding to feedback and self-correcting	• Check through all feedback from your teacher. • Highlight what was right or wrong. • Attempt to identify where you have errors and rework the answer to get it right.

Examination preparation

In the weeks before the examination, begin preparing. The earlier you begin revising, the easier it will be. It is also helpful to begin practising exam-style questions as early as possible, not just in the weeks before the exam.

Like most skills, practice will improve your ability to do exams and to handle different types of exam questions. Doing practice exams is vital because you gain experience in:

- using reading time effectively
- allocating the right amount of time to each question
- working to a time limit
- reading and interpreting questions
- understanding what is required for each question
- planning answers
- deciding on relevant information
- proofreading/checking your answers
- writing efficiently for the duration of the exam.

Use your practice exam experience to revise, to analyse your strengths and weaknesses, and to assess how you managed your time.

Use the following checklist as a reminder of your study program.

Study program checklist	Tick ✔
Have I:	
• revised all areas of the course?	
• highlighted important points?	
• made a summary of the important points in each topic?	
• read over my revision notes?	
• looked at and worked through practice exam papers?	
• answered practice exam questions within the appropriate time limit?	

EXAMINATION STRATEGIES

Familiarise yourself with the conditions of the examination well before the day you sit the exam. You should know:

- the number of exams for the subject
- the amount of reading time allowed in the exam before writing begins
- the amount of writing time allocated
- any particular equipment allowed or required, such as a calculator, pencils, pens and ruler
- strategies to tackle the exam.

Exam strategies are listed in the following table.

Exam strategies
Reading time • You will be given reading time at the beginning of the exam (usually 15 minutes). • Remember that no writing at all is allowed during this time—no note-taking, no highlighting or underlining. • Read the instructions. • Read through the short-answer questions first—this will give you an overall sense of the themes of questions that require written responses. • Read the multiple-choice questions next. • Decide the order in which you will answer questions. Start with what you consider to be the easiest question to build confidence.
Writing time • You will be given 2.5 hours of working time. • Begin with the multiple-choice questions. • Answer every multiple-choice question, even if you can only make an educated guess. • If you are unsure of an answer to a multiple-choice question, mark it so you can come back to it if time allows. • Attempt the short-answer questions next. • Attempt the easiest short-answer questions first and work your way to the more challenging questions.
Tips for answering questions • Carefully read each question, underlining key words. • Be aware that most questions are structured so they become more challenging towards the end. You may not be able to answer the last part of a question but you will have earned most of the marks by answering earlier parts. • Look carefully at any diagrams, pictures, tables and graphs and make sure you understand their relevance to the questions involved. • For questions with graphs, read the graph title and the labels on the axes carefully so that you can establish the relationship the graph is showing. • For questions with tables, read the headings on the columns and rows carefully so that you can analyse the content of the table effectively. • Check for key words in a question. Highlight them but do not colour the whole question. • Use correct spelling—it can mean the difference between scoring a point and not scoring a point. • Plan your answers before you write, remembering to address the exam criteria. • For questions with parts, read the whole question first. This gives you an overall picture of the question. It will also help to ensure that you do not repeat yourself in subsequent parts of the question. • Make sure you actually answer the question that is asked. • Once you have answered the question, re-read your answer and then re-read the question to ensure that you have actually answered all of the question. • When writing a definition, avoid using the word you are defining in your definition. • If giving values from a graph, use a ruler to line up points with the axes so you can be accurate, and always include units in your answer. • Be sure to attempt all questions. • Read over your answers to pick up careless errors—the mind is faster than the hand and you may not always write what you intend (especially when you have limited time). • Write legibly. Exams are scanned and marked online. If the assessor can't read your answer, they can't mark it as correct. • Keep an eye on the time. • Never leave an exam early. Use any spare time to re-read and check your answers.
Exam cues • The number of marks allocated to a question provides a clue about how much you are expected to write. Two marks usually means you need to make a minimum of two points. • The number of lines allowed for the answer indicates the length of the expected answer. If your writing is large, you may need to turn the page over and continue on the back. Make sure you indicate to the examiner that they must turn to the back of the page for the rest of the answer. Where the answer continues, clearly state that it is the continuation of the question and state the question number.

 ISBN 978 0 6557 0016 6

UNIT 1

How is energy useful to society?

AREA OF STUDY 1

How are light and heat explained?

Outcome 1

Model, investigate and evaluate the wave-like nature of light, thermal energy and the emission and absorption of light by matter.

Key knowledge

Electromagnetic radiation

- identify all electromagnetic waves as transverse waves travelling at the same speed, *c*, in a vacuum as distinct from mechanical waves that need a medium to propagate
- identify the amplitude, wavelength, period and frequency of waves
- calculate the wavelength, frequency, period and speed of travel of waves using: $\lambda = \frac{v}{f} = vT$
- explain the wavelength of a wave as a result of the velocity (determined by the medium through which it travels) and the frequency (determined by the source)
- describe electromagnetic radiation emitted from the Sun as mainly ultraviolet, visible and infrared
- compare the wavelength and frequencies of different regions of the electromagnetic spectrum, including radio, microwave, infrared, visible, ultraviolet, x-ray and gamma, and compare the different uses each has in society
- investigate and analyse theoretically and practically the behaviour of waves including:
  - refraction using Snell's Law: $n_1 \sin(\theta_1) = n_2 \sin(\theta_2)$ and $n_1 v_1 = n_2 v_2$
  - total internal reflection and critical angle including applications: $n_1 \sin(\theta_c) = n_2 \sin(90°)$
- investigate and explain theoretically and practically colour dispersion in prisms and lenses with reference to refraction of the components of white light as they pass from one medium to another
- explain the formation of optical phenomena: rainbows; mirages
- investigate light transmission through optical fibres for communication

Thermal energy

- convert between degrees Celsius and kelvin scales
- describe how an increase in temperature corresponds to an increase in thermal energy (kinetic and potential energy of the atoms) of a system:
  - distinguish between conduction, convection and radiation with reference to heat transfers within and between systems
  - explain why cooling results from evaporation using a simple kinetic energy model
- investigate and analyse theoretically and practically the energy required to:
  - raise the temperature of a substance: $Q = mc\Delta T$
  - change the state of a substance: $Q = mL$

Interaction of thermal energy and electromagnetic radiation

- calculate the peak wavelength of the radiated electromagnetic radiation using Wien's Law: $\lambda_{max}T = \text{constant}$
- compare the total energy across the electromagnetic spectrum emitted by objects at different temperatures
- apply concepts of energy transfer, energy transformation, temperature change and change of state to climate change and global warming.

KEY KNOWLEDGE

- **You will now be able to complete Worksheet 1.**

Waves and electromagnetic radiation

TRANSVERSE AND LONGITUDINAL WAVES

Waves transfer energy from one point to another. They do not transfer matter, although matter may move as the wave passes through it. They are classified according to what they move through. A **mechanical wave** is any wave that travels through vibrations in a medium. Waves travelling through water, along a spring or through the air (such as sound waves) are examples of mechanical waves. **Electromagnetic waves** (light waves) can travel without the need for a medium, but can also travel through a medium. For example, light from the Sun reaches Earth through the vacuum of space, but also travels through Earth's atmosphere.

A wave may be a single pulse, continuous or periodic. Periodic waves have a pattern that repeats (oscillates) over time as the wave energy moves. Depending on the direction of the oscillation, a wave is described as either transverse or longitudinal. Mechanical waves can be either transverse or longitudinal, while electromagnetic waves are only transverse.

In a **transverse** wave, the oscillations are perpendicular to the direction in which the wave energy is travelling. The particles in the medium move transversely (sideways) in peaks and troughs as the wave passes (Figure 1.1.1a). Ripples on a pond are an example of a transverse wave. In a **longitudinal** wave, the oscillations are parallel to the direction the wave energy is travelling. The particles in the medium move longitudinally (back and forth) in compressions and rarefactions as the wave passes (Figure 1.1.1b). Sound is an example of a longitudinal wave.

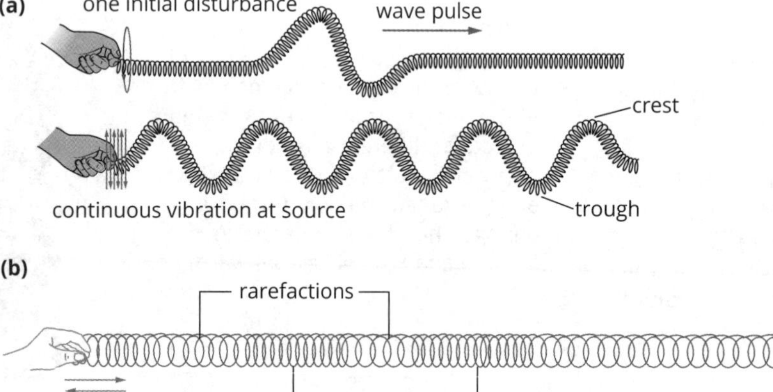

Figure 1.1.1 (a) A transverse wave and (b) a longitudinal wave

MEASURING WAVES

Waves can be represented by displacement–distance graphs and displacement–time graphs. From a displacement–distance graph, it is easy to determine the amplitude and wavelength.

The **amplitude** of a wave is the maximum displacement (movement) of the particles from the rest position (when displacement is zero).

The **wavelength**, denoted by the Greek letter lambda (λ) is the distance between any two repeating points, also called a cycle. Wavelength is measured in metres.

Figure 1.1.2 illustrates an example of a displacement–distance graph.

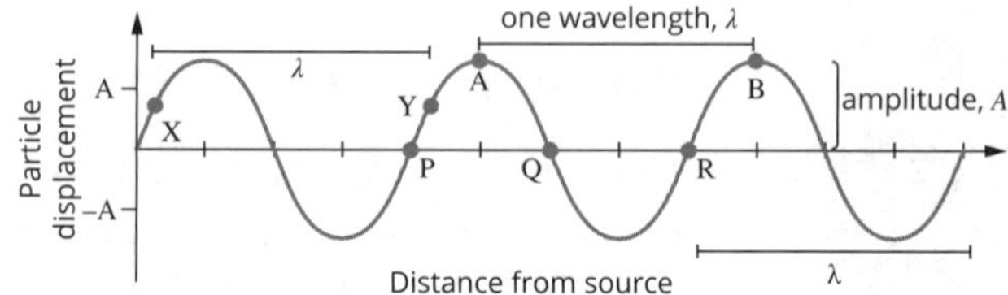

Figure 1.1.2 Displacement–distance graph showing amplitude and wavelength

The **period**, T, of a wave is the time it takes for any point on the wave to go through one complete cycle and the **frequency**, f, is the number of complete cycles that pass a given point per second. The period of a wave has an inverse relationship to the frequency, according to the relationship:

$$T = \frac{1}{f}$$

The rate at which energy can travel can also be determined, if either frequency (or period) and wavelength is provided. The speed of a wave can be calculated using the wave equation:

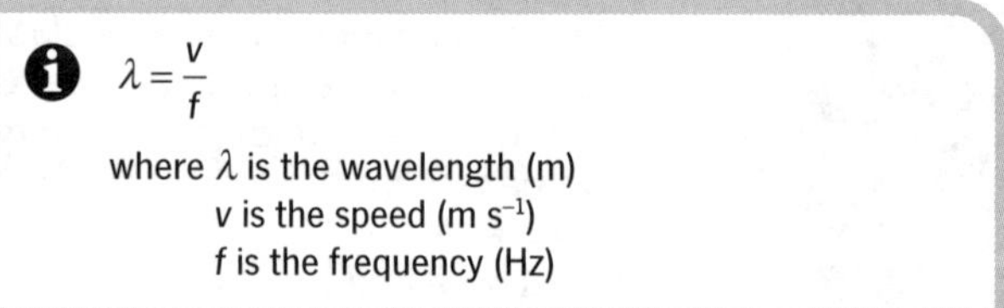

$$\lambda = \frac{v}{f}$$

where λ is the wavelength (m)
v is the speed (m s^{-1})
f is the frequency (Hz)

ISBN 978 0 6557 0016 6

KEY KNOWLEDGE

Amplitude, wavelength, frequency and period can all be determined from a displacement–time graph. The amplitude and period can be read straight from the graph (Figure 1.1.3).

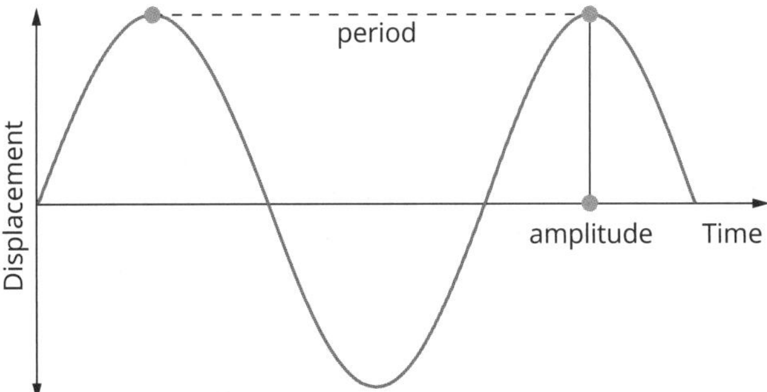

Figure 1.1.3 Reading amplitude and period from a displacement–time graph

- **You will now be able to complete Worksheet 2 and conduct Practical activity 1.**

THE ELECTROMAGNETIC SPECTRUM

Electromagnetic radiation includes ultraviolet, visible and infrared light, which are each a part of the **electromagnetic spectrum** (Figure 1.1.4). So, electromagnetic radiation behaves as we know light to behave: i.e. it travels at the speed of light, *c*, and it can be reflected and **absorbed**. Different types of electromagnetic radiation are described in Table 1.1.1.

Electromagnetic radiation, or light, travels at the speed of light in a vacuum. Light travels through a vacuum at approximately $c = 3.0 \times 10^8\,\text{m}\,\text{s}^{-1}$. The speed of light is so reliable that it is a fixed SI unit. The wave equation can therefore be changed to:

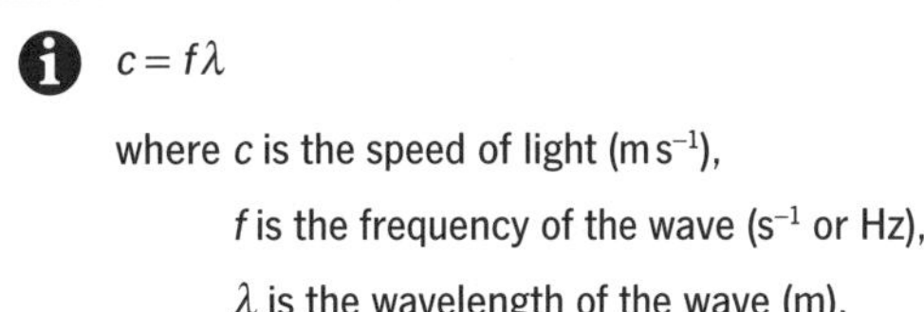

$c = f\lambda$

where c is the speed of light ($\text{m}\,\text{s}^{-1}$),

f is the frequency of the wave (s^{-1} or Hz),

λ is the wavelength of the wave (m).

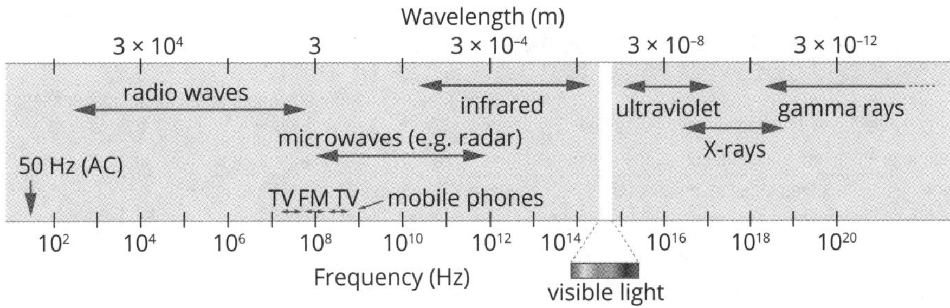

Figure 1.1.4 The electromagnetic spectrum

Table 1.1.1 Types of electromagnetic radiation

Gamma rays (γ-rays)	The highest energy, shortest wavelength energy, which is produced within the nucleus of an atom. Gamma rays are one of the three types of emissions that come from radioactive (unstable) atoms.
X-rays	When fast-moving electrons are fired into an atom, X-rays are produced. X-rays got their name as a result of scientists at first not knowing what they were, hence the letter 'X'.
Ultraviolet (UV)	UV light has a shorter wavelength than visible violet light and is less energetic than gamma rays or X-rays. It is known to cause skin cancer, particularly with frequent exposure. Wavelengths are less than 10 nm (1 nm = 10^{-9} m).
Visible light	This is the small portion of wavelengths around the middle of the electromagnetic spectrum that can be detected by human eyes. Many other life forms, for example insects and birds, can perceive wavelengths well into the ultraviolet range.
Infrared (IR)	Infrared or heat radiation is emitted by all objects that are not at a temperature of absolute zero. The hotter the object, the more radiation emitted, and the shorter the wavelength within the IR band.
Microwaves	Microwaves are produced by the spin of electrons or nuclei. They can be used to heat your dinner and allow remote communications and radar to work. Wavelengths range from about 1 nm to 10 cm.
Radio and television waves	Electrons oscillating in a conducting wire, such as an antenna, produce the radio and television waves that bring music and pictures to your home and carry voice and data to your phone. Long wavelength, low-energy electromagnetic radio and television waves can be transmitted across very long distances.

KEY KNOWLEDGE

Light

REFLECTION AND REFRACTION

When light reflects off a surface, the angle from the normal at which the wave strikes a surface will equal the angle from the **normal** to the reflected wave. The normal is an imaginary line at 90° (i.e. perpendicular) to the surface.

The **angle of incidence** and **angle of reflection** from the normal are labelled θ_i and θ_r, respectively (Figure 1.1.5). This is referred to as the law of reflection.

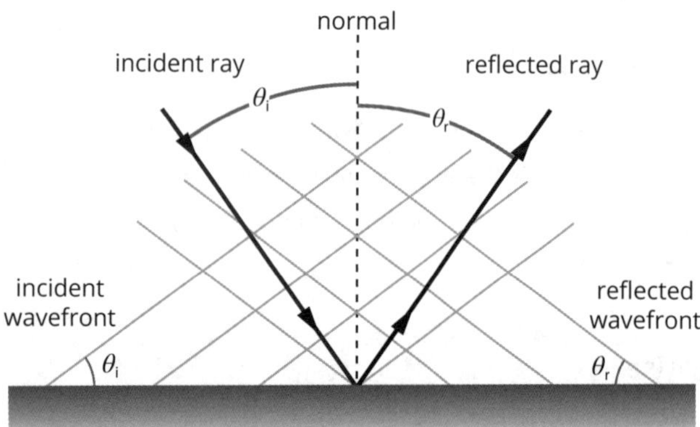

Figure 1.1.5 The law of reflection. The angle between the direction of the incident wave and the normal (θ_i) is the same as the angle between the normal and the reflected wave (θ_r).

Refraction is a change in the direction of light when it moves from one medium to another. Refraction is caused by changes in the speed of light rays. A convenient way to describe the change in speed of a wave is a property called the **refractive index.** The refractive index determines how far light is refracted when entering a material.

The refractive index, n, in a medium is given by the following formula:

$$n = \frac{c}{v}$$

where n is the refractive index (Note that n is dimensionless; i.e. it has no units, it is just a number.)
c is the speed of light in a vacuum ($3.0 \times 10^8\,\text{m s}^{-1}$)
v is the speed of light in the medium.

When light moves from one medium to another, the changes in speed can be calculated using the following formula:

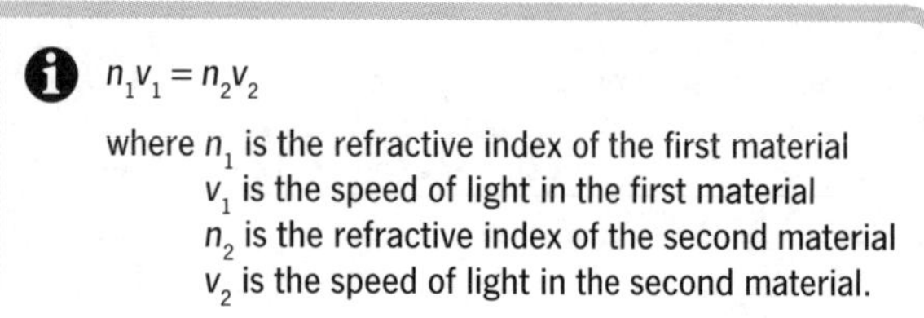

$$n_1 v_1 = n_2 v_2$$

where n_1 is the refractive index of the first material
v_1 is the speed of light in the first material
n_2 is the refractive index of the second material
v_2 is the speed of light in the second material.

This relationship can be linked to **Snell's law**. Snell's law relates to the geometry of the situation when a light ray refracts as it moves from one medium to another.

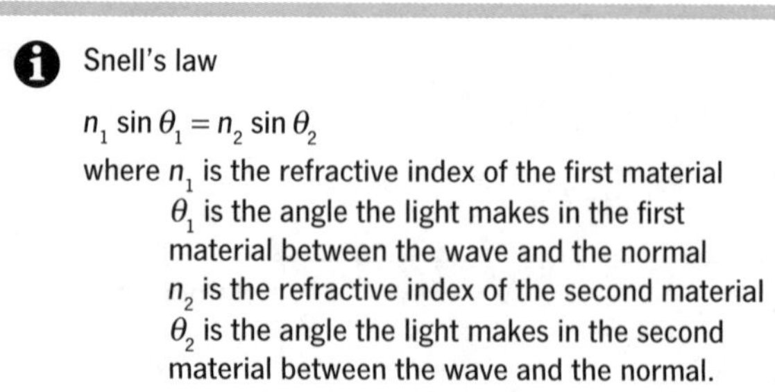

Snell's law

$$n_1 \sin\theta_1 = n_2 \sin\theta_2$$

where n_1 is the refractive index of the first material
θ_1 is the angle the light makes in the first material between the wave and the normal
n_2 is the refractive index of the second material
θ_2 is the angle the light makes in the second material between the wave and the normal.

When waves travel from a medium with a high refractive index to one with a lower refractive index, **total internal reflection** can occur. Total internal reflection is when a light ray does not undergo refraction when it hits the boundary between two mediums; instead, the light ray is reflected back into the original medium, as if it was striking a mirror. Figure 1.1.6 shows internal reflection at an air–water boundary.

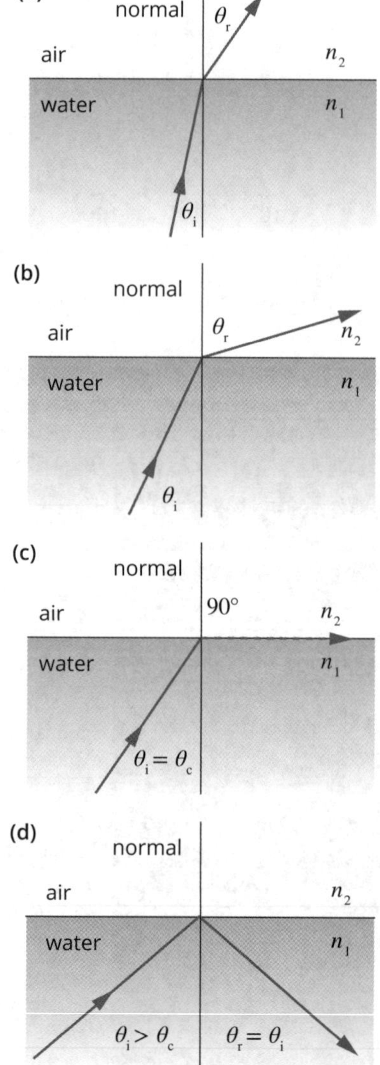

Figure 1.1.6 Internal reflection at an air–water boundary

ISBN 978 0 6557 0016 6

KEY KNOWLEDGE

Total internal reflection occurs when the incident angle is equal to or greater than what is known as the critical angle. The critical angle can be calculated by the following formula:

> $n_1 \sin\theta_c = n_2 \sin 90°$
>
> Since $\sin 90° = 1$, then $n_1 \sin\theta_c = n_2$, or $\sin\theta_c = \frac{n_2}{n_1}$.

Fibre-optic cables and total internal reflection

Optical fibres take advantage of total internal reflection. To make a fibre-optic cable for communication systems, a clear, central fibre (or bundle of fibres) is coated with a material of a different refractive index. This causes light travelling along the fibre to totally internally reflect at this change in medium, and therefore propagate (spread) down the length of the fibre.

The fibre-optic cables used in modern communication systems have many advantages over conventional older copper cables. Fibre-optic cables carry more information at a higher speed and with less interference. However, copper cables are stronger and cheaper.

Mirages

On a very hot day, the atmosphere heats up. Hotter (less dense) layers of air form and rise above colder (denser) layers of air, which sink down. The variation in temperature and density produces a variation in the refractive index of the air, which effectively curves the direction of the light. This can result in light from the sky being refracted upwards towards you, creating a mirage. For example, when you are out driving on a hot day it may look like the road is wet ahead of you. But when you arrive at that point, the ground is dry.

DISPERSION

White light is a mixture of light waves with many different wavelengths. When white light passes through a triangular glass prism (Figure 1.1.7), it disperses (separates) into its component colours of red, orange, yellow, green, blue, indigo and violet. **Dispersion** is a result of refraction.

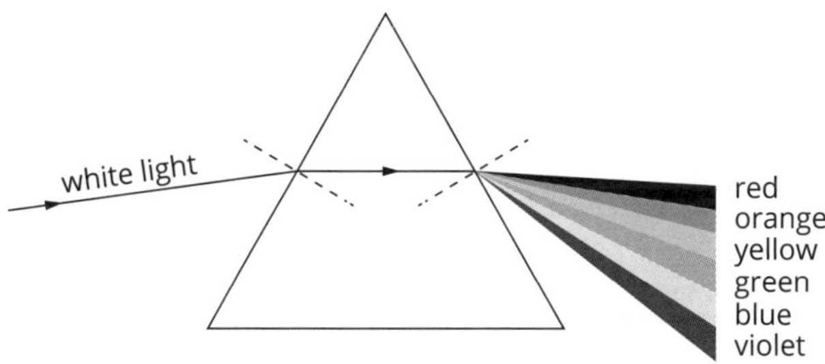

Figure 1.1.7 Dispersion is the splitting of white light into its component colours.

Each colour of light represents a wave of a different wavelength (Table 1.1.2).

Table 1.1.2 Approximate wavelength ranges for the colours in the visible spectrum. 1 nm = 10^{-9} m

Colour	Wavelength (nm)
red	780–622
orange	622–597
yellow	597–577
green	577–492
blue	492–455
violet	455–390

When white light passes from one material to another and the light waves slow down, the wavelength shortens as the waves bunch up. The wavelengths of each colour also change by different amounts. This means that each colour travels at a slightly different speed in the new medium, and that each colour is refracted by a slightly different amount. In other words, each colour of light has a different refractive index in a material.

Longer wavelengths, such as red, are refracted the least. Shorter wavelengths, such as violet, are refracted the most.

The formation of rainbows

After rain, light waves can enter a raindrop. Because the refractive index of water is higher than the refractive index of air, the light is refracted as it enters the raindrop. Like a prism, the refractive index of water varies with wavelength. Therefore, dispersion occurs in the raindrop, so the angle of refraction is higher for red light than for blue light (Figure 1.1.8).

Total internal reflection occurs at the back of the raindrop. The light is refracted once more as it leaves the raindrop. This leads to an angular spread of colour from blue through to red, which gives the rainbow its circular shape. We don't see the full circle, because Earth gets in the way. We see only the semicircle, which we call a rainbow.

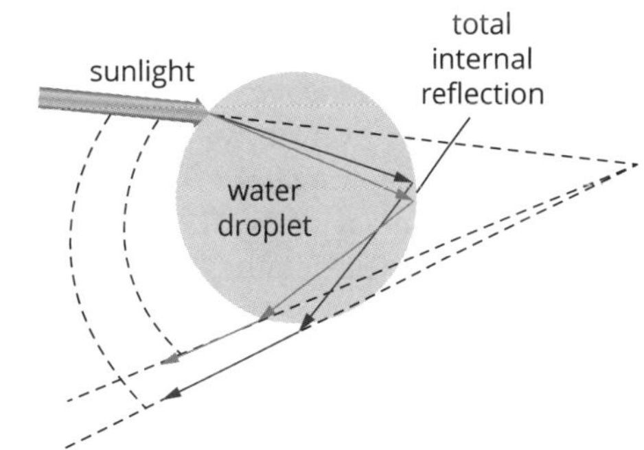

Figure 1.1.8 Rainbows form due to a combination of reflection and dispersion in raindrops.

- **You will now be able to complete Worksheet 3 and conduct Practical activities 2 and 3.**

KEY KNOWLEDGE

Thermal energy

HEAT AND TEMPERATURE

The **kinetic particle model** (or kinetic theory) assumes that all matter is made of lots of small particles (atoms or molecules) in constant motion. The particles feel forces of attraction and repulsion, and when they collide, no kinetic energy is lost or gained.

All states of matter (solids, liquids and gases) follow the kinetic particle model. The distances between particles change for each state: e.g. the distance between particles is much greater for a gas than a solid.

Heat is a measure of the **internal energy** of a system. The internal energy is the sum of all the **kinetic energy** and **potential energy** of the particles within a substance. Heat is measured in joules (J). As a substance is heated, particles will gain either kinetic energy or potential energy, and its **temperature** will increase. The temperature is a measure of the average kinetic energy of the particles. Heat (or **thermal energy**) will always travel from a hotter object to a colder one.

Temperature is generally measured using the arbitrary scales of Fahrenheit and Celsius. In contrast to these scales is the absolute scale known as **kelvin** (K). Absolute scales can't have negative values, so the lowest value must be 0 K. The kelvin scale was developed using the triple point of water (where all three states of water can coexist). The freezing point of water (0°C) is equivalent to 273.15 K. This is often approximated to 273 K.

- To convert a temperature from degrees Celsius to kelvin, add 273.15.
- To convert a temperature from kelvin to degrees Celsius, subtract 273.15.

For energy to be transferred between two objects, they need to be in **thermal contact**. For example, if an ice cube is placed into a cup of hot coffee, the ice's atoms are in thermal contact with the coffee's atoms. As the coffee is warmer than the ice, thermal energy will transfer from the coffee to the ice.

This system will eventually reach **thermal equilibrium** when the transfer of energy between objects in thermal contact ends. At this stage, both objects will be the same temperature.

Internal energy

Energy only changes from one form to another. Therefore, the amount of internal energy in a system remains constant. Changes in internal energy can occur by heating, by cooling or by work being done on or by the system.
The change in the internal energy (ΔU) can be calculated from the amount of energy added ($+Q$) or removed ($-Q$), and whether work was done on the system ($-W$) or by the system (+W).

$\Delta U = Q - W$

The internal energy (U) of a system is defined as the total kinetic and potential energy of the system. The average kinetic energy of a system is related to its temperature, and the potential energy of the system is related to its state. Therefore, a change in the internal energy of a system means that either the temperature changes or the state changes.

For example, while cooking a pot of soup, a chef does 200 J of work on the soup while stirring it. The pot also increases in temperature and gains 80 J of thermal energy from the surroundings. The change in energy of the soup will then be $\Delta U = Q - W = 80 - (-200) = 280$ J.

- **You will now be able to conduct Practical activity 4.**

SPECIFIC HEAT CAPACITY

The heat needed to raise the temperature by a certain amount will be proportional to the mass of the substance: $\Delta Q \propto m$. If you heat the same mass but use a different material, then you find that different materials require different amounts of energy to increase in temperature. The **specific heat capacity**, c, of a substance allows you to compare the energy required by different materials to change in temperature. Specific heat capacity is equal to the amount of energy that must be transferred to change the temperature of 1 kg of the material by 1°C or 1 K.

$Q = mc\Delta T$

where Q is the heat energy transferred in joules (J),
m is the mass in kilograms (kg),
ΔT is the change in temperature in °C or K, and
c is the specific heat capacity of the material ($J\,kg^{-1}\,K^{-1}$).

Table 1.1.3 lists the specific heat capacities for some common materials.

Table 1.1.3 Approximate specific heat capacities of common substances

Material	c ($J\,kg^{-1}\,K^{-1}$)
human body	3500
methylated spirits	2500
air	1000
aluminium	900
glass	840
iron	440
copper	390
ice (water)	2100
liquid water	4200
steam (water)	2000

- **You will now be able to complete Worksheet 4 and conduct Practical activity 5.**

ISBN 978 0 6557 0016 6

KEY KNOWLEDGE

LATENT HEAT

As a substance goes through a change of state, such as when ice turns into water, the temperature does not change. The energy required to undergo this change is called the **latent heat**, L.

Latent heat is calculated using the equation:

$Q = mL$

where Q is the heat energy transferred in joules (J)
m is the mass in kilograms (kg)
L is the latent heat ($J\,kg^{-1}$).

Figure 1.1.9 shows the different changes of state for water: from ice to liquid water to steam. As the water changes from solid ice to liquid water, the energy required to melt the ice is called the **latent heat of fusion**. Then, as it changes from liquid water to a gas when the water boils into steam, the energy required is known as the **latent heat of vaporisation**.

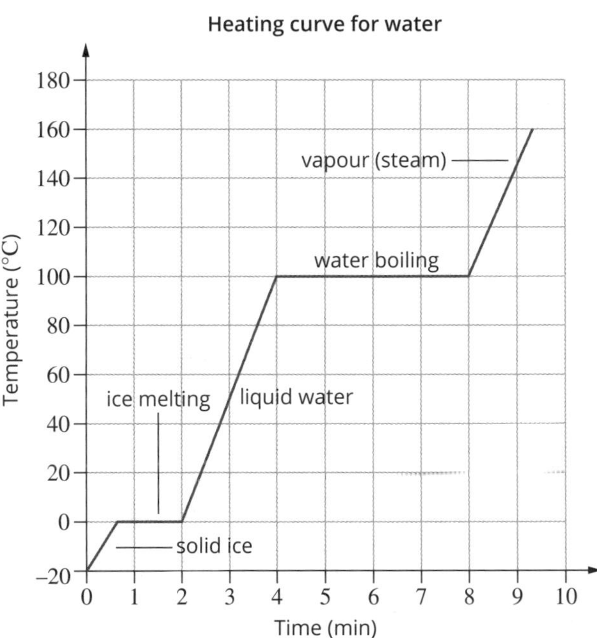

Figure 1.1.9 Heating curve for water showing changes of state

Table 1.1.4 lists a few values for the latent heat of different materials.

Table 1.1.4 The latent heats of fusion and vaporisation for some common materials

Substance	Melting point (°C)	L_{fusion} ($J\,kg^{-1}$)	Boiling point (°C)	L_{vapour} ($J\,kg^{-1}$)
water	0	3.34×10^5	100	22.5×10^5
oxygen	−219	0.14×10^5	−183	2.2×10^5
lead	327	0.25×10^5	1750	9.0×10^5
ethanol	−114	1.05×10^5	78	8.7×10^5
silver	961	0.88×10^5	2193	23.0×10^5

Evaporation

When a liquid changes into a vapour at room temperature, it is said to have evaporated. Evaporation occurs when the liquid's particles have enough energy to escape from the surface of the liquid. Eventually, no liquid remains.

Evaporation cools a liquid. This is because the higher-energy (and hence higher-temperature) molecules are the first to evaporate, leaving behind lower-energy, lower-temperature molecules.

How quickly a liquid will evaporate depends on the:

- volatility of the liquid—volatile liquids, such as methylated spirits, have weaker surface bonds and so evaporate faster
- surface area—larger surface areas create more evaporation
- temperature—at higher temperatures (higher-energy molecules) evaporation is faster
- humidity—less evaporation occurs in more humid conditions
- air movement—if a breeze is blowing over the liquid's surface, evaporation is faster.

● **You will now be able to complete Worksheet 5 and conduct Practical activity 6.**

CONDUCTION, CONVECTION AND RADIATION

When heat is moved from one place (or material) to another without the movement of particles, then the heat is said to be transferred by **conduction**. If a material readily conducts heat, it is said to be a good **conductor.** If it is a poor conductor, it is referred to as an **insulator**. Some examples of conductors and insulators are given in Table 1.1.5.

Table 1.1.5 Conductors and insulators

Conductor	Insulator
iron	wood
copper	plastic
steel	polystyrene

When you boil an electric kettle, the heating filament at the bottom of the kettle heats the water. The particles of water gain kinetic energy, pushing them apart. This changes the density of the heated water, so that the hot water rises. The colder fluid at the top of the kettle will be denser and hence will sink, causing a current to form (Figure 1.1.10). This type of energy transfer is known as **convection**. Convection currents occur in all types of fluid: from upwelling in oceans to wind and weather patterns.

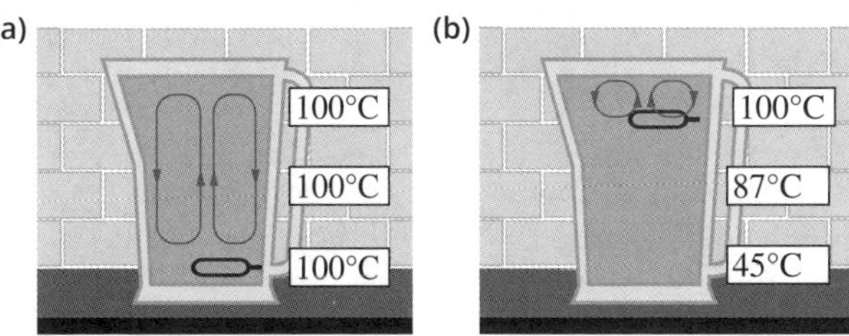

Figure 1.1.10 Convection currents in an electric kettle

KEY KNOWLEDGE

Conduction and convection both require a medium to transfer heat energy. Electromagnetic **radiation** is different, because it transfers heat without the movement of particles. For example, the Sun's energy travels through the vacuum of space to reach Earth.

Thermal energy, electromagnetic radiation and Earth's climate

WIEN'S LAW AND BLACK-BODY RADIATION

If an object's temperature is above absolute zero (0 K), then it will emit electromagnetic radiation. The peak wavelength of the emitted radiation is dependent on the internal energy of the object.

Wilhelm Wien, a German physicist, discovered that the peak wavelength at which an object will emit the maximum intensity of radiation is dependent on the object's surface temperature.

Wien's displacement law, more commonly known just as **Wien's law**, states that:

> $\lambda_{max} T = 2.898 \times 10^{-3}$ m K
> where λ_{max} is the peak wavelength of the emitted radiation in metres (m)
> T is the surface temperature of the object in kelvin (K).

For example, the 6000 K curve in Figure 1.1.11 will have a peak wavelength at 483 nm (as shown below), which is within the visible light range.

$$\lambda_{max} T = 2.898 \times 10^{-3} \text{ m K}$$

$$\lambda_{max} = \frac{2.898 \times 10^{-3}}{6000}$$

$$= 483 \text{ nm}$$

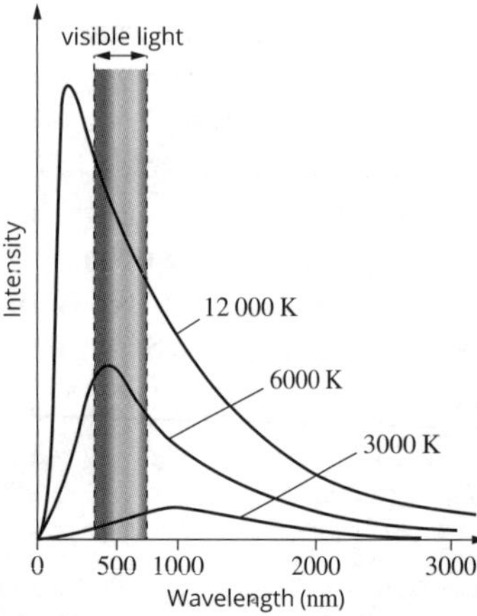

Figure 1.1.11 The spectrum of wavelengths at different temperatures (kelvin)

Black-body radiation

Wien's work on the relationship between temperature and wavelength of the radiation emitted by an object was based initially on a hypothetical object called a **black body**. A black body is a perfect absorber or emitter of radiation. In other words, it completely absorbs all the electromagnetic radiation that reaches it, regardless of the wavelength of the radiation, and therefore does not reflect any radiation.

The radiation emitted from a black body is known as **black-body radiation**. A black body does not necessarily have to be black, and black objects are not necessarily black bodies.

- **You will now be able to complete Worksheet 6.**

RADIATION AND THE ENHANCED GREENHOUSE EFFECT

The vast majority of the thermal energy received by Earth is short-wave radiant energy from the Sun. Most of this is within or close to the visible spectrum. The radiant energy that is absorbed by Earth's surface transforms to thermal energy. This increases the temperature of the absorbing surfaces and the air touching them. Over time, very little of this energy is retained. Almost all of the energy is re-radiated by the surface as long-wavelength radiant energy (Figure 1.1.12).

Even though Earth's surface is re-radiating heat from the Sun out towards space, it still stays warm due to the **greenhouse gases** in the atmosphere. Greenhouse gases absorb the wavelengths of radiant energy that are re-radiated from Earth's surface and re-radiate them down to Earth's surface again. This is known as the **greenhouse effect.**

The greenhouse effect is what gives Earth the consistent temperatures that have allowed life to evolve. Other planets in our solar system have no atmosphere, and therefore have no greenhouse effect. On Mercury, for example, the lack of atmosphere leads to extreme swings in temperature from 100 K to 700 K (−170°C to 430°C).

In more recent years, research has been conducted into what has been termed the **enhanced greenhouse effect**. The increased production of greenhouse gases coincides with the industrialisation of modern society. Evidence suggests that the atmosphere is now absorbing and retaining more of the long-wavelength infrared radiation emitted from Earth's surface.

The most abundant gases in Earth's atmosphere are, in order of abundance:

- water vapour (H_2O)
- carbon dioxide (CO_2)
- methane (CH_4)
- nitrous oxide (N_2O)
- ozone (O_3)
- chlorofluorocarbons (CFCs).

 ISBN 978 0 6557 0016 6

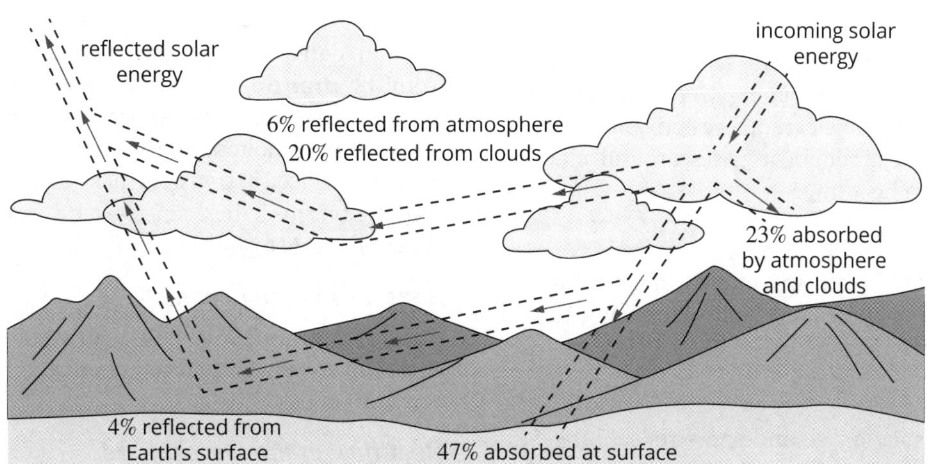

Figure 1.1.12 Radiant energy reaches Earth from the Sun. Only 47% of the radiant energy is eventually absorbed by Earth's surface. The remainder is reflected back into space or absorbed by the atmosphere.

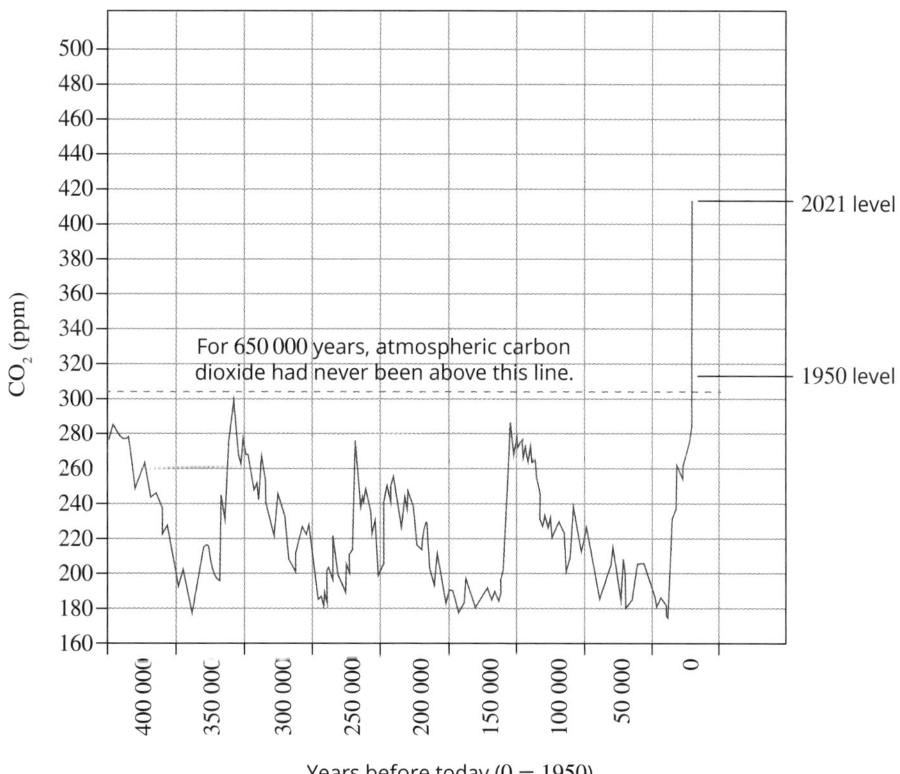

Figure 1.1.13 Carbon dioxide levels over the last 400 000 years, based on ice-core samples

Over the last 400 000 years, all the way up to the Industrial Revolution, the levels of carbon dioxide in the atmosphere stayed relatively constant (Figure 1.1.13) at levels lower than 300 parts per million (ppm). In recent times, levels have increased at a rapid rate. In 2014 the carbon dioxide levels passed 400 ppm and by 2021 had reached an average of just over 419 ppm. This increase has mainly been caused by humans, through burning **fossil fuels** and large-scale land clearing.

Human activities and energy re-radiated by Earth

The rate at which energy is re-radiated by Earth's surface depends on the surface material. Changing the surface of Earth affects how readily it can absorb and re-radiate thermal energy. Three ways in which Earth's surface can be changed are building, land clearing and melting ice.

KEY KNOWLEDGE

Building

The materials used to build cities, such as concrete and asphalt, re-radiate thermal energy into the atmosphere at a higher rate than uncleared, forested land. Increased concentrations of greenhouse gases around cities can also act as urban heat traps.

Land clearing

Land is cleared to create areas for farming or building. Land clearing contributes approximately 12% of Australia's total emissions.

Melting ice

The bright surface of ice and snow reflects the Sun's radiation, which passes through the atmosphere back into space. Ice can only absorb 10% of the radiation that hits it, whereas water can absorb 94%. Increasing temperatures cause ice to melt. In turn, this causes more heat to be absorbed, which causes more ice to melt.

How heat moves around Earth

The main mechanisms for moving heat around Earth are conduction, convection and radiation. Evaporation also moves heat energy around Earth's atmosphere and is sometimes considered a fourth process. More correctly, evaporation is a product of heat transfer due to conduction, convection and radiation.

Heat flow inside Earth

Although most of the thermal energy needed to support life on Earth comes from the Sun, a small proportion comes from **geothermal energy** (the internal heat of Earth itself). Heat flow inside Earth is mainly through convection of this geothermal energy. Heat from the **mantle** (the layer of rock between the crust and the outer core) moves towards the surface. When hot magma (molten rock) from the mantle reaches Earth's surface, it transfers heat to the crust through conduction, and then sinks back towards the centre. Where the crust is thinnest, conduction is higher.

Heat flow in the oceans

Ocean currents move massive amounts of thermal energy over very large distances through the process of convection.

Heat flow in the atmosphere

Energy is transferred within the atmosphere by radiation, conduction and convection.

- Radiant energy largely comes from the Sun as short-wavelength radiation and, to a lesser degree, long-wavelength reflection and emission from Earth's surface. Greenhouse gases retain radiant energy within the atmosphere.
- Conduction happens only in the very low levels of Earth's atmosphere, as air is a very poor conductor of thermal energy.
- Convection is the major process by which thermal energy is moved around Earth's atmosphere.

● **You will now be able to complete Worksheets 7, 8 and 9.**

ISBN 978 0 6557 0016 6

WORKSHEET 1

Knowledge review—waves and energy

1 Recall the comparative wavelength of each of the following radiation types and use that information to re-order them in increasing wavelength.

green light, infrared, radio, ultraviolet, blue, red, X-rays, microwaves

2 State the temperature, in Celsius, and in Fahrenheit, of melting ice.

3 Explain why the sound from a lightning strike is always heard after it is seen.

4 Explain the difference between transverse and longitudinal waves.

5 When a mirror is placed vertically, halfway along a letter, some capital letters (such as A) look the same.

Deduce which other letters would look the same in that mirror.

Identify letters that would look the same when the mirror is placed horizontally. (You may want to try this one with a mirror yourself!)

6 Define the attributes that make something a wave. Write a single, short sentence that summarises the key properties of a wave.

7 The following are examples of types of wave:

sound, string, radio, visible light, beach breaks, microwaves, X-ray, stadium, earthquake, slinky.

Classify these as either mechanical or electromagnetic in the table below.

Mechanical	Electromagnetic

8 For each of the situations in the table below, identify the correct process from the following list:

condensation, transformation, freezing, boiling, combustion, melting.

Change of state	Process
gas changes to liquid	
liquid changes to solid	
liquid changes to gas	

9 Of the three methods of heat transfer (conduction, convection and radiation), recall the one that describes each situation in the table below.

Situation	Method
lighter-coloured clothes keep you cooler in summer	
a drink cooler is made from polystyrene foam	
the air near the ceiling of a room is warmer than near the floor	
a saucepan has a plastic handle	

10 Recall how heat is transferred by selecting the correct option in each statement below.

a Heat always flows from an object of higher temperature to one of lower/higher temperature.

b Insulators are good/poor conductors of heat.

c Gases are good/poor conductors of heat.

d On a warm day, a house is warmer upstairs because of conduction/convection currents.

e The element of a hot water system will be located near its top/base and the heat is spread by convection.

 ISBN 978 0 6557 0016 6

WORKSHEET 2

Literature review

Interpreting graphs of waves

The graph for wave A shows the variation with distance (in m) of the displacement (in cm) of a particular transverse wave at a point in time. The frequency of the wave is 5.0 Hz. The wave is directed to the right.

The graph for wave B shows the variation with time (in s) of the displacement (in cm) of a particular longitudinal wave at a point in time. The wavelength is 0.45 m.

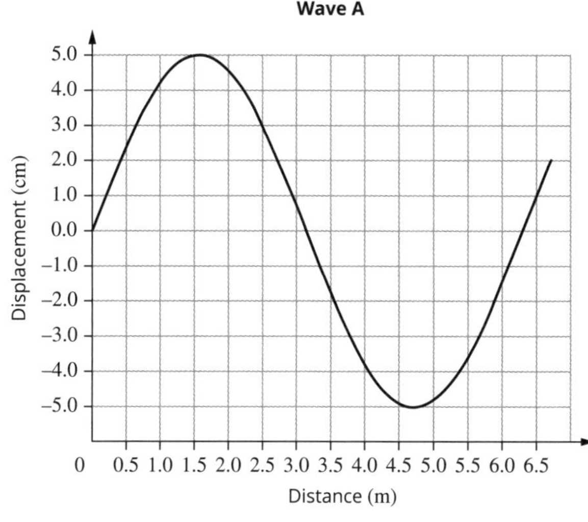

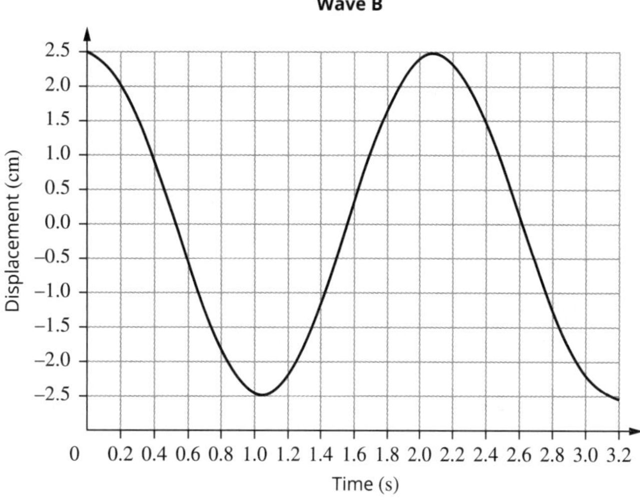

1 What is the amplitude of each wave?

2 Determine the wavelength of wave A.

3 Mark a point on the waves where the speed of a particle in the wave is at a maximum.

4 Calculate the frequency of wave B.

5 Calculate the period of both waves.

6 Calculate the speed of both waves.

WORKSHEET 3

Literature review

Waves and light

1 The speed of sound in air is about 330 m s^{-1}. If the thunder created by a lightning bolt is heard 12 s after the lightning is noticed, how far away was the lightning?

____

2 What is the difference between transverse and longitudinal waves?

____

3 Put the following radiation types into order of increasing wavelength.

green	infrared radio	ultraviolet	blue	red	X-rays	microwaves

4 Use the following word list to complete the text below. Some words may be used more than once.

sound	longitudinal	energy	parallel
matter	pulse	mechanical	perpendicular
transverse	guitar string	periodic	

- A wave may be a single _______________ or it may be continuous or _______________. A wave only transfers _______________ from one point to another. There is no net transfer of _______________. _______________ waves can be either _______________ or _______________. In a transverse wave, the oscillations are _______________ to the direction in which the wave energy is travelling. A vibrating _______________ is an example of a transverse wave. In a _______________ wave the oscillations are _______________ to the direction the wave energy is travelling. _______________ is an example of a longitudinal wave.

5 Use the following word list to complete the text below. Not every word will be used and some may be used more than once.

transmitted	fixed	reflected	phase
incident	absorbed	boundary	free

- A wave reaching the _______________ between two materials in which it can travel will be partly _______________ and partly _______________, and may be partly _______________. This incoming wave can be split into three different waves: an _______________ wave, a _______________ wave and a _______________ wave.

The reflected wave will respond in one of two ways when it reaches a boundary:

- Waves reflect with a 180° phase change from _________ boundaries.
- Waves reflect with no phase change from __________ boundaries.

6 Use the following word list to complete the text below.

speed	medium	frequency	refraction
wavelength	propagation	speed	

- When waves pass from one _______________ to another, further properties of waves can be observed. _______________ is the same; however, _______________ and _______________ differ. _______________ is the change in direction of _______________ of a wave that occurs when there is a change in _______________ of the waves.

ISBN 978 0 6557 0016 6

WORKSHEET 4

Modelling

Specific heat capacity

A student performed an experiment to measure the specific heat capacity of lead. A 2.5 cm cube of lead with a density of 11.34 g cm^{-3} was placed in a beaker of boiling water and left to come to thermal equilibrium at 98.6°C. The temperature was measured using a digital thermometer.

1 The student was expecting the temperature of the boiling water to be 100°C. Explain why the thermometer did not reach 100°C.

The student also had a polystyrene calorimeter holding 100 mL of tap water at a temperature of 20.5°C. The lead cube was removed from the boiling water with tongs and quickly placed in the calorimeter. The lid was returned to the calorimeter, which was then gently shaken about for 3 or 4 min until its temperature stabilised at 24.0°C.

2 Complete the specific heat calculation below. (c_{water} = 4.2 kJ kg^{-1} K^{-1})

$\Delta Q_{lead} + \Delta Q_{water} = 0$

$m_{lead} c_{lead} \Delta T_{lead} + m_{water} c_{water} \Delta T_{water} = 0$

3 The answer obtained is lower than the accepted value of 0.1256 kJ kg^{-1} K^{-1}. Explain why this is the case.

4 The student had heard that the rate of cooling of an object depended on its surface area. She thought that she could try to verify this by means of a similar experiment. She asked some of the metalwork students to take some of the same-sized cubes of lead and hammer them into bricks, cylinders and a sphere. They returned with the objects listed in the table below. Calculate the surface area of each of these objects. Use the formulas given on the left.

sphere: SA = πd^2

brick: SA = $2(hl + lw + hw)$

cylinder: SA = $\pi d\left(h + \frac{1}{2}d\right)$

Object	Dimensions (cm)	Surface area (cm²)	Time (s)	$t \times$ SA
sphere	d = 2.3		25.2	
brick 1	3.0 × 3.0 × 0.7		15.2	
brick 2	4.1 × 3.1 × 0.5		11.8	
cylinder 1	h = 2.0, d = 2.0		21.8	
cylinder 2	h = 1.1, d = 2.7		19.0	

She then repeated the experiment above with the same initial conditions. However, this time she placed a small, perforated platform in the bottom of the calorimeter so that the water could circulate easily. The time it took to raise the temperature of the water by 1.0°C was recorded. These times appear in the table above.

5 If the rate of cooling of the lead is proportional to the surface area, determine the relationship between the warming time (t) and the surface area (SA). Describe what is significant about the product $t \times$ SA. Use the last column of the table to test your hypothesis.

6 State, in your own words, whether the data confirms that the rate of cooling is proportional to the surface area.

WORKSHEET 5

Modelling • Simulation

Thermal equilibrium

If two objects are in thermal contact, energy can transfer between them. For example, if an ice cube is placed in a copper pan, the ice molecules are in thermal contact with the copper atoms. Assuming that the copper is warmer than the ice, thermal energy will transfer from the copper to the ice: i.e. from the higher average energy level to the lower average level.

Thermal equilibrium is when two objects in thermal contact stop having a transfer of energy between them.

1 A 200 g sample of water initially at 80°C is mixed with 200 g of water at 10°C. Assuming no heat is lost to the surroundings, determine the final temperature of the mixture.

2 A 400 g sample of liquid ethanol at 16°C ($c = 2460\,\mathrm{J\,kg^{-1}\,K^{-1}}$) is mixed with 500 g of water at 85°C. Assuming no heat is lost to the surroundings, determine the final temperature of the mixture.

3 A 100 g cube of aluminium initially at 100°C is dropped into a container of 1.00 L of water. Then, 2700 J of energy is transferred to the water as the aluminium cools down by 30°C.

a Determine the specific heat capacity of aluminium.

b Determine the original temperature of the water.

c Explain why the change in the temperature of the water was very small.

ISBN 978 0 6557 0016 6

4 A 30 g piece of iron is dropped into a container of water and transfers 700 J to the water in cooling. Calculate the iron's temperature change. Use $c_{iron} = 444\,J\,kg^{-1}\,K^{-1}$.

5 1.0 kg of ice is dropped into a bucket of water containing 4.0 L of water initially at 28°C. Calculate the final temperature of the mixture.

WORKSHEET 6

Modelling • Simulation

Electromagnetic radiation

1 Based solely on colour, identify the star below that is likely to be the hottest.

A An orange-looking star

B A yellow dwarf star similar to our Sun

C A red giant

D A blue giant

E There's insufficient information to make a decision

2 State the relationship between temperature and frequency for an energy-emitting body.

____

3 For an energy-emitting body, the wavelength of maximum intensity will get _____ as an object gets _____.

A hotter, shorter

B longer, hotter

C shorter, colder

D shorter, hotter

The following diagram describes the energy density versus wavelength curves for black-body radiation at various temperatures.

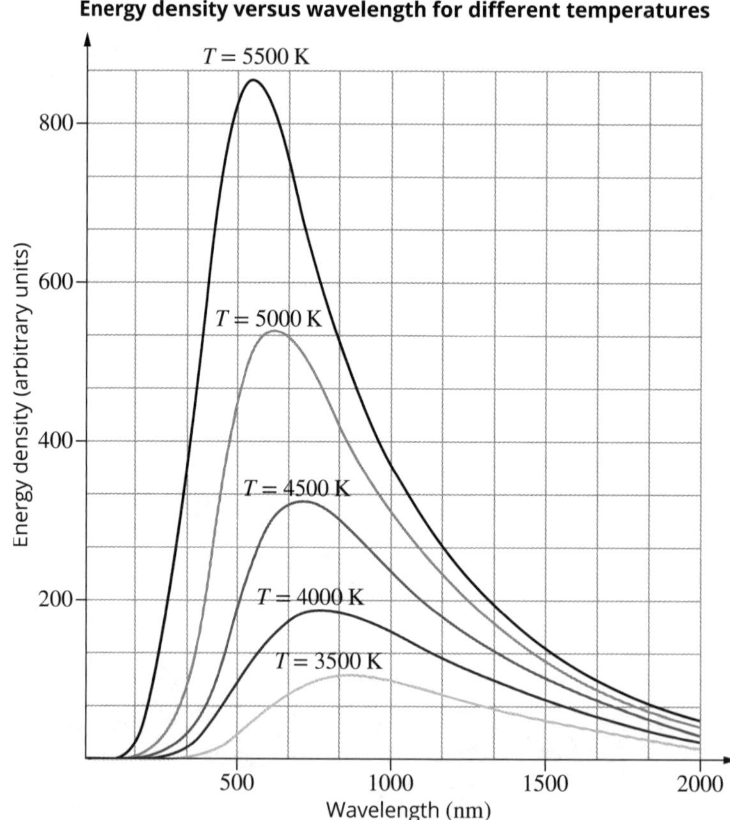

ISBN 978 0 6557 0016 6

4 Using Wien's law, calculate the expected peak wavelength for:

a 3500 K

b 4500 K

c 5500 K

5 Our Sun has a surface temperature of 5777 K. Calculate the peak wavelength and frequency of the Sun and describe what sort of light this is.

6 Wien's law is often referred to as 'Wien's displacement law'. Explain the reference to 'displacement' in this description.

7 The temperature of a healthy human body is approximately 37°C. Determine the wavelength of peak intensity emitted by the human body.

8 Three metal discs (A, B and C) of the same material and thickness, having a radius of 2 m, 4 m and 6 m, respectively, are coated with a non-reflective, black, graphite-based paint on the outer surface. The wavelengths of the emitted electromagnetic radiation from each disc, corresponding to the maximum intensity, are 300 nm, 400 nm and 500 nm, respectively. Based on the wavelengths:

A Disc A is at the highest temperature.

B Disc B is at the highest temperature.

C Disc C is at the highest temperature.

D The temperature of each is the same. It's unrelated to the emitted wavelength.

ISBN 978 0 6557 0016 6

WORKSHEET 7

Literature review • Modelling

Climate in the balance—the role of oceans and air in climate control

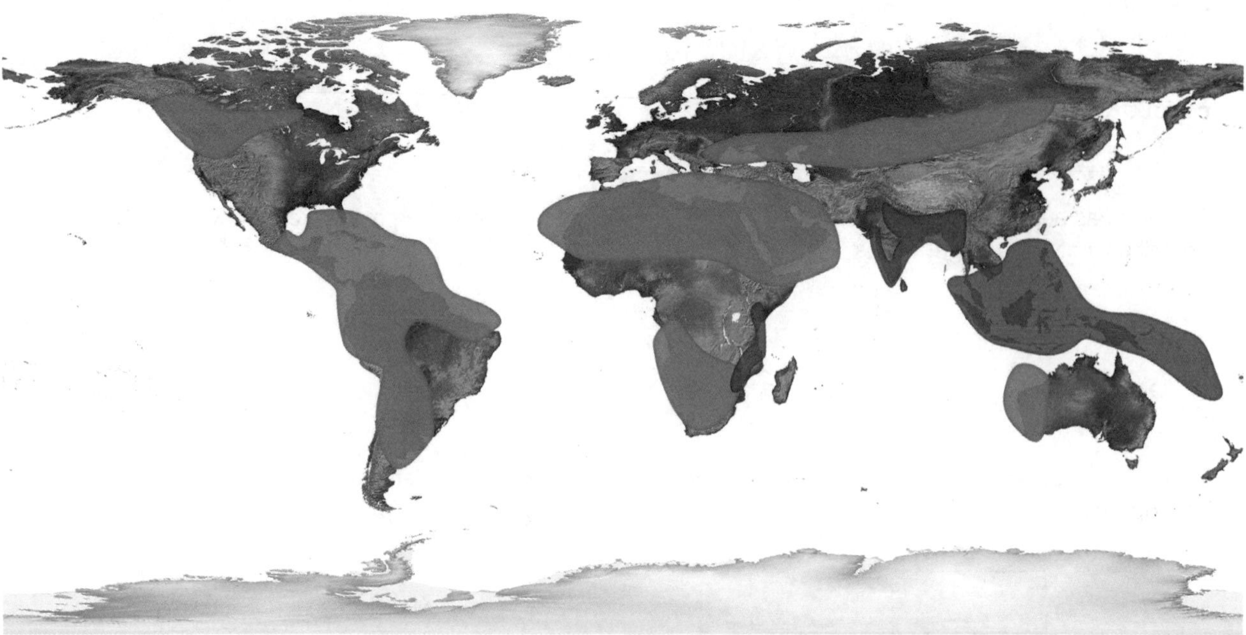

Water has a surprisingly high specific heat capacity: 10 times higher than most metals. The specific heat capacity of water is higher than for all but a very few uncommon materials. As a result, water makes a very useful cooling and heat storage agent. For example, it is used in generator cooling towers and car engine radiators.

Life on Earth depends on the specific heat capacity of water. About 70% of Earth's surface is covered by water, and our oceans are the primary regulator of global climate through absorption, storage and transport of heat energy.

To a large degree, our ability to understand what might happen to Earth's climate in the future depends on understanding the role of the oceans in maintaining and moderating climate change.

The following questions look at how much energy can be stored and transferred by the oceans.

1 How much energy does it take to heat 1 L of water by 1°C?

2 The oceans around the equator are exposed to direct sunlight for around 12 h every day. If the temperature of the top 1 cm of water over 1000 km^2 increases by an average 2°C from 26°C to 28°C in one day, how much heat energy has the water absorbed?

3 If this heat energy were to be released into the atmosphere overnight, calculate the volume of air that could be warmed by 1°C. Assume that all of the energy is transferred. Check suitable references to find out the volume of 1 kg of air and the specific heat capacity of air.

ISBN 978 0 6557 0016 6

4 The total mass of Earth's atmosphere has been estimated at 5.1×10^{18} kg. Assuming the air was of uniform composition, determine the change in temperature for the whole atmosphere from the release of this heat energy.

5 Since 1950, the temperature of the top 300 mm of the ocean's surface has risen by about 0.3°C. Over the last 50 years, more than 90% of the excess heat energy from human activities has been stored as excess energy in the ocean, amounting to a total of 2×10^{23} J. If this energy were to be suddenly released, calculate the average temperature change in Earth's atmosphere.

6 Assume now that this heat energy was instead used to heat ice from 0°C to water at 0°C. Determine the mass of melted ice.

7 A number of moderating influences mean these massive changes are not likely to happen. From your understanding of the movement of heat energy, explain the mechanisms behind heat transfer in Earth's atmosphere.

WORKSHEET 8

Classification and identification

Literacy review—energy

1 Complete the paragraph comparing electromagnetic radiation to wave behaviour using the word list supplied. A term may be used more than once.

speed	medium	frequency	refraction	wavelength	propagation

- When light passes from one _______________ to another, one property of electromagnetic radiation behaving as a transverse wave can be observed. _______________ is the same; however, _______________ and _______________ differ. _______________ is the change in direction of _______________ of a wave that occurs when there is a change in _______________ of the waves.

2 Complete the paragraph relating to thermodynamics using the word list supplied. Not every word will be used and some may be used more than once.

kinetic	potential	kelvin	Celsius	Fahrenheit	velocity	temperature	heat	energy

- Two common temperature scales used in science are the _______________ and _______________ scales. _______________ is related to the average _______________ energy of the particles in a material. _______________ energy depends upon the mass and _______________ of particles.

3 Complete the paragraph relating to thermodynamics using the word list supplied. Not every word will be used and some may be used more than once.

kinetic energy	thermal energy	cold	hot	transfer

- The word 'heat' is loosely used in common language. However, in science it specifically relates to the _______________ of _______________ from one material to another. Sometimes the term 'heat' is used interchangeably with the term '_______________'. _______________ is in fact the total amount of energy contained in a material. Heat is transferred spontaneously from a _______________ object to a _______________ object.

4 From the key knowledge of this area of study, your text or other suitable source, define each of the following means of heat transfer.

Conduction:

Convection:

Radiation:

5 The following paragraph explains the application of latent heat of vaporisation to variation in climate. Complete the paragraph from words and background found in the key knowledge section of this area of study.

- The transfer of _______________ during a _______________ change between liquid water and water vapour has a profound effect on our environment. The temperature doesn't cool much at night in regions of _______________ humidity. However, the temperature in deserts (_______________ humidity) quickly drops after the sun goes down. This is because regions of high humidity have lots of _______________ _______________ in the air. _______________ _______________ condensing back into a liquid releases _______________ to the air.

 ISBN 978 0 6557 0016 6

WORKSHEET 9

Reflection—How are light and heat explained?

The following table lists the key knowledge covered in this area of study.

1 Reflect on how well you understand the concepts listed. Rate your learning by shading the circle that corresponds to your current level of understanding for each one.

Key knowledge	Not confident ◄				► Very confident
Wave properties: the wave equation $\lambda = \frac{v}{f} = vT$, speed, frequency, period and wavelength	○	○	○	○	○
Electromagnetic waves: transverse waves, speed of light *c*, the electromagnetic spectrum	○	○	○	○	○
Refraction: Snell's law, total internal reflection, dispersion	○	○	○	○	○
Optical effects: rainbows, mirages	○	○	○	○	○
Temperature: units of measurement Celsius and kelvin, the kinetic energy model	○	○	○	○	○
Heat transfer: Conduction, convection and radiation	○	○	○	○	○
Specific heat capacity: $Q = mc\Delta T$	○	○	○	○	○
Latent heat: $Q = mL$, change of state	○	○	○	○	○
Internal energy: work done on or by the system	○	○	○	○	○
Wien's law: black-body radiation, $\lambda_{max}T$ = constant	○	○	○	○	○
Climate change and global warming: energy transfer, energy transformation, temperature change	○	○	○	○	○

2 Consider the points you have shaded from Not confident to Very confident. List specific ideas you can identify that were challenging.

____

____

____

3 Write down two different strategies that you will apply to help further your understanding of these ideas.

____

____

____

PRACTICAL ACTIVITY 1

Experiment • Modelling

Waves in slinky springs and ropes

SUGGESTED DURATION

- 50 minutes

MATERIALS

- springs of various diameters and materials (e.g. different types of slinky spring)
- 1 to 2 m length of string or light rope
- strings or light ropes between 5 m and 10 m in length and of varying mass per metre

INTRODUCTION

The particles affected by the motion of a transverse waves move perpendicular to the direction of the wave. Particles affected by a longitudinal wave move in the same direction as the movement of the wave. The transfer of energy through a longitudinal or transverse wave is affected by the medium in which it travels.

AIM

To investigate some simple properties of longitudinal and transverse waves and the effect of different mediums on the propagation of the wave.

Safety

Metal slinky springs can be easily damaged by use that is too vigorous or tangling. Handle with care.

Take care to avoid catching hair or fingers in the coils of the springs. Complete a risk assessment before starting the activity.

METHOD

1. Lay the larger or heavier slinky spring flat on the floor in a clear space. With each end held by a student, stretch the spring until it is taut but not overly stretched.
2. One student generates a transverse pulse by whipping their hand out and back along the floor and at right angles to the line of the spring. Observe and comment on what happens to the pulse as it travels down the spring and reflects from the fixed end.

   ____

   ____

   ____

3. Repeat with the smaller spring and describe what happens. Pay particular attention to any difference between the movement and reflection of the pulse in the smaller and larger springs.

   ____

   ____

   ____

4. Now attach the piece of string to the end of the heavier spring. Stretch the spring and string out between two people without over-stretching the spring. Send a single pulse down the spring. Describe what you observe at the join between the spring and the string.

   ____

   ____

5. Remove the string and stretch out one of the springs between two students.

 ISBN 978 0 6557 0016 6

6 ▪ Create a longitudinal pulse by asking one student to move their hand holding the spring sharply back and forth along the length of the spring (longitudinally). Observe what happens as the pulse travels down the spring and reflects off the fixed end. Compare your observations with the behaviour of the transverse wave.

7 ▪ Join the two springs together and stretch them out along the floor.

8 ▪ Keeping the end of the heavier spring fixed, generate a transverse pulse in the smaller spring. Observe and sketch what happens to the pulse as it reaches the point where the two springs join.

9 ▪ Repeat the previous step, this time generating the pulse in the heavier spring while keeping the end of the smaller spring fixed. Describe the differences you observe.

10 ▪ Fix one end of a long rope. For example, tie it to a nail in a wall or the handle of a door. Hold the other end with your hand and take up the slack in the rope without pulling it tight. Tie a small ribbon or rubber band anywhere along the rope. (It doesn't have to be in the centre, but don't make it too close to either end.)

11 ▪ Moving your hand up and down sharply, flick the rope to produce a single transverse pulse that travels along the rope. Observe closely the movement of the point in the rope that you have marked with the ribbon. Describe the movement of the ribbon.

12 ▪ Repeat the activity with ropes of varying mass per metre and composition.

13 ▪ Describe what happens to the pulse in the rope when it reaches the fixed end.

14 ▪ Now tie a loop at the end of the rope around a thin, upright object such as the leg of a desk so that the rope is free to move up and down. Once again, flick the rope to produce a single transverse pulse that travels along the rope.

15 ▪ Describe what you observe when the pulse in the rope reaches the fixed end.

PRACTICAL ACTIVITY 1

DISCUSSION

1 In this practical activity, the waves generated have been referred to as pulses. Explain why the term 'pulse' is appropriate.

2 Try holding the rope at different tensions. Discuss whether the tension in the rope has any effect on the speed of the pulse along the rope.

3 Based on your observations, determine whether the speed of the pulse is affected by the mass or diameter of the rope.

4 Determine whether the direction of travel of the point marked with the ribbon is different from the direction of propagation of the pulse itself. Describe your observations.

5 List examples of naturally occurring transverse and longitudinal waves.

CONCLUSION

ISBN 978 0 6557 0016 6

PRACTICAL ACTIVITY 2

Experiment • Modelling

Dispersion and refraction

SUGGESTED DURATION

- 50 minutes

INTRODUCTION

This method provides a higher-level option to determining the refractive index of particular colours of light for a material based on dispersion through a triangular prism.

A prism is an optical element with polished, flat edges that refract light. When light travels from air to the material of the prism, it is refracted or bent from its original path. The degree of bending of the light's path depends on the angle that the incident beam of light makes with the surface of the prism, and on the ratio between the refractive indices of the air and the prism material. This is referred to as Snell's law. That is:

$n_1 \sin \theta_i = n_2 \sin \theta_r$

where:

n_1 is the refractive index of the first material
θ_i is the angle of incidence (°)
n_2 is the refractive index of the second material
θ_r is the angle of refraction (°).

The refractive index of many materials varies with the wavelength of the light used. This phenomenon is called dispersion. It causes light of different colours to be refracted differently and can be used to separate a beam of white light into its constituent spectrum of colours.

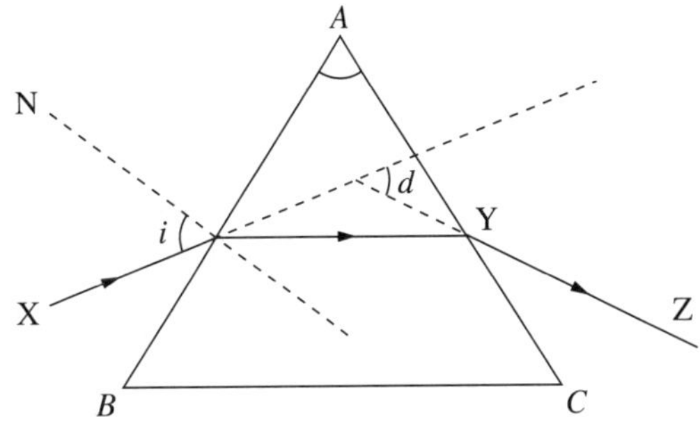

A ray of light refracts twice on passing through a prism: once on entry and again on exit. The angle through which the final ray deviates from the direction of the original incident ray is called the angle of deviation, *d*, and is a measure of the overall refraction through the prism. The figure to the right shows how this can be measured.

Because the different wavelengths of visible light have different refractive indices, the angle of deviation will vary with wavelength. Shorter wavelengths (e.g. blue) will deviate more from their original path than colours with longer wavelengths (e.g. red).

As the angle of incidence is increased, the angle of deviation, *d*, will decrease until it reaches a minimum value. If the angle of incidence is increased further, the angle of deviation will increase. At the minimum angle of deviation:

- the angle of incidence of the light ray, *i*, will be identical to the angle of refraction of the exit angle of the light ray
- a plane mirror placed at right angles to the exiting light ray will cause the reflection to exactly retrace its original path
- the ray of light passing through the prism is parallel to the base of the prism.

If *D* is the angle of minimum deviation, then the refractive index, *n*, for the particular wavelength of light for the material of the prism can be found from:

$$n = \frac{\sin\frac{(A+D)}{2}}{\sin\frac{A}{2}}$$

where *A* is the internal angle at the corner of the prism between the incident and deviated light.

Hence, by finding the minimum angle of deviation, the refractive index can be found for particular colours of light.

PRACTICAL ACTIVITY 2

AIM

To determine the refractive indices of a triangular prism for red and blue light by the dispersion of white light.

Safety

Laser-based light boxes or pen lasers can give more consistent results. However, take care to not shine the light directly into a person's eyes. Complete a risk assessment before starting the activity.

MATERIALS

- light box and power supply
- glass and/or Perspex triangular prisms
- lightly sticking masking tape or 'magic tape'
- grid paper
- plane mirror
- ruler
- protractor

METHOD

1. Connect the ray box to the power supply, turn it on and adjust it so that the ray box produces one thin ray of white light. The ray should be as thin as possible.
2. Set the prism on a sheet of plain white, grid or graph paper. A grid is helpful for tracing the rays and measuring angles. A suitable grid is included in the Results section. Make sure that the prism is flat and stable, and that the base of the prism is parallel to the grid. Stick the prism to the paper to maintain this orientation.
3. Using a protractor or from the information supplied with the prism, record the angle A, in the diagram of the prism. This is the internal angle of the prism for the corner between the incident and refracted light.
4. Using a protractor, draw a normal (right-angle line) from around the centre of the prism on one side of the prism. It should look similar to line N in the diagram. This will help you measure the angle of incidence.
5. Align the ray box to shine the single beam through the prism so that the light passes right through the prism at the point where the normal line meets the prism. Describe the effect the prism has on the beam of white light.

6. Identify the colour of visible light that is deviated the least and the colour that is deviated the most. Recall whether this is what you would expect from theory.

7. Starting with the light from the ray box incident on the prism at an incident angle close to 90° below the normal, slowly move the ray box so that the incident angle decreases until it is at 0° to the prism (i.e. normal to the prism). Continue until the beam is close to 90° above the normal. Describe what happened to the light as it passed through the prism as the angle of incidence was changed.

8. Return the ray box to a position where the incident angle is close to 90° below the normal. Slowly move the ray box, keeping the ray of light incident on the normal line, until the red (top) side beam through the prism is parallel to the base of the prism. Use the grid lines on the paper to assist in determining that the beam is parallel. Recall the significance of this angle.

ISBN 978 0 6557 0016 6

PRACTICAL ACTIVITY 2

9. Draw a line marking the line of the incident beam through the prism and the line of the exiting beam back through the prism. Measure the angle of minimum deviation, *D*, in the diagram, and record it in the results table for red light. Record the uncertainty in the measurement.
10. Repeat steps 8 and 9 at least three times to confirm the angle.
11. Repeat steps 8 and 9 for the blue (bottom) side of the beam. Measure and record the angle of minimum deviation, *D*, in the results table as the minimum angle of deviation for blue light. Record the uncertainty in the measurement.
12. Keeping the ray box in position at the minimum angle of deviation for blue light, hold a plane mirror at right angles to the emergent ray such that the mirror reflects the emergent beam back into the prism. Describe the path that the light takes back through the prism.

____

RESULTS

List the variables in this experiment:

Independent: ______________________________

Dependent: ______________________________

Controlled: ______________________________

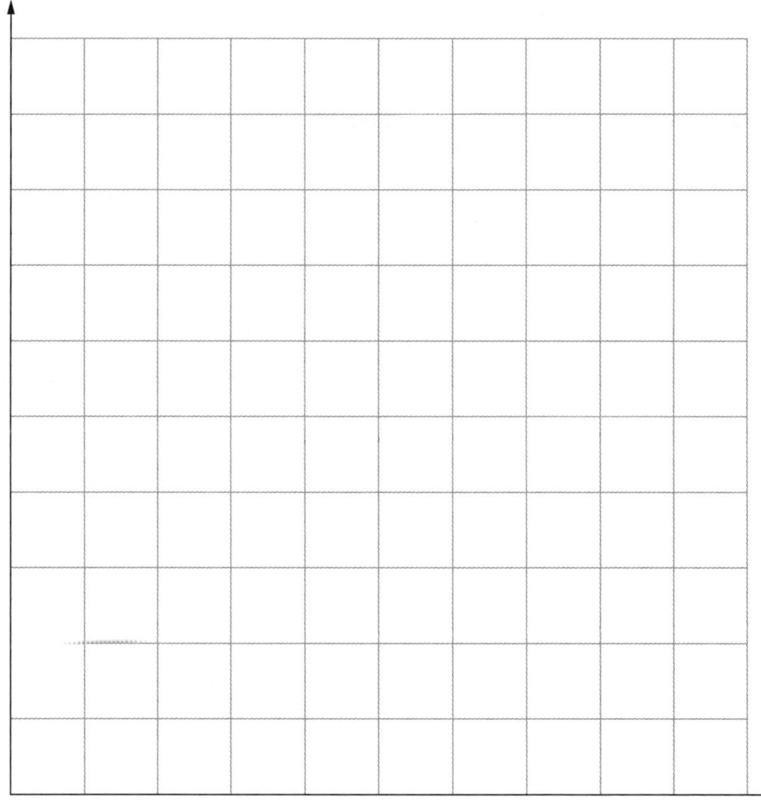

PRACTICAL ACTIVITY 2

Colour	Angle A of the prism	$\frac{A}{2}$	Minimum angle of deviation D_1 (°)	Minimum angle of deviation D_2 (°)	Minimum angle of deviation D_3 (°)	Minimum angle of deviation D_4 (°)	Average D (°)	$\frac{A+D}{2}$	n_λ
red	±	±	±	±	±	±	±	±	±
blue	±	±	±	±	±	±	±	±	±

1 Using the angle A and the average angle of deviation of the four trials, D, calculate and record in the results table values for $\frac{A}{2}$ and $\frac{A+D}{2}$, including the uncertainty in each ratio.

2 Calculate the refractive index for the prism for both red and blue light and record it in the results table.

Note: While outside the general scope of this course, the uncertainty in sin x can be found by multiplying cos x (in radians) by the uncertainty in the angle. Consult your calculator's instruction manual for using angles in radians. Don't forget to change back to degrees for other calculations!

DISCUSSION

1 Find out the expected refractive index for the material of the prism used in the experiment. This is usually quoted for a particular colour of light. Compare your results with the accepted value.

2 Compare the experimentally determined refractive indices of red and blue light. Discuss the extent to which the experimental values compare with those expected from theory.

3 Describe the major sources of error in this experiment and suggest methods by which they could be reduced.

CONCLUSION

ISBN 978 0 6557 0016 6

PRACTICAL ACTIVITY 3

Experiment • Modelling • Simulation

Measuring the speed of light

SUGGESTED DURATION

- 50 minutes

MATERIALS

- microwave oven with a turntable
- packet or two of marshmallows—you can also use a large chocolate block or choc chips
- microwave-safe plate or dish
- ruler
- heatproof gloves

INTRODUCTION

Today, manufacturers of high-quality science equipment produce apparatus for the laboratory measurement of the speed of light. These rely on the high-speed measurement of the reflection of monochromatic light over a measured distance or Foucault's method of rotating and fixed mirrors.

There is a simpler method which, while making some assumptions, can determine the speed of light with reasonable precision based on light's wave-like behaviour.

AIM

To determine the speed of light based on light's wave-like behaviour.

Since microwaves are a form of electromagnetic radiation, as is visible light, the speed of microwave radiation can be used to determine the speed of light.

Safety

Take care to ensure the microwave is closed before turning on. Do not leave metal objects inside. Carefully follow all other manufacturer's safety guidelines.

Materials will be very hot when being removed. Use appropriate safety apparatus, including heatproof gloves.

METHOD

1. Remove the turntable from the microwave.
2. Open the bag of marshmallows and arrange them in the base of the dish, completely covering it with one layer of the marshmallows. If you're using chocolate blocks, break the block up and arrange the individual squares in a similar way.
3. Place the dish in the microwave and cook on a low power level. Microwaves don't heat evenly and normally require something like a turntable to ensure that the heat is distributed evenly. As the dish isn't being rotated, the marshmallows will begin to melt unevenly, melting more quickly in the 'hottest' parts of the oven. Continue to heat the marshmallows or chocolate until around four or five distinct, melted spots are observed.
4. Carefully remove the dish from the microwave using the heatproof gloves to avoid being burnt. Allow the dish to cool.
5. Using the ruler, measure the distance between two nearby melted spots and record them in the following table. Repeat this for the distance between two different melted spots until you have filled the table.
6. Record an estimate of the error in each of your distance measurements. Record your results in the table.
7. Recall that the velocity of a wave is given by $v = f\lambda$, or for the speed of light, $c = f\lambda$. The frequency of the microwaves in the oven will be recorded on the specifications panel fixed to the back or side of the microwave oven. Record this in the table.

RESULTS

Distance between melted spots (cm)	Measurement uncertainty (cm)	Distance between melted spots × 2 (m)	Microwave frequency (Hz)	Speed of light c (m s^{-1})

ISBN 978 0 6557 0016 6

PRACTICAL ACTIVITY 3

1 The distance between melted spots corresponds to half the wavelength of the microwaves. Explain why this is the case. Use a diagram to support your explanation.

2 Using twice the distance between melted spots as the wavelength of the microwaves, in metres, calculate the speed of light for each pair of melted spots. Record the average value.

DISCUSSION

1 Compare your determination of the speed of light with the currently accepted value for the speed of light in air.

2 Comment on the reliability of conclusions you can draw from this investigation.

CONCLUSION

ISBN 978 0 6557 0016 6

PRACTICAL ACTIVITY 4

Experiment

The relationship between temperature and heat

SUGGESTED DURATION

- 50 minutes

INTRODUCTION

Heat is defined as energy that is transferred between two or more objects by way of thermal interaction (conduction, radiation or convection). The heat energy in an object is a representation of the total kinetic energy of all the particles that make up the object.

Temperature is a physical measurement of how 'hot' or 'cold' a substance is based on the average kinetic energy of particles in the substance. The amount of heat energy in an object is related to temperature, but temperature by itself is not a measure of the thermal energy (heat) in an object. Identical thermometers in two pots of water on a hotplate will show different temperatures if the amount of water in each pot is different, even if the pots have been on the hotplate for the same time.

AIM

To examine the relationship between temperature and heat.

Safety

Do not directly touch hot items, such as the hotplate, beaker or water.

Keep boiling water away from other electrical equipment, such as computers.

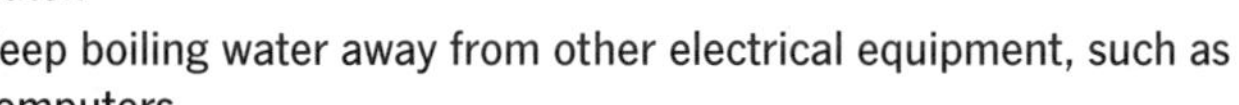

Wear a lab coat, goggles and gloves as recommended by your teacher.

MATERIALS

- digital thermometer or temperature sensor and data logger (use 2 or more temperature sensors for concurrent measurement)
- electronic balance (1 per classroom)
- 2 × 100 mL beakers, such as Pyrex or calorimeter
- hotplate or heating coil
- 250 mL water
- stopwatch (not required with data logger)
- heatproof gloves
- retort stand and clamp (2 required if measuring concurrently)

METHOD

1. Using the electronic balance, measure and record the mass of each beaker in the space provided in the Results section. Preheat the hotplate. If the plate has a temperature control, set it to a maximum of around 80°C. There's no need for higher temperatures in this experiment.
2. Fill one beaker with around 40 mL of water and the other with 60 mL of water.
3. Measure and record the mass of each of the beakers, including the water.
4. Carefully place the beaker containing 40 mL of water on the hotplate. Use the retort stand and clamp to secure the digital thermometer or temperature sensor so that the tip of the thermometer can be submerged in the water without touching the wall or bottom of the beaker.
5. Using a stopwatch or the options in your data logger, note and record the temperature of the water at 30 s intervals in the table below for 5 min. Alternatively, print out the data from your data logger and paste it over the table.
6. Stop recording data and turn off the hotplate after the 5 min heating period.
7. Using the heatproof glove, carefully remove the first beaker and repeat steps 1 and 2 for the beaker containing 60 mL of water. Record your data in Table 1. Note: if you have two thermometers or temperature sensors, you can record both beakers at the same time.

PRACTICAL ACTIVITY 4

RESULTS

Mass of beaker in test 1: ______

Mass of beaker and water in test 1: ______

Mass of beaker in test 2: ______

Mass of beaker and water in test 2: ______

Time (s)	Temperature 1 (°C)	Temperature 2 (°C)
0		
30		
60		
90		
120		
150		
180		
210		
240		
270		
300		
330		
360		
390		

1 Calculate the mass of the water for each test.

______

2 Plot the data for each test on the same set of axes in the graph space below, with time on the horizontal axis and temperature on the vertical axis. Label the axes, include units and add a title for your graph. If you're using a data logger, you may prefer to print out your graph and stick it over the space provided.

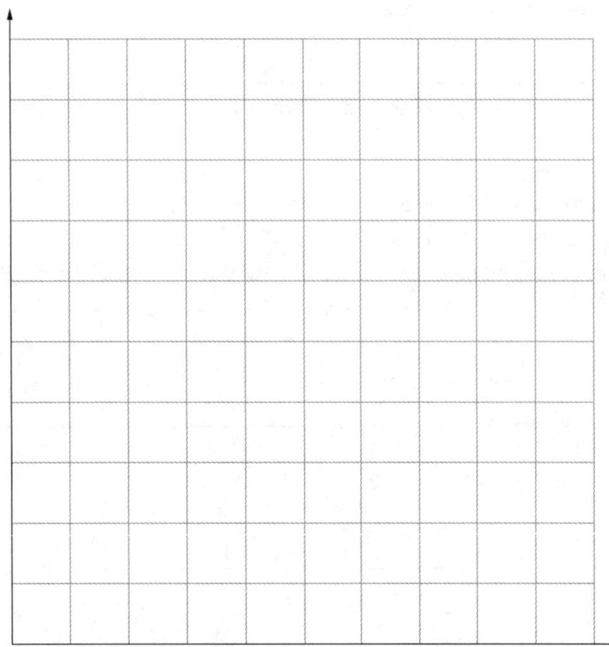

ISBN 978 0 6557 0016 6

3 Draw a line of best fit for each graph and calculate the gradient for each line.

4 Assess how the gradient and temperature change for test 1 (40 mL of water) compares with test 2 (60 mL of water).

5 Considering your answer to the previous question, explain why the final temperature of test 1 is higher than that for test 2.

DISCUSSION

1 The aim of the experiment was to determine the relationship between temperature and heat. Summarise your findings, including the relationship between time and temperature for each test.

2 Considering your analysis and conclusion, appraise the experimental method you followed as a means of determining the relationship between heating time and temperature of the water.

3 Devise an alternative method to improve the experiment.

CONCLUSION

PRACTICAL ACTIVITY 5

Experiment

Determining the specific heat capacity of a substance

SUGGESTED DURATION

- 50 minutes

MATERIALS

- thermometer or temperature sensor and data logger
- electronic balance (1 per classroom)
- hotplate
- 600 mL beaker
- crucible tongs
- 3–5 calorimetry cups
- 1 L water
- 5 metal samples (at least 5 different masses of the same metal)
- 5 × 15-cm pieces of string
- retort stands and clamps

INTRODUCTION

The amount of energy added to (or taken away from) a substance is proportional to the change in its temperature, its mass and its specific heat capacity.

The mathematical relationship between the heat energy transferred, Q, and temperature change, ΔT, for a substance of mass m is given by:

$Q = mc\Delta T$

where:

Q is the heat energy transferred in joules (J)
m is the mass of material being heated in kilograms (kg)
ΔT is the change in temperature (°C or K)
c is the specific heat capacity of the material ($J\,kg^{-1}\,K^{-1}$).

In this experiment, a metal sample is heated by placing it in a beaker of boiling water. The temperature of the metal will increase as it absorbs energy from the water. The metal sample is then placed in a calorimeter cup and the temperature logged as the water in the cup and the sample reach equilibrium.

By measuring the change in temperature in the water before the metal is added, and as it comes to equilibrium, it is possible to find the heat energy given to the metal by the water. By measuring the metal's mass and change in temperature, its specific heat capacity can be found.

AIM

To derive the specific heat capacity of an unknown metal.

Safety

When using the hotplate, be very careful not to burn your hands or fingers.

Use a 600 mL borosilicate glass beaker for boiling water. Other beakers may shatter when exposed to high heat.

Boiling water can cause severe burns. Be very careful when using boiling water, and do not carry the beaker without insulated gloves or tongs when it is hot.

All glass beakers can break when dropped. Be very careful not to drop any of the glassware used in this lab. If an accident does occur, follow the proper cleaning and disposal procedure instituted by your teacher.

Before you commence this practical activity, conduct a risk assessment.

METHOD

1 ▪ Create a hot-water bath by filling the beaker three-quarters full of water and placing the beaker on the hotplate. Note: To speed up this step, fill the beaker with hot water from a kettle or classroom system.

2 ▪ Set the hotplate temperature to boil the water in the beaker.

3 ▪ Use the balance to measure the mass and its uncertainty for the empty calorimetry cups. Record these measurements in the first table in the Results section.

4 ▪ Add equal amounts of cold water to the calorimetry cups (so they are approximately three-quarters full), and record the mass and its uncertainty of each calorimeter cup and water in the Results section. Note: Do not overfill the calorimeter. If you do, water will spill over the edge of the cup when you submerge the metal sample.

5 ▪ Record the mass of each metal sample, and its uncertainty, in the first table in the Results section.

ISBN 978 0 6557 0016 6

6 ▪ Tie a 15-cm piece of string to each metal sample. Tie the other end of the string to a retort stand so that the metal samples are suspended in the hot water in the beaker, rather than touching the bottom of the beaker. Allow them to equilibrate for 5–10 min. Explain why this is important.

____

7 ▪ Set up your data logger following the manufacturer's instructions (if available) and, using the temperature sensor or thermometer, measure the temperature of the hot water and metal samples. Record the temperature and the uncertainty in temperature measurement in the first table in the Results section.

8 ▪ Place the thermometer or sensor in the first calorimeter and let it stabilise. Measure the temperature of the water and record it in the first table in the Results section.

9 ▪ Start recording the temperature and then, quickly but carefully, transfer the first metal sample to the first calorimeter cup, being careful not to directly touch the sensing end of the thermometer or sensor. Record the temperature for around 2 min (at 10 s intervals if doing this manually) until the temperature reaches equilibrium. Record the final temperature in the first table in the Results section.

10 ▪ Repeat steps 8 and 9 for the remaining metal samples and calorimeters, recording the final temperature for each, once the temperature stabilises. Note: If you do not have sufficient calorimeters to go around, empty out the warmed water and metal sample, refill with cold water and record the mass as before, then once again transfer the metal samples and record the temperature change.

RESULTS

List the variables in this experiment

Independent: _______________

Dependent: _______________

Controlled: _______________

Uncertainty in measurement of mass: ± _______________ kg

Uncertainty in measurement of temperature: ± _______________ °C

1 Calculate the mass of the water in the calorimeter for each sample:

mass of water = mass of water & cup – mass of cup

2 Calculate the uncertainty in the mass from the uncertainty in the individual measurements. For VCE physics you do not need to calculate the uncertainty in Q.

Sample	m_{cup} (kg)	$m_{water + cup}$ (kg)	m_{water} (kg)	Uncertainty in m (kg)	$T_{initial}$ (°C)	T_{final} (°C)	ΔT (°C)	Uncertainty (°C)	Q (J)
1									
2									
3									
4									
5									

3 Use the mass and temperature data to find the energy gained by the water for each sample and complete the table above. Use $c_{water} = 4200\,\text{J kg}^{-1}\,\text{K}^{-1}$ and $Q = mc\Delta T$.

ISBN 978 0 6557 0016 6

4 Based on the energy gained by the water, complete the table below by calculating the specific heat capacity for the metal for each sample and the average of the five samples.

Sample	m (kg)	Uncertainty in m (kg)	$T_{initial}$ (°C)	T_{final} (°C)	ΔT (°C)	% uncertainty in ΔT	Q_{water} (J) (from previous table)	c_{metal} (J kg^{-1} K^{-1})
1								
2								
3								
4								
5								
Average								

DISCUSSION

1 The aim of the experiment was to determine the specific heat capacity of the five metal samples and hence the average. State the average value. Based on the value you found, and the table of known specific heat capacities in the key knowledge section on page 6, determine the type of metal.

2 Assess the reliability of your result based on the comparison with the known value for the particular metal. Discuss other attributes of the metal that helped your decision.

3 Explain some of the factors that may have caused your calculated values for specific heat, c, to be different from the accepted figure.

ISBN 978 0 6557 0016 6

4 Discuss some options for improving the methodology for this experiment.

CONCLUSION

PRACTICAL ACTIVITY 6

Experiment

Latent heat of fusion

SUGGESTED DURATION

- 50 minutes

MATERIALS

- data logger and temperature sensor (or thermometer and stopwatch)
- 600 mL beaker
- calorimetry cup
- electronic balance (one per class)
- hotplate
- stirring rod (temperature sensor can be used instead) or stir station
- 300 mL water
- 3 or 4 ice cubes
- paper towel

INTRODUCTION

Heat is the energy that is transferred from one substance to another as a result of a difference in their temperature. In addition to changing the temperature of a substance, heat can also break intermolecular bonds, causing the substance to change phase. When this happens, no energy goes into changing the temperature of the substance; it is all used to alter the intermolecular bonds within the substance. The heat energy required for a substance to change phase from a solid to a liquid is given by:

$$\Delta Q = mL_{\text{fusion}}$$

where:

ΔQ is the change in energy (J)
m is the mass of the substance changing phase (kg)
L_{fusion} is the latent heat of fusion of the substance (J kg^{-1}).

The latent heat of a substance is the amount of energy required to turn the substance from a solid to a liquid. Like the specific heat of a substance, the latent heat of fusion depends on the type of substance and its ability to absorb heat while it changes phase.

AIM

To determine the latent heat of fusion of water.

Safety

Keep water away from sensitive electronic equipment.
Be careful using the hotplate. Always be aware that it is on, and be conscious of any loose clothing or papers that could accidently melt or catch fire if left in contact with the hotplate.

METHOD

1. Heat 300 mL of water to approximately 40°C in the beaker on the hotplate.
2. If you are using a data logger, start a new experiment, connect the temperature sensor to the data logger, and choose a digital display of temperature.
3. Carefully measure the mass of the calorimetry cup, and record this value in the table in the Results section.
4. Fill the calorimetry cup three-quarters full with hot water (at approximately 40°C), then quickly, but accurately, measure the mass of the filled cup, and record this in the table in the Results section.
5. Insert the thermometer or temperature sensor into the calorimetry cup and allow the temperature to stabilise. Record the initial temperature (as accurately as possible with your equipment) in the table in the Results section. Include an estimate of the uncertainty.
6. Dry off 3 or 4 ice cubes with the paper towel and then place the ice cubes into the cup, stirring slowly until the ice completely melts. Continue stirring for an additional minute to ensure that the water has reached equilibrium. Record the final temperature of the water in the cup in the table.
7. Remove the thermometer or temperature sensor from the calorimetry cup and use the balance to measure the total mass of the cup, initial water and melted ice. Record this value in the table along with the uncertainty in each measurement.

ISBN 978 0 6557 0016 6

RESULTS

Item	Value	Uncertainty
mass of calorimetry cup	kg	± kg
mass of calorimeter and initial water	kg	± kg
mass of initial water, m_{water}	kg	± kg
mass of cup, initial water and melted ice	kg	± kg
mass of ice, m_{ice}	kg	± kg
initial temperature of water in the cup, $T_{initial}$	°C	± °C
final temperature of water in the cup, T_{final}	°C	± °C
initial temperature of ice	°C	± °C
temperature of melted ice	°C	± °C
temperature change of water	°C	± °C
temperature change of melted ice	°C	± °C

1 Identify the sign (positive or negative) of the temperature change calculated. Identify what the sign signifies.

2 Assuming that the specific heat capacity of water, *c*, is $4200\,J\,kg^{-1}\,K^{-1}$, use the values from the above table to find the heat energy transferred from the water initially in the cup.

3 Using the values calculated in the table, determine how much of the heat transferred out of the water in the cup went into warming the melted ice to the final temperature.

4 If the energy needed to warm the melted ice does not account for all the heat transferred from the water, deduce where the additional heat went. Using the results of your previous calculations, determine the amount of additional energy lost by the water that did not go into warming the melted ice.

5 Assume instead that all of the remaining energy can be attributed to the melting ice. Using the mass of the ice, calculate the latent heat of fusion of water.

6 If the theoretical value for the latent heat of fusion for water is $3.34 \times 10^5\,J\,kg^{-1}$, calculate the percentage difference between the experimentally determined value and the theoretical value. Use the following formula:

$$\text{percentage difference} = \frac{\text{theoretical value} - \text{experimental value}}{\text{theoretical value}} \times 100\%$$

DISCUSSION

1 Compare the experimentally determined value for the latent heat of fusion for water with the accepted theoretical value. Comment on the reliability of your answer with reference to the calculated percentage difference.

2 Explain why you dried the ice cubes before you placed them in the beaker.

3 Identify the source of the heat energy that melted the ice.

4 Discuss the assumption made in this experiment about the initial temperature of the ice.

5 Identify other assumptions that were made about energy transfer in conducting this experiment, and assess their likely effect on your final result.

6 Keeping these assumptions in mind, discuss improvements to the procedure that could lead to a more reliable experimental result.

CONCLUSION

ISBN 978 0 6557 0016 6

EXAM-STYLE QUESTIONS

Multiple-choice questions

Question 1

Identify which of the following forms of electromagnetic radiation has the *shortest* wavelength in a vacuum.

A. radio

B. ultraviolet

C. X-ray

D. microwave

Question 2

The following statements describe what happens to key properties of electromagnetic radiation as a wave, as light passes from a less dense medium to a denser medium. Identify the correct statement.

A. The wavelength is reduced, while the frequency and velocity remain the same.

B. The wavelength and velocity are reduced, while the frequency remains the same.

C. The frequency is reduced, while the wavelength and velocity remain the same.

D. The frequency is reduced, while the wavelength and velocity increase.

Question 3

The diagram below shows a ray of light, X, reaching the boundary between water and glass.

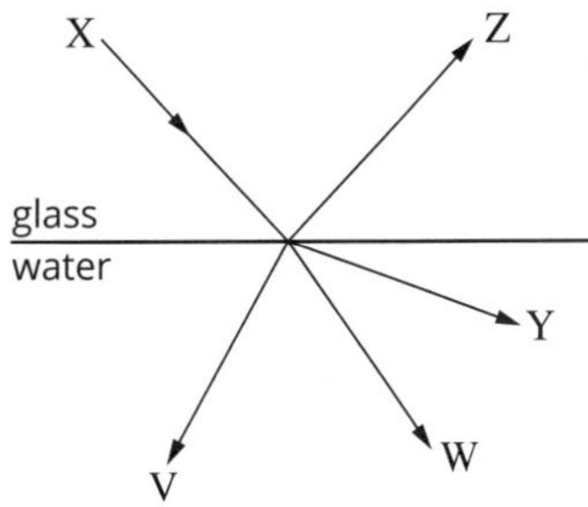

Identify which of the following paths could be taken by rays of light that have reached the water–glass boundary.

A. Y only

B. Y and V

C. Y and Z

D. W and Z

Question 4

A vacuum flask has a reflective coating of aluminium on the internal surfaces of a sealed vacuum space. This 'silvered' surface reduces heat transfer by:

A. radiation

B. convection

C. conduction

D. all of the above

EXAM-STYLE QUESTIONS

Question 5

Identify which of the following is the best example of heat transfer by conduction.

A. heat transfer from the Sun to Earth

B. heat transfer from the bottom of the ocean to the top

C. heat transfer from Earth's crust to the layer below (the mantle)

D. heat transfer from Earth's surface to the upper atmosphere

Question 6

Water is poured into a stainless-steel pot, which is heated over a gas flame. As the water at the bottom of the pan is heated, it begins to rise to the surface. Identify the correct order of heat transfer during this entire process.

A. conduction, convection, radiation

B. convection, conduction, radiation

C. radiation, convection, conduction

D. radiation, conduction, convection

Short-answer questions

Question 1 (3 marks)

Isaac Newton famously passed white light through a prism and showed that light was composed of many different colours. This phenomenon is known as dispersion and is due to different colours of light having slightly differing refractive indices in most transparent materials. For example, in crown glass, violet light ($\lambda = 400$ nm) has a refractive index of 1.53, whereas red light ($\lambda = 700$ nm) has a refractive index of 1.51.

The diagram below depicts the ideal image formation of a star on a white screen using a lens made of crown glass.

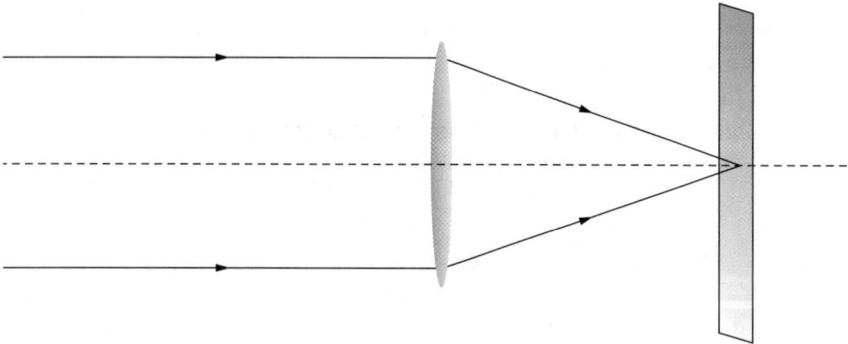

a. If we assume that the rays depicted are produced by a wavelength of 450 nm, draw the paths taken by the red and the violet light. (You will need to exaggerate the rays.) 2 marks

b. Describe the effect this will have on the star's image. 1 mark

 ISBN 978 0 6557 0016 6

EXAM-STYLE QUESTIONS

Question 2 (4 marks)

Light travels down a fibre-optic cable by reflecting repeatedly off the walls at a shallow angle that is less than the critical angle for the material. The light travels through the core of the fibre. Bonded around the core is another layer called the cladding, which ensures that the light stays within the core. The cladding does this because it is made of glass with a lower refractive index than the glass core.

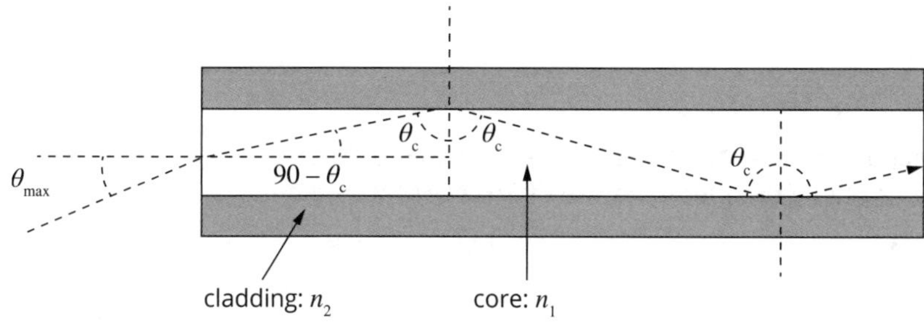

The core of a particular glass fibre-optic cable has a refractive index of 1.48. The cladding material has a lower refractive index of 1.46. Determine the sharpest angle at which the fibre-optic cable can be bent and the light still remain in the cable.

Question 3 (2 marks)

Another fibre-optic cable has a core with a refractive index of 1.65. Around this core, the cladding has a refractive index of 1.35. Calculate the critical angle for this fibre-optic cable.

Question 4 (2 marks)

Based on your answers to questions 2 and 3, decide on the cable that would be the most flexible for use in a general-purpose communications network. Justify your answer with reference to the previous answers. Suggest other considerations that would need to be given to the choice of cable.

Question 5 (1 mark)

If the particles within two objects have the same average kinetic energy, explain whether the two objects will be at the same temperature.

EXAM-STYLE QUESTIONS

Question 6 (2 marks)

A thermometer is supplied with no markings. Describe the process you would go through to produce a calibrated scale. State whether your scale would be arbitrary or absolute.

Question 7 (3 marks)

Determine how much energy, in joules, is needed to raise the temperature of 100 kg of water from a room temperature of 20.0°C to a comfortable bath temperature of 35.0°C. (Assume no losses to the surrounding environment.)

Question 8 (1 mark)

Energy must be supplied to ice for it to melt. The temperature of the resulting water is no higher than the temperature of the original ice. Explain.

Question 9 (10 marks)

A 200 g sample of naphthalene is heated carefully in a closed glass vessel, in which all the fumes can be safely contained and the energy inputs can be accurately measured. The heating curve below was produced as a result of the measurements.

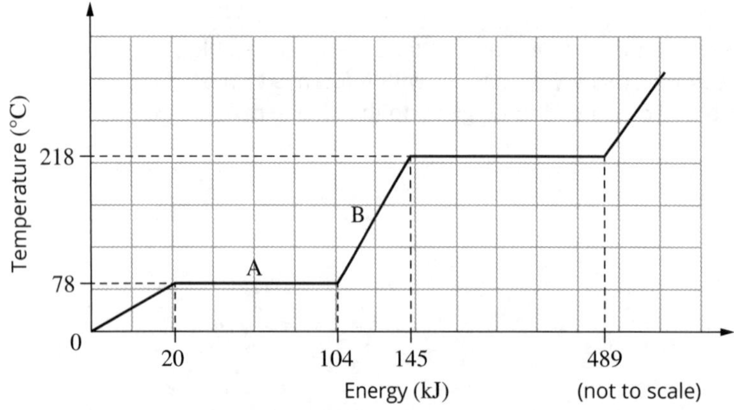

a. Recall the states of matter of the naphthalene in sections A and B. 2 marks

 ISBN 978 0 6557 0016 6

EXAM-STYLE QUESTIONS

Use the information on the graph to complete parts b to e by calculating the following values for naphthalene:

b. specific heat capacity as a solid 2 marks

c. specific heat capacity as a liquid 2 marks

d. latent heat of fusion 2 marks

e. latent heat of vaporisation. 2 marks

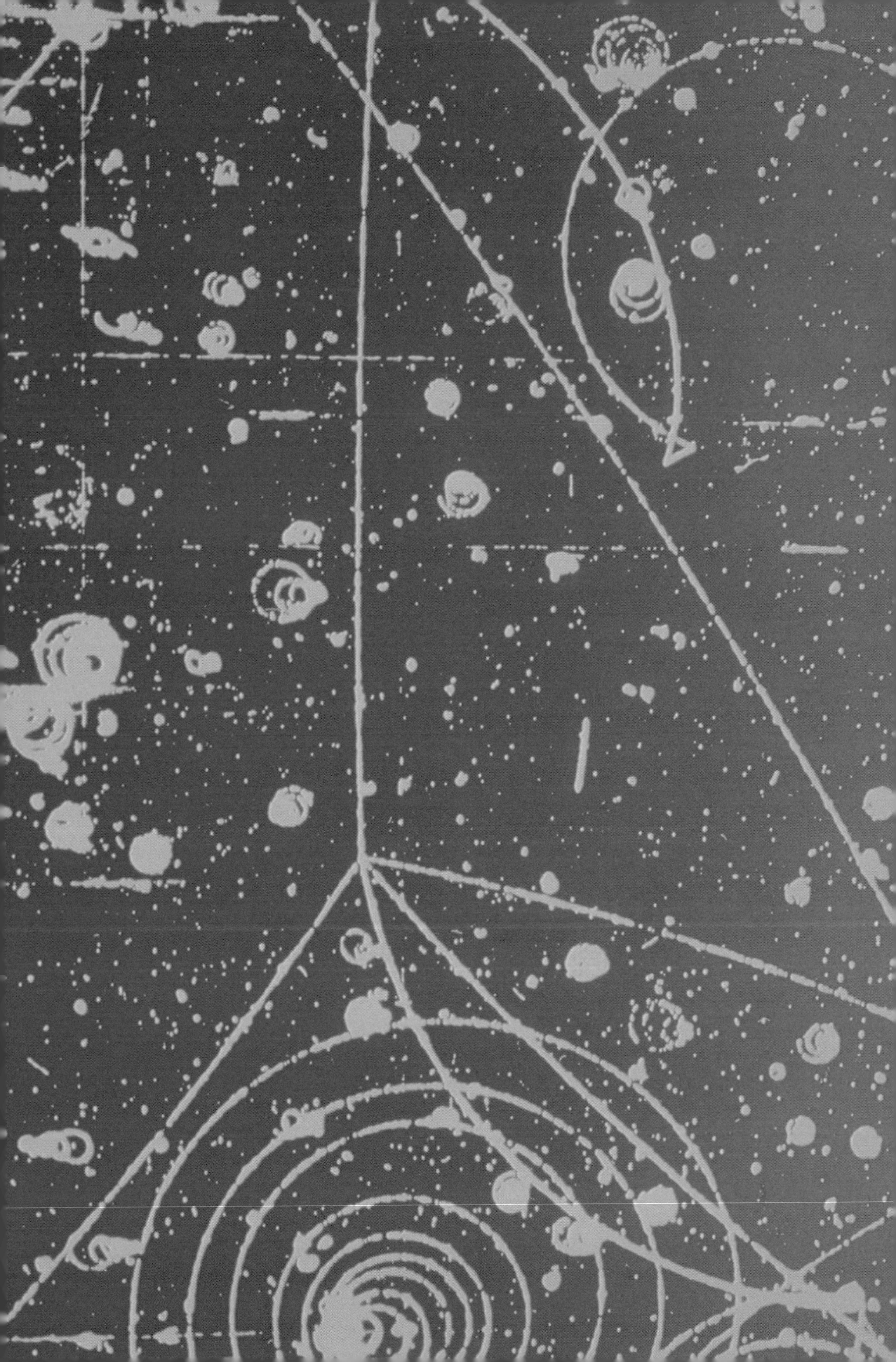

UNIT 1

How is energy useful to society?

AREA OF STUDY 2

How is energy from the nucleus utilised?

Outcome 2

Explain, apply and evaluate nuclear radiation, radioactive decay and nuclear energy.

Key knowledge

Radiation from the nucleus

- explain nuclear stability with reference to the forces in the nucleus including electrostatic forces, the strong nuclear force and the weak nuclear force
- model radioactive decay as random decay with a particular half-life, including mathematical modelling with reference to whole half-lives
- describe the properties of α, β^-, β^+ and γ radiation
- explain nuclear transformations using decay equations involving α, β^-, β^+ and γ radiation
- analyse decay series diagrams with reference to type of decay and stability of isotopes
- explain the effects of α, β and γ radiation on humans, including:
  - different capacities to cause cell damage
  - short- and long-term effects of low and high doses
  - ionising impacts of radioactive sources outside and inside the body
  - calculations of absorbed dose (gray), equivalent dose (sievert) and effective dose (sievert)
- evaluate the use of medical radioisotopes in therapy including the effects on healthy and damaged tissues and cells

Nuclear energy

- explain, qualitatively, nuclear energy as energy resulting from the conversion of mass
- explain fission chain reactions including:
  - the effect of mass and shape on criticality
  - neutron absorption and moderation
- compare the processes of nuclear fusion and nuclear fission
- explain, using a binding energy curve, why both fusion and fission are reactions that release energy
- investigate the viability of nuclear energy as an energy source for Australia.

KEY KNOWLEDGE

- **You will now be able to complete Worksheet 10.**

Radiation from the nucleus

ATOMS, ISOTOPES AND RADIOISOTOPES

Atomic notation, shown in Figure 1.2.1, helps to identify a particular atom.

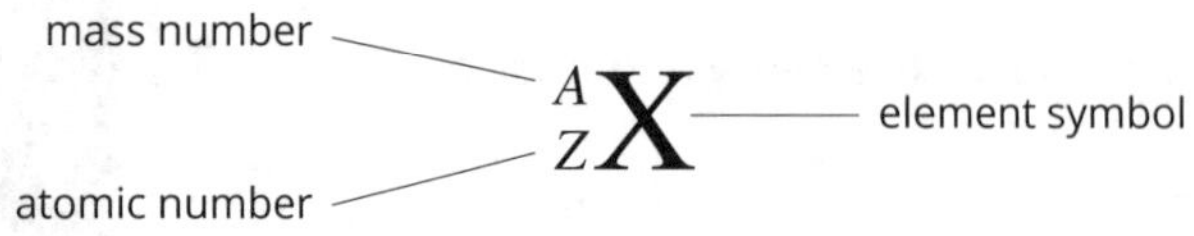

Figure 1.2.1 Atomic notation

The total number of protons and neutrons in the nucleus is known as the **mass number** (A).

The number of protons in the nucleus is known as the **atomic number** (Z).

Atoms with the same number of protons belong to the same element. The number of neutrons does not affect which element the atom is, but does affect the mass of the atom. If an atom has the same number of protons but a different number of neutrons, it is called an **isotope** of that atom.

An unstable nucleus may spontaneously become more stable by emitting a particle, and so change into a different element or isotope. Unstable atoms are radioactive. An individual radioactive isotope is known as a **radioisotope**. Radioactive substances in storage are identified by the radiation warning symbol shown in Figure 1.2.2.

Figure 1.2.2 The symbol used to identify a radioactive source

Figure 1.2.3 shows that every isotope of every element with an atomic mass greater than that of bismuth ($Z = 83$) is radioactive. The first 92 elements are naturally occurring.

RADIOACTIVITY

Radioactivity comes in different forms and should not be confused with electromagnetic radiation. In this area of study, we are concerned with particle physics: specifically, the particles and radiation emitted during radioactive decay. Three forms of radiation are identified: alpha, beta and gamma.

Group

Period	1	2	3	4	5	6	7	8	9	10	11	12	13	14	15	16	17	18
Period 1					1 H 1.008													2 He 4.003
2	3 Li 6.941	4 Be 9.012											5 B 10.81	6 C 12.01	7 N 14.01	8 O 16.00	9 F 19.00	10 Ne 20.18
3	11 Na 22.99	12 Mg 24.31											13 Al 26.98	14 Si 28.09	15 P 30.97	16 S 32.07	17 Cl 35.45	18 Ar 39.95
4	19 K 39.10	20 Ca 40.08	21 Sc 44.96	22 Ti 47.87	23 V 50.94	24 Cr 52.00	25 Mn 54.94	26 Fe 55.85	27 Co 58.93	28 Ni 58.69	29 Cu 63.55	30 Zn 65.38	31 Ga 69.72	32 Ge 72.64	33 As 74.92	34 Se 78.96	35 Br 79.90	36 Kr 83.80
5	37 Rb 85.47	38 Sr 87.61	39 Y 88.91	40 Zr 91.22	41 Nb 92.91	42 Mo 95.96	43 Tc (98)	44 Ru 101.1	45 Rh 102.9	46 Pd 106.4	47 Ag 107.9	48 Cd 112.4	49 In 114.8	50 Sn 118.7	51 Sb 121.8	52 Te 127.60	53 I 126.9	54 Xe 131.3
6	55 Cs 132.9	56 Ba 137.3	57 La 138.9	72 Hf 178.5	73 Ta 180.9	74 W 183.9	75 Re 186.2	76 Os 190.2	77 Ir 192.2	78 Pt 195.1	79 Au 197.0	80 Hg 200.6	81 Tl 204.4	82 Pb 207.2	83 Bi 209.0	84 Po (210)	85 At (210)	86 Rn (222)
7	87 Fr (223)	88 Ra (226)	89 Ac (227)	104 Rf (261)	105 Db (262)	106 Sg (263)	107 Bh (264)	108 Hs (267)	109 Mt (268)	110 Ds (271)	111 Rg (272)	112 Cn (285)	113 Nh (284)	114 Fl (289)	115 Mc (289)	116 Lv (292)	117 Ts (294)	118 Og (294)

Lanthanides

57 La 138.9	58 Ce 140.1	59 Pr 140.9	60 Nd 144.2	61 Pm (145)	62 Sm 150.4	63 Eu 152.0	64 Gd 157.3	65 Tb 158.9	66 Dy 162.5	67 Ho 164.9	68 Er 167.3	69 Tm 168.9	70 Yb 173.1	71 Lu 175.0

Every isotope of these elements is radioactive

Actinides

89 Ac	90 Th 232.0	91 Pa (231.0)	92 U 238.0	93 Np (237)	94 Pu (244)	95 Am (243)	96 Cm (247)	97 Bk (247)	98 Cf (251)	99 Es (252)	100 Fm (257)	101 Md (258)	102 No (259)	103 Lr (262)

Figure 1.2.3 The periodic table of the elements

ISBN 978 0 6557 0016 6

KEY KNOWLEDGE

Alpha (α) decay

An **alpha particle** (symbol α) is a positively charged particle consisting of two protons and two neutrons. This is identical to a helium nucleus, so it can also be written as ${}^{4}_{2}He$.

When an unstable nucleus undergoes alpha decay, it will eject an alpha particle. The unstable nucleus is known as the **parent nucleus**. Once it has ejected the alpha particle, the remaining element is known as the **daughter nucleus**. For example, once the parent nucleus of uranium-238 (${}^{238}_{92}U$) emits an alpha particle, it changes into a completely different element, and the daughter nucleus is now thorium-234 (${}^{234}_{90}Th$).

When an atom changes into a different element, it is said to undergo a **nuclear transmutation**. In nuclear transmutations, electric charge is conserved.

Beta (β) decay

There are two types of **beta particles**: beta minus (β^-) and beta plus (β^+).

Beta minus is written as ${}^{0}_{-1}\beta$. This type of beta particle is an electron that is emitted from the nucleus of a radioactive atom.

Beta plus, also known as a positron, is written as ${}^{0}_{+1}\beta$. These particles are similar to electrons except they have a positive charge instead of a negative charge. A positron is emitted when a nucleus has too many protons. In this case, a proton may spontaneously change into a neutron and emit a neutrino (ν) and a positively charged beta particle.

Gamma (γ) decay

After alpha or beta decay, the protons and neutrons in the daughter nucleus rearrange to remove excess energy. This energy is released as a **gamma ray**, written as ${}^{0}_{0}\gamma$.

Gamma rays are high-energy electromagnetic radiation. They have no mass or charge. They travel at the speed of light ($3.0 \times 10^8\,m\,s^{-1}$).

Comparing alpha, beta and gamma radiation

Table 1.2.1 compares the properties of alpha, beta and gamma radiation.

HALF-LIFE AND DECAY SERIES

The **half-life** ($t_{1/2}$) of a radioisotope is the time that it takes for half of the nuclei of the sample radioisotope to decay.

The number of nuclei (N) remaining after a particular number of half-lives (n) can be found mathematically using:

$$N = N_0\left(\frac{1}{2}\right)^n$$

where N is the number of radioactive nuclei remaining
N_0 is the initial number of radioactive nuclei
n is the number of half-lives elapsed.

This equation is shown graphically in Figure 1.2.4.

The number of half-lives in a period of time (T) can be found using:

$$n = \frac{T}{t_{1/2}}$$

where n is the number of half-lives elapsed
T is the period of time that the radioactive nuclei has decayed
$t_{1/2}$ is the half-life of the radioactive nuclei.

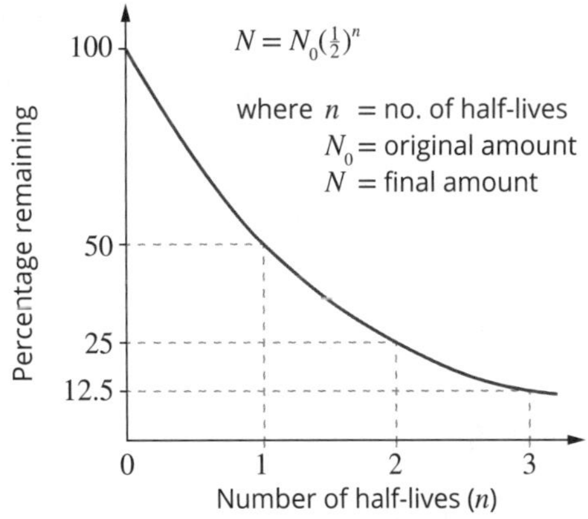

Figure 1.2.4 A decay curve

Table 1.2.1 Summary of the differences between alpha, beta and gamma radiation

Property	α-particle	β-particle	γ-ray
mass	heavy	light	none
speed	up to 20 000 km s^{-1} or about 10% of the speed of light	about 90% of the speed of light	the speed of light
charge	+2	−1 or +1	0
range in air	a few centimetres	1 or 2 m	many metres
penetration in matter	~10 μm–2 mm	a few mm	high

- **You will now be able to conduct Practical activity 7.**

KEY KNOWLEDGE

A Geiger counter can be used to record the number of radioactive decays occurring in a sample each second. This is known as the activity of the sample and it is measured in becquerels, Bq. One disintegration per second is equal to 1 becquerel.

The activity (A) of the nuclei after a number of half-lives n can be found using:

$$A = A_0\left(\frac{1}{2}\right)^n$$

where A is the activity of radioactive nuclei remaining
A_0 is the initial activity of radioactive nuclei
n is the number of half-lives elapsed.

A **decay series** describes how a radionuclide reaches a stable isotope. Generally, the daughter nucleus after decay is not completely stable. It is still radioactive and will undergo further decay until a stable isotope is reached and the sequence ends. An example of a decay series is shown in Figure 1.2.5 where uranium-238 (shown at the top of the chart) decays into lead-206 (shown at the bottom of the chart).

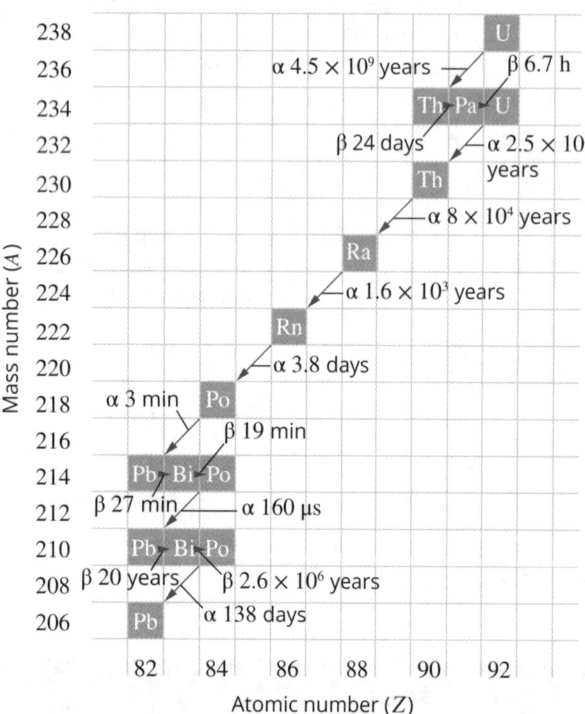

Figure 1.2.5 The uranium decay series

- **You will now be able to complete Worksheets 11 and 12 and conduct Practical activity 8.**

RADIATION AND THE HUMAN BODY

Alpha particles are highly ionising because of their double positive charge, relatively large mass and relatively slow speed. They can cause multiple ionisations within a very small distance, giving them the potential to do more biological damage. Alpha particles, being the least penetrating of α, β and γ radiation, can't penetrate the layer of dead cells on the skin. They are normally only a safety concern if the radioactive decay occurs inside the body or a cell.

Beta particles are less ionising than alpha particles, and so can travel through millimetres of skin or tissue. A sufficient intensity of beta radiation can cause burns, similar to sunburn. Breathing in beta-emitting radionuclides can damage internal cells and organs.

Gamma radiation has the highest penetration power of the three types, and can cause an effect throughout the body. Gamma ionisation is significantly less than that of alpha particles. High exposures can cause direct acute effects through immediate damage to cells. Low levels of exposure over a long time increase the probability of cancer.

Radiation doses

Dose is a measure of the amount of energy from an ionising radiation deposited in body tissue. The radiation energy absorbed per kilogram of tissue is called the **absorbed dose**. The SI unit used to measure absorbed dose is the gray (Gy). 1 Gy is equivalent to 1 J of energy per kilogram of mass. The mass could be anything: air, water or human tissue.

$$\text{Absorbed dose} = \frac{\text{energy absorbed by tissue}}{\text{mass of tissue}}$$

The absorbed dose is measured in joules per kilogram ($J\,kg^{-1}$) or grays (Gy), i.e. $1\,Gy = 1\,J\,kg^{-1}$.

The absorbed dose is not widely used when measuring the radiation dose, because it does not take into account the type of radiation involved. **Equivalent dose**, which does take the type of radiation involved into account, is the most common way of measuring radiation doses.

The biological impact different types of radiation have is given a weighting called the **quality factor** (QF).

Equivalent dose = absorbed dose × quality factor

$$ED = AD \times QF$$

The equivalent dose is measured in sieverts (Sv).

One sievert (Sv) is also equal to 1 joule per kilogram. The sievert represents the equivalent biological effect of one joule of radiation energy transferred to a kilogram of human tissue. Large doses of radiation to the whole body (10 sieverts and above), received over a short time, significantly damage internal organs and tissues. Bodily systems cease to function and death may result within days or weeks. Very high doses (between about 1 sievert and 10 sieverts) kill large numbers of cells, which can impair the function of vital organs and systems. Nausea, vomiting, skin and deep tissue burns may result within hours, days or weeks. The extent of the damage increases with dose.

ISBN 978 0 6557 0016 6

Doses below these thresholds may cause cellular damage, but this does not necessarily harm a person. The effects are referred to as probabilistic; that is, the chance of adverse effect is increased by exposure time. Evidence suggests that a dose accumulated over a long period carries less risk.

Effective dose takes into account the sensitivity of the organ to ionising radiation. Effective dose is found by calculating the sum of the equivalent doses multiplied by the **weighting factor**, W, for each organ affected. In physics, the symbol sigma (Σ) is used to represent the 'sum of'.

Effective dose = Σ(equivalent dose × W)
Effective dose is measured in sieverts (Sv)

Nuclear energy

ENERGY FROM MASS

The energy of subatomic particles and radiation is usually given in **electron volts** (eV). One electron volt is an extremely small amount of energy.

An electron volt is the energy that an electron would gain if it was accelerated by an electrical potential difference of 1 volt and is equal to 1.6×10^{-19} J.

To convert from eV to joules: multiply by 1.6×10^{-19} J.

To convert from joules to eV: divide by 1.6×10^{-19} J.

If a given, intact nucleus could be disassembled into its individual protons and neutrons, then the sum of the masses of the individual protons and neutrons would be slightly higher than the mass of the nucleus itself. The difference between the mass of the nucleus as a whole and the sum of the individual nucleons is called the **mass defect**, Δm.

The mass defect is calculated as:

Δm = total mass of individual protons and neutrons − actual mass of nucleus

This 'missing' mass might seem to violate conservation laws. However, when the individual protons and neutrons come together to form a nucleus, some of their mass is converted into the energy needed to bind them into a nucleus. This is called the binding energy, ΔE. It is defined as the energy that would need to be given to a nucleus to separate it into its individual nucleons.

Einstein developed a mathematical rule that linked energy and matter. The rule was based on the fact that matter can be converted entirely into energy, and energy can be converted entirely into matter. His equation is known as the mass–energy equivalence relationship. It has many applications, but in this case, it relates the binding energy, ΔE, to the mass defect, Δm, by:

The mass–energy equivalence relationship:

$$\Delta E = \Delta mc^2$$

where ΔE is the energy content produced in a nuclear reaction (J)
Δm is the difference in mass before and after a nuclear reaction has taken place (kg)
c is the speed of light in a vacuum (3.0×10^8 m s^{-1}).

In Unit 4 you will see this written simply as $E = mc^2$.

- **You will now be able to complete Worksheet 13.**

FISSION, FUSION AND THE FUTURE OF NUCLEAR ENERGY IN AUSTRALIA

When one element changes into another, the process is called nuclear transmutation. Nuclear transmutation can be either artificial or natural. Artificial transmutation is changing one element by bombarding it with some fundamental particles, while natural transmutation is due to the unstable nuclei.

Within a nucleus, the forces of attraction and repulsion are acting. The long-distance, electrostatic force of repulsion acts between the protons. The short-distance, strong nuclear force of attraction acts between every nucleon.

Nuclear fission and nuclear fusion are the two different types of reactions that release energy. They occur due to either the repulsion or attraction of overcoming the other force.

Fission

Nuclear fission occurs when a nucleus is made to split and release a number of neutrons. A relatively large amount of energy is released during this process. Fission can be induced by striking a fissile nucleus with a neutron. Fissile nuclei are generally heavy atoms with large numbers of nucleons. The fission process can occur when their nuclei are struck by neutrons, or due to electrostatic repulsion created by their large numbers of protons.

Every time neutrons are released by fission, an additional fission occurs in at least one further nucleus. This causes a fission chain reaction. For example, if a stray neutron strikes an atom of U-235, it absorbs the neutron and becomes an unstable atom of U-236. It then undergoes fission. More neutrons are released, and they can strike other U-235 atoms to initiate their fission.

ISBN 978 0 6557 0016 6

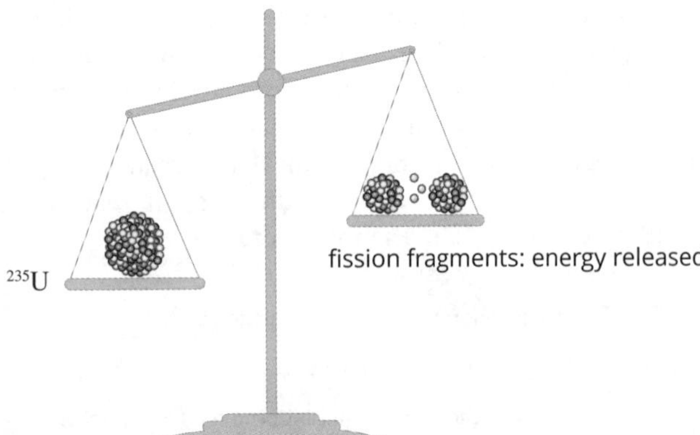

Figure 1.2.6 The mass of the products (the fission fragments) is less than the mass of the original sample (in this example, U-235).

The **fission fragments**, as demonstrated in Figure 1.2.6, have less combined mass than the original nucleus.

Fusion

Nuclear fusion occurs when two light nuclei are combined to form a larger nucleus. Similar to nuclear fission, the product of the reaction has less mass than the reactants (Figure 1.2.7). The energy from the mass defect can again be calculated using Einstein's equation: $E = mc^2$.

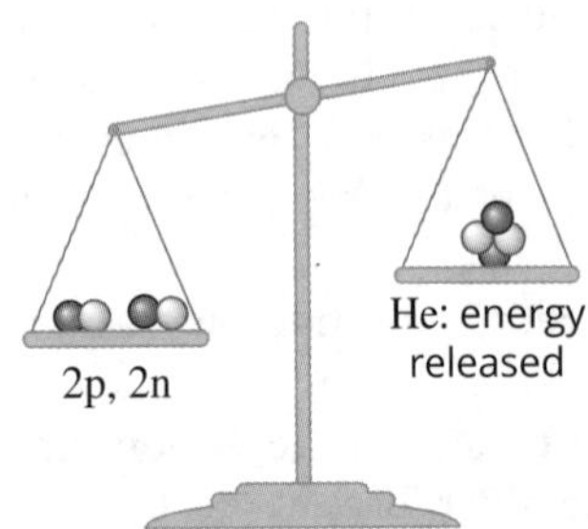

Figure 1.2.7 The mass of the products (in this example, helium) is less than the mass of the reactants (shown here as two protons and two neutrons).

Because nuclei are positively charged, they exert an electrostatic force of repulsion on each other. This means it is very difficult to force nuclei together. For nuclei to get close enough for the strong nuclear force of attraction to bind them together, a large amount of energy is needed.

Slow-moving nuclei with small amounts of kinetic energy will not be able to get close enough for fusion to occur. The nuclei need to be travelling at higher speeds to have enough kinetic energy to overcome the electrostatic repulsive force.

Nuclear energy in Australia

The use of nuclear power to help replace fossil fuels has long been debated. More than 50 countries use some form of nuclear fission reaction to produce electricity or heating, and about 10% of the world's electricity is generated by nuclear fission. France leads the world in nuclear-power generation, with almost three-quarters of its electricity produced by nuclear fission reactors.

Australia is one of the world's largest producers of uranium, with around one-third of the world's uranium deposits. Despite this abundance, Australia has never had a nuclear power station, instead relying on low-cost coal and natural gas reserves (fossil fuels). As a result, the production of electricity is our highest contributor to enhanced global warming due to the high emissions of carbon dioxide.

Nuclear fission produces almost no carbon dioxide. In that respect, nuclear fission will not harm the environment. Fission power is also much more efficient than burning fossil fuels. For instance, 1 kg of uranium-235 fuel in a nuclear reactor produces millions of times more energy than 1 kg of coal, oil or natural gas. Despite these advantages, many countries have not adopted nuclear fission as a source of energy because of the risks it carries. These include:

- risk of accidents
- disposal of waste products
- security issues with transportation.

- **You will now be able to complete Worksheets 14, 15 and 16 and conduct Practical activity 9.**

 ISBN 978 0 6557 0016 6

WORKSHEET 10

Knowledge review—the properties of matter

Check on your current knowledge of nuclear radiation by responding to each statement, and indicating whether it is true and false. For statements marked as false, provide a short explanation of the correct alternative.

Statement	True/false	Explanation
All beta-minus radiation is negatively charged.		
The atomic number of an element is the number of protons in a nucleus of that element.		
The mass number of an isotope is the number of neutrons in a nucleus of that element.		
Marie Curie invented the Geiger counter.		
The nuclear reaction taking place in the Sun's core is fusion.		
Gamma and beta radiation are both types of electromagnetic radiation.		
Carbon dating only works on the remains of living organisms.		
Smoke detectors commonly use a radioactive isotope.		
In every atom the number of protons equals the number of neutrons.		
Both atomic bombs and nuclear reactors use a fission reaction.		
The atomic symbol for carbon-12 is ${}^{12}_{7}C$.		
Gamma rays have a longer wavelength than ultraviolet rays.		

ISBN 978 0 6557 0016 6

Half-life in radioactive decay

1 Thorium-231 decays to protactinium-231 with a half-life of 25 h. For a sample with 5×10^{22} nuclei of thorium-231, plot the number of thorium-231 nuclei against time from 0 h to 150 h.

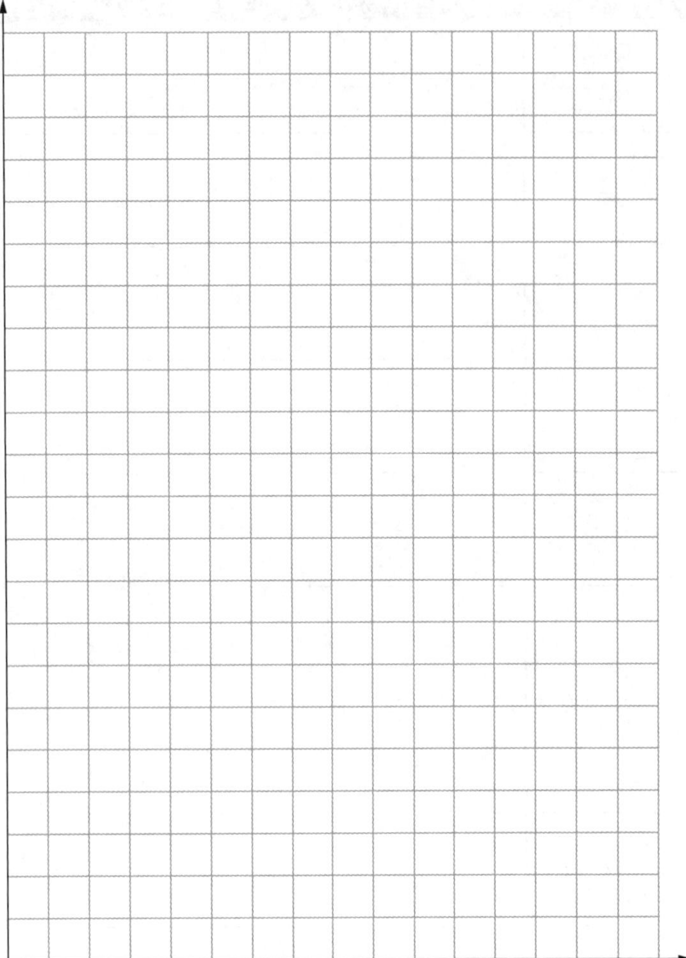

2 From the graph, determine the expected number of atoms at:

a $t = 30$ h

b $t = 70$ h

Show your working on the graph.

3 ^{215}Po decays to ^{215}At with a half-life $t_{1/2} = 3.9$ s. If a sample with 5×10^{22} nuclei starts off with 100% ^{215}Po, calculate the number of ^{215}Po at:

a $t = 7.8$ s

b $t = 15.6$ s

c $t = 39$ s

d $t = 3.9$ min

ISBN 978 0 6557 0016 6

4 **a** A sample of ^{208}Tl measures 1200 counts in 5 s. Calculate the count rate in Bq.

b Determine the expected count rate at 6.2 min given its half-life is 3.1 min.

c Calculate its expected activity at 15.5 min.

d Determine its expected activity at 31 min.

5 A sample initially has 400 g of radioactive nuclei. Ten minutes later it only has 25 g of radioactive nuclei. Determine the half-life of the sample.

Igneous rocks are formed by the cooling of molten magma, often from volcanic eruptions. The age of igneous rocks can be determined by measuring the ratio of parent radioactive atoms and daughter atoms. To determine the age of samples less than 70 000 years old, geologists can use the radioactive decay of carbon-14 to nitrogen-14. For rock samples older than this—right back to Earth's formation 4.3 billion years ago—geologists use the radioactive decay of potassium-40 to argon-40. The technique assumes that at the time of formation of the igneous rock, only potassium-40 was present.

Archaeologists also use radiometric dating to determine the age of fossil samples. Fossils are found in sedimentary rocks. Sedimentary rocks are formed from the accumulation of broken-up rock, chemical weathering and debris from organic processes. Sedimentary rock can be deposited on igneous rock, and more igneous rock can be deposited on top later on, as shown in the diagram below. To determine the age range of the fossil, archaeologists determine the age of the older igneous rock below the fossil, and the younger igneous rock above the fossil.

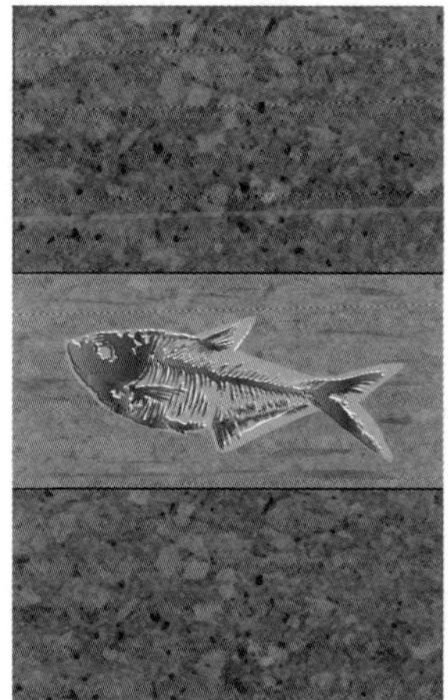

ISBN 978 0 6557 0016 6

6 a Given that the half-life for the decay of ^{14}C to ^{14}N is 5730 years and for the decay of ^{40}K to ^{40}Ar is 1.29×10^9 years, explain why carbon-14 dating is not used to determine the age of samples greater than 70 000 years.

b In the figure on page 57, ^{40}K dating is used to determine the age of the fossil. In the lower layer, a small sample is found to have 0.30 g of ^{40}K and 0.20 g of ^{40}Ar.

i Calculate the proportion of ^{40}K to the total mass of ^{40}K and ^{40}Ar; i.e. $\frac{N}{N_0}$

ii Determine the number of half-lives and hence the age of the lower igneous rock. You will need to rearrange your equation to be $\frac{N}{N_0} = \left(\frac{1}{2}\right)^n$ then express as a logarithm such as $n = \log_{\frac{1}{2}}\left(\frac{N}{N_0}\right)$ and solve for n. Your teacher can also provide guidance.

c The upper igneous rock sample had 0.32 g of potassium-40 and 0.18 g of argon-40. Calculate the age of the upper igneous rock and hence determine the age range of the fossil.

 ISBN 978 0 6557 0016 6

WORKSHEET 12

Decaying away

The stability of the nucleus of an atom depends on electrostatic forces, the strong nuclear force and the weak nuclear force.

1 Explain the importance of the strong nuclear force and neutrons in maintaining stability in nuclei with more than one proton.

2 A $^{212}_{84}Po$ nucleus undergoes alpha-decay. State the atomic number and the mass number of the daughter nucleus. Use a periodic table to determine the daughter isotope.

3 Explain the difference between β^- and β^+ decay.

4 Explain how a β^- particle and a β^+ particle are related to each other, and what will happen if they interact with each other.

5 A particular atomic nucleus produces gamma radiation. Describe the change that takes place in the nucleus when this happens.

6 Explain the difference between the terms 'isotope' and 'nuclide'.

7 Explain the difference between a stable isotope and a radioisotope.

8 $^{4}_{2}He$ is a very stable nuclide and contains two protons and two neutrons. $^{197}_{79}Au$ is also a very stable nuclide, yet it contains many more neutrons than protons. Explain why both nuclides can be stable, even though they have a very different ratio of protons to neutrons in each nucleus.

9 For the unknown nuclides X and Y in each of these decay equations, determine the atomic number and mass number. Then use the periodic table to identify the unknown elements.

a $^{235}_{92}U \rightarrow {}^{4}_{2}He + X$

b $^{228}_{88}Ra \rightarrow Y + {}^{0}_{-1}\beta + {}^{0}_{0}\bar{\nu}$

10 State what is missing from the decay equation $^{45}_{20}Ca \rightarrow {}^{45}_{21}Sc + ?$.

 ISBN 978 0 6557 0016 6

WORKSHEET 13

Modelling

Nuclear energy

As the mass of protons and neutrons is very small, scientists often don't want to use the kilogram as the measurement unit. Instead, you may sometimes see the use of the unified atomic mass unit (u). One unified atomic mass unit (1 u) is defined as $\frac{1}{12}$ of the mass of a carbon-12 atom (6 protons, 6 neutrons and 6 electrons), which is 1.66054×10^{-27} kg.

Useful information:

Particle	Mass (u)
proton	1.0072766
neutron	1.0086554
electron	0.00054858

1 Consider a carbon-12 nucleus, which has a mass of exactly 12.00 u.

a Calculate the mass of all the individual nucleons in the carbon-12 nucleus.

b Calculate the mass defect Δm between that of the individual nucleons and the carbon-12 nucleus.

c Where does this difference in energy go?

d Calculate this energy in J and MeV using Einstein's famous equation.

e One way of determining the stability of a nucleus is to look at the binding energy per nucleon. Calculate the binding energy per nucleon for carbon (in units MeV nucleon^{-1}) and compare it to the graph in question 2 of binding energy per nucleon versus number of nucleons.

ISBN 978 0 6557 0016 6

2 Consider the binding energy curve below.

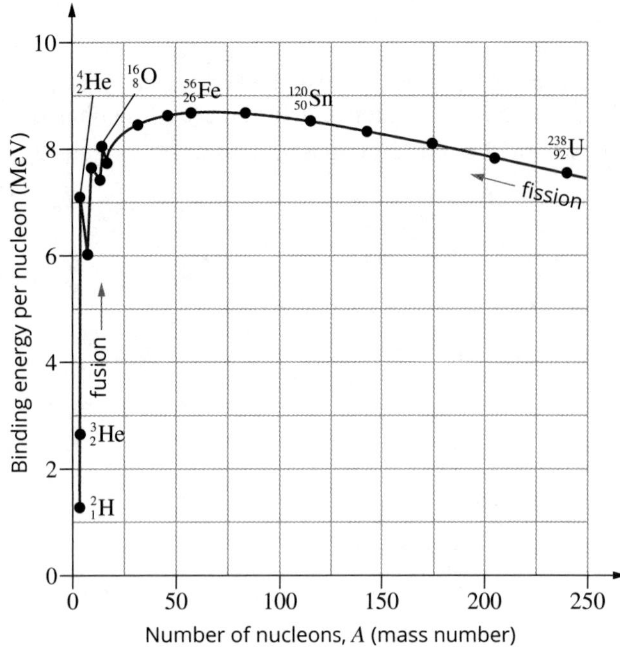

a Calculate the binding energy per nucleon (in MeV) for the isotope $^{3}_{2}$He, given that its mass is 3.016029 u.

b Calculate the binding energy per nucleon (in MeV) for the isotope ^{235}U, given its mass is 235.043923 u.

c Determine the most stable nuclei on the graph.

d Deduce which elements are most suitable for fusion, and explain why.

e Deduce which elements are most suitable for fission, and explain why.

ISBN 978 0 6557 0016 6

WORKSHEET 14

Modelling

Fission versus fusion

1 Nuclear fission is produced by firing a neutron at uranium-235. In this case, the fission products are rubidium-93 and caesium-140.

a Write a balanced nuclear equation and hence determine how many neutrons are released.

b Explain why a neutron is used instead of an alpha or a beta particle.

c Compare the energy of the incident neutron with the energy of the released neutrons.

d Explain what needs to happen for the released neutrons to cause fission in other uranium nuclei.

2 **a** Natural uranium contains both uranium-238 and uranium-235. State the percentage of uranium-235 found in natural uranium and describe the process needed to use the uranium in a nuclear reactor.

b Describe the difference between a controlled nuclear chain reaction and an uncontrolled chain reaction that occurs in an explosion.

c Explain the measures taken to control nuclear reactions in a reactor.

d Identify the safety precautions that need to be taken in a nuclear reactor.

3 **a** Scientists have been trying create fusion reactors, but have not succeeded yet. Identify the constraints that make this a difficult process to emulate on Earth.

b Discuss the advantages a fusion reactor would have over fission reactors.

 ISBN 978 0 6557 0016 6

WORKSHEET 15

Literacy review—the terminology of ionising radiation

Complete the following table by defining each term, taking care to clearly distinguish each one from similar-sounding terms. You will find similar-sounding terms grouped together, rather than being listed alphabetically.

Term	Definition
alpha particle	
beta particle	
gamma ray	
decay series	
fissile	
fission	
fusion	
half-life	
atomic number	
mass number	
nucleon	
neutron	
neutrino	
nuclide	

WORKSHEET **16**

Reflection—How is energy from the nucleus utilised?

The following table lists the key knowledge covered in this area of study.

1 Reflect on how well you understand the concepts listed. Rate your learning by shading the circle that corresponds to your current level of understanding for each one.

Key knowledge	Not confident ◄				► Very confident
Nuclear stability—strong nuclear force, weak nuclear force, electrostatic force	○	○	○	○	○
Half-life—random decay, mathematical modelling of half-life	○	○	○	○	○
Alpha, beta and gamma radiation—properties, decay equations, effects on humans	○	○	○	○	○
Medical applications—radioisotopes	○	○	○	○	○
Energy from the conversion of mass	○	○	○	○	○
Fission reactions—chain reaction, mass of material, neutron absorption	○	○	○	○	○
Fusion reactions	○	○	○	○	○

2 Consider the points you have shaded from Not confident to Very confident. List specific ideas you can identify that were challenging.

3 Write down two different strategies that you will apply to help further your understanding of these ideas.

 ISBN 978 0 6557 0016 6

PRACTICAL ACTIVITY 7

Modelling

Detecting radiation with a G–M tube

SUGGESTED DURATION

- 90 minutes

MATERIALS

- G–M tube, counter and stopwatch or data logger
- power supply and counter or computer interface
- base and support rod
- radioactive sources (alpha, beta, gamma)
- right-angle clamp
- shielding material—lead, paper, plastic and aluminium—in 5 cm squares

INTRODUCTION

This is an introductory activity.

The nuclear decay process seems to be both random and predictable. It is impossible to say which nucleus will become unstable enough to decay next. However, it is fairly easy to use a Geiger–Müller (G–M) tube to count the number of nuclei that decay per second in a radioactive sample. If you record the nuclear decay of a radioactive sample with a G–M tube and counter (or nuclear sensor) and plot the counts per time interval over a period of time, the results will look like a standard distribution curve.

In many ways, nuclear radiation behaves as though the radiation were tiny bullets. So it makes sense that different materials absorb different amounts of nuclear radiation energy in different ways, depending on the nature of the material.

AIM

To investigate the penetrating ability of three common types of nuclear radiation, and the ability of different materials to absorb the nuclear radiation.

Safety

The radioactive sources used in this experiment are very low level, but may be dangerous if not handled properly. Handled as follows, laboratory samples provide little or no cause for concern.

Do not touch sources with a bare hand.

Pick up sources with forceps or tongs.

Do not point a source towards human bodies.

Maintain a distance of about half a metre from samples when possible.

Wash hands thoroughly after performing an experiment.

Complete a risk assessment before starting the activity.

METHOD

1. In the first part of this activity, you will measure the background radiation. In the second part of the activity, you will compare the radiation from three different sources that are shielded with different thicknesses of three different materials. The measurements are made from a fixed distance over equal intervals of time.
2. Connect the G–M tube to its power supply and counter as per the instructions supplied with the equipment, or connect the G–M tube to your data-collection system according to the manufacturer's instructions. Clamp the G–M tube securely in a retort stand pointing downwards so the distance from each source is controlled.

PART A • BACKGROUND RADIATION

1. Move all radiation sources at least 3 m from the G–M tube. Turn on the power supply/counter and zero the counter; then start the counter or start data collection with your data-collection system.
2. Allow the counter to record for 60 s and record the number of counts. Repeat three or four times during the course of the entire activity to enable a reliable average background count. Make sure the samples are away from the G–M tube or are shielded each time a background check is taken.
3. Record the background counts in Table 1 of the Results section.

PART B • RADIATION SHIELDING

1 ▪ Position the sealed alpha source under the G–M tube without any shielding. Turn on the power supply and counter, if they are not already on, or connect your data-collection system. Measure and record the number of counts over 60 s. Record this in Table 2 of the Results section.

2 ▪ Measure the radiation counts from the alpha source with it shielded by one layer of paper. Repeat for two, three, four and five layers of paper. In each case, record the count for 60 s.

3 ▪ Replace the sealed alpha source with a sealed beta source. Repeat the steps, recording counts for the unshielded beta source and then for the beta source shielded by one to five layers of paper as per step 2. Record the number of radiation counts per 60 s for each trial.

4 ▪ Replace the sealed beta source with a sealed gamma source. Repeat the data-recording process again with no shielding and then with one to five sheets of paper.

5 ▪ Repeat steps 1–4 for each radiation source, using thin squares of plastic as the shielding material. Record the number of radiation counts per 60 s for each trial.

6 ▪ Repeat the entire process of data collection for each source, using thin squares of lead as the shielding material. Record the number of radiation counts per 60 s for each trial.

7 ▪ Repeat the entire process of data collection for each source using thin squares of aluminium as the shielding material. Record the number of radiation counts per 60 s for each trial.

RESULTS

1 Calculate the average background count and the uncertainty in the average count:

Table 1 Background radiation count

Sample	Count per 60 s
1	
2	
3	
4	
Average count:	±

 ISBN 978 0 6557 0016 6

For each of the counts per 60s, make a note of the value excluding the average background radiation count:

Table 2 Radiation shielding

Source	No shielding (# counts)	Shielding material	One layer (# counts per 60 s)	Two layers (# counts per 60 s)	Three layers (# counts per 60 s)	Four layers (# counts per 60 s)	Five layers (# counts per 60 s)
alpha		paper					
alpha		plastic					
alpha		lead					
alpha		aluminium					
beta		paper					
beta		plastic					
beta		lead					
beta		aluminium					
gamma		paper					
gamma		plastic					
gamma		lead					
gamma		aluminium					

2 In this experiment, an estimate of the uncertainty wasn't recorded for the measurement of counts. Justify this aspect of the experimental data recording.

3 Construct a graph using the number of layers of shielding versus the count for each type of radiation and shielding material. Graph all tests for one type of shielding material clearly on one set of axes so that comparisons can easily be made between sources.

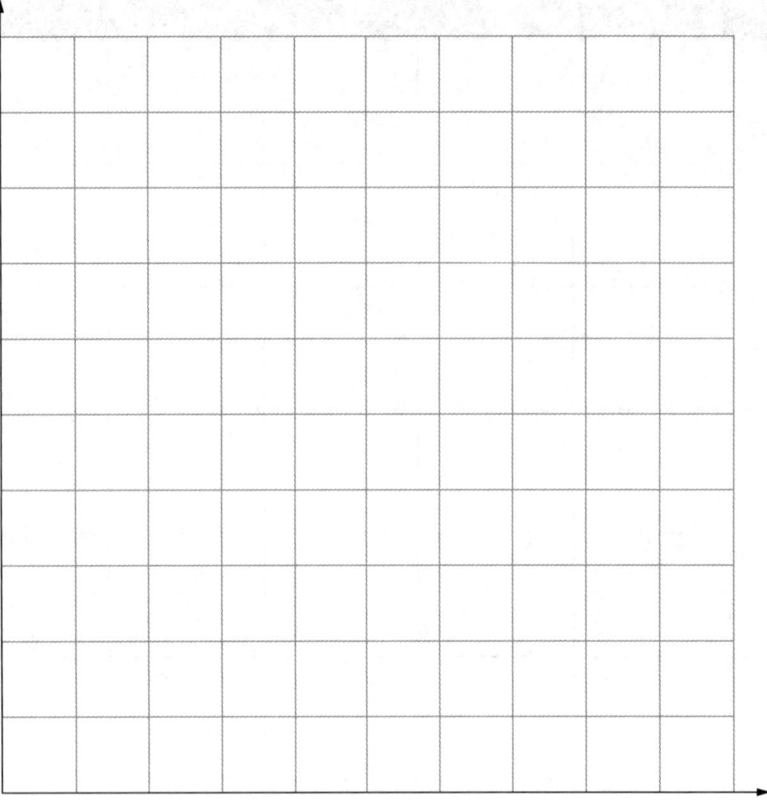

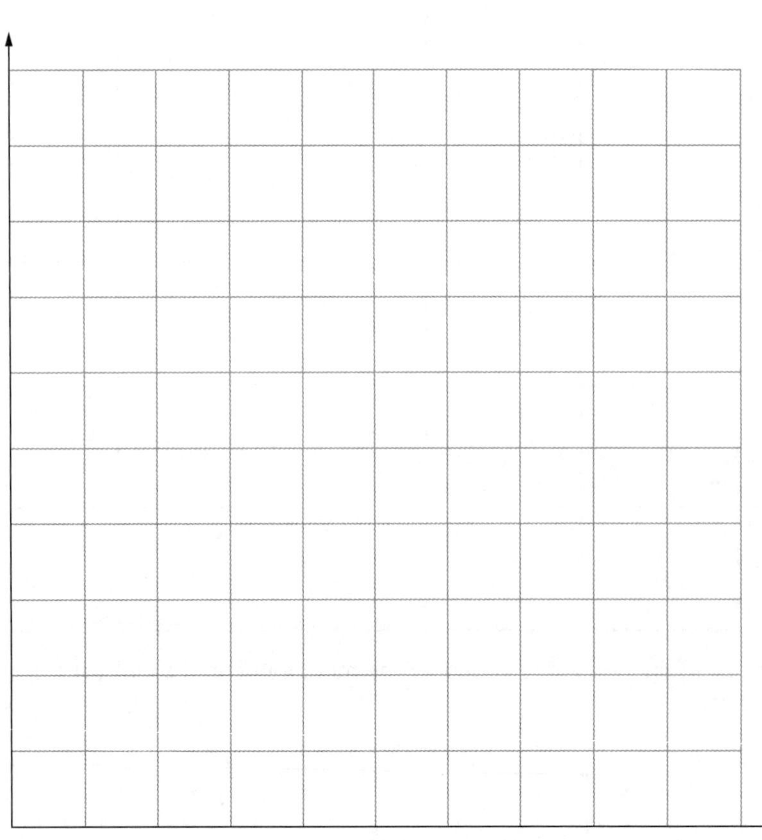

 ISBN 978 0 6557 0016 6

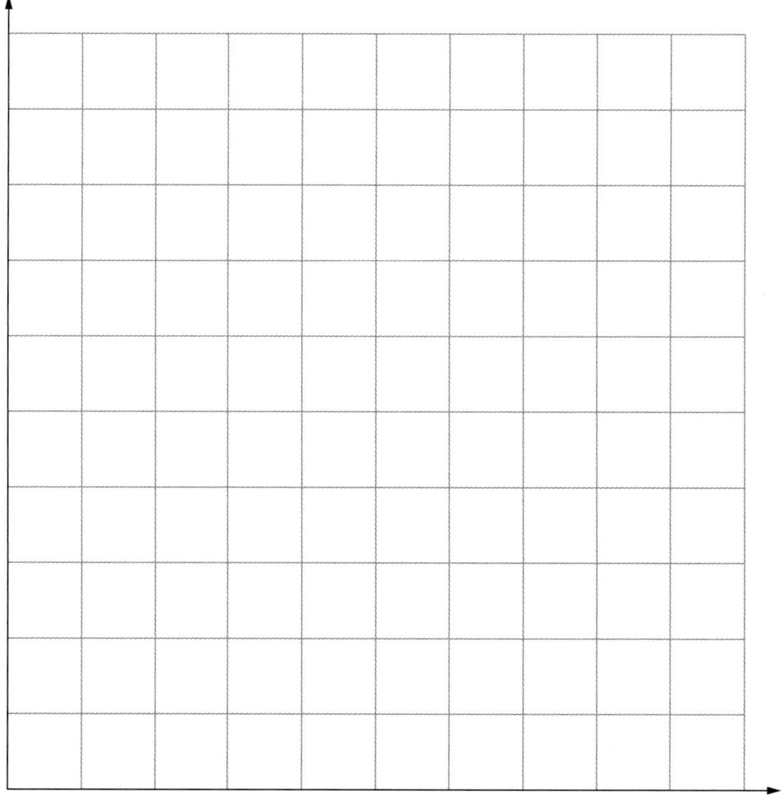

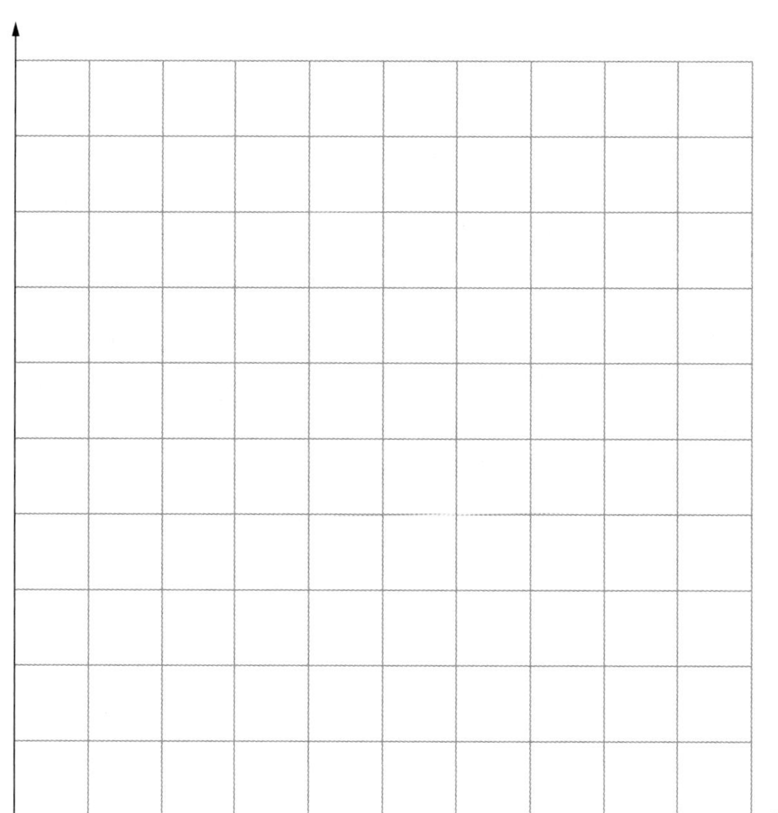

ISBN 978 0 6557 0016 6

DISCUSSION

1 Discuss your results, commenting on the penetration of each source and the effect of shielding.

2 Evaluate the effect of the thickness of the shielding material on the count rate.

3 Assess the effect of the density of the shielding material on the count rate.

4 You measured the background radiation before measuring the counts from the radioactive material. Discuss the reasons for this and whether it would be justified to take additional measurements throughout the experiment.

CONCLUSION

ISBN 978 0 6557 0016 6

PRACTICAL ACTIVITY 8

Modelling

An analogue model of radioactive decay

SUGGESTED DURATION

- 50 minutes

INTRODUCTION

This activity illustrates the randomness of radioactive decay and shows how to generate data upon which theory can effectively be developed. In the activity, you will record results as a class group and note them down for your own analysis.

MATERIALS

- class of students
- 1 coin per student
- 1 standard 6-sided die per student (optional as time allows)

AIM

To model the randomness of radioactive decay.

METHOD

1. All students stand up, holding a coin. Each student represents a radioactive nucleus within a sample.
2. On the word 'go' or 'decay' from the teacher or group leader, start shaking the coin in your cupped hands.
3. Every 10 s, the teacher will give a signal. Stop shaking and look at the coin. If your coin shows heads, sit down. You represent a decayed nucleus.
4. Count the number of students that remain standing each time, and record the value on a whiteboard or other group recording device for later transfer to Table 1.
5. Continue until all students have 'decayed'.
6. Repeat two or three times as total lesson time permits.
7. Repeat the activity with each student shaking a die instead of a coin. Sit down if the die shows the number 1 facing upwards.

RESULTS

Table 1 Decay rates for a coin

Time (s)	Standing students trial 1	Standing students trial 2	Standing students trial 3
0			
10			
20			
30			
40			
50			
60			
70			
80			
90			
100			

PRACTICAL ACTIVITY 8

1 Graph the results for each coin trial on the graph space provided. Show all trials on one graph.

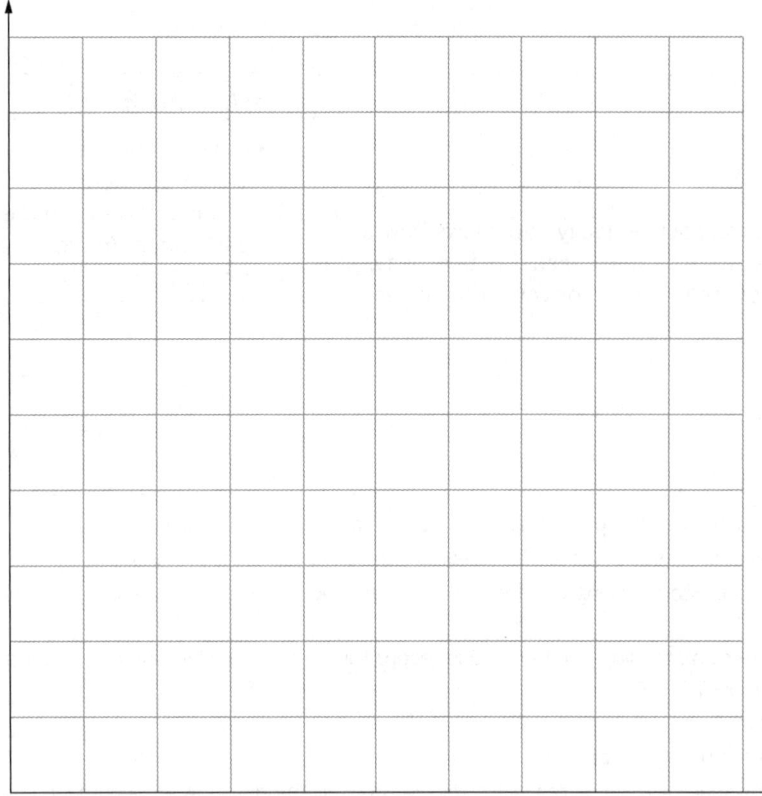

Table 2 Decay rates for a 6-sided die

Time (s)	Standing students trial 1	Standing students trial 2	Standing students trial 3
0			
10			
20			
30			
40			
50			
60			
70			
80			
90			
100			

ISBN 978 0 6557 0016 6

PRACTICAL ACTIVITY 8

2 Graph the results for each die trial on the graph space provided. Show all trials on one graph.

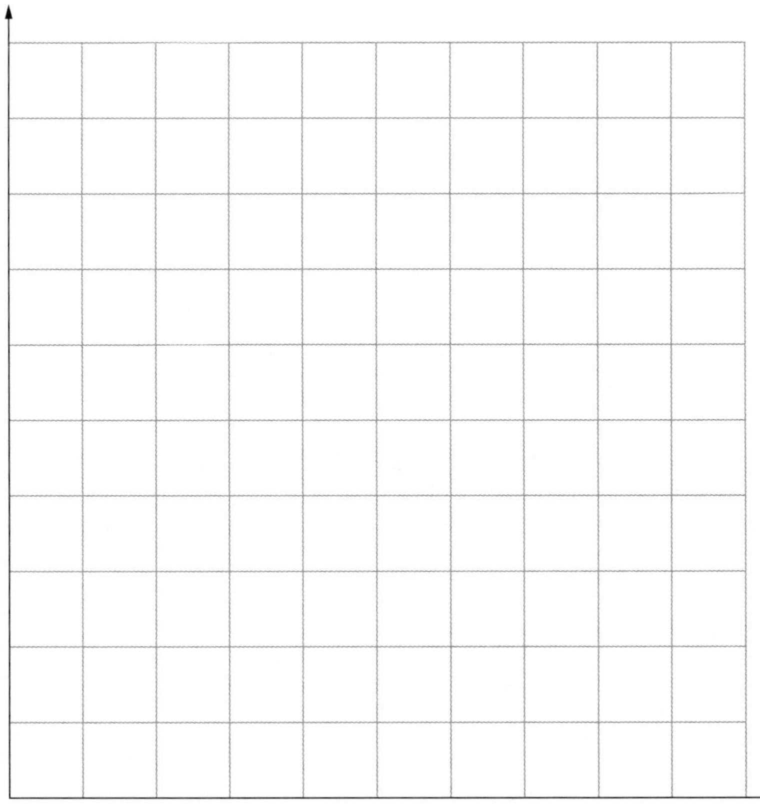

DISCUSSION

1 Comment on the relative decay rates for coins and dice. State whether the rate of decay is the same for each trial.

2 Discuss whether the process of sitting down is purely random.

3 Based on the graphs, decide how the number of 'radioactive nuclei' remaining decreases with time. Evaluate whether they fit any standard graphical form covered in maths. Suggest suitable models.

4 The time for half of the 'radioactive nuclei' to disintegrate is constant. From the data obtained, assess whether you think that this statement is true or false for this experiment.

5 When the statement in question 4 is true, the time for half of the nuclei to disintegrate may be called the half-life. Calculate the half-life for the class results.

6 If 1000 students were to take part in this experiment instead of one class, discuss the likelihood of the experimental results providing a more constant or less constant outcome.

CONCLUSION

 ISBN 978 0 6557 0016 6

PRACTICAL ACTIVITY 9

Case study • Literature review

The OPAL research reactor, Lucas Heights—How can the energy of the atomic nucleus be harnessed?

SUGGESTED DURATION

- 4 hours

INTRODUCTION

Beginning in the late nineteenth and early twentieth centuries, experimental discoveries revolutionised the accepted understanding of the nature of matter on an atomic scale. The work of Thompson, Rutherford, Bohr, de Broglie and others developed a more complex model on which the experimental investigations of the late twentieth and early twenty-first centuries built our current understanding of the atomic model.

This task requires you to investigate and collect valid and reliable data and information on the operation of the OPAL research reactor located at the Australian Nuclear Science and Technology Organisation, Lucas Heights, Sydney. You will develop an inquiry question that requires research to develop an informed hypothesis, plan a research or experimental investigation, analyse secondary data and information from appropriate sources, and use problem-solving techniques to determine the validity of the data or sources. You will evaluate secondary data to form conclusions by considering the quality of the data. You will select and process the data and information to communicate your findings in a fact sheet of approximately 500 words. The fact sheet should be aimed at the general public and communicate scientific understanding using suitable language and terminology, scientific notation and nomenclature, and graphs and diagrams. The fact sheet should also include evidence-based arguments supporting the role of OPAL, developed following peer evaluation of your arguments and conclusions.

Inside the OPAL research reactor. The core containing the reactor fuel can be seen in the centre, with ports for irradiating targets surrounding the core.

AIM

Research an aspect of the development, operation or function of the OPAL research reactor and report on your knowledge and understanding of the topic based on an analysis of secondary-sourced data. Your final analysis should be peer reviewed and adapted based on feedback to ensure clear communication of your conclusions.

PRACTICAL ACTIVITY 9

TOPIC REQUIREMENTS AND CONSTRAINTS

Your research must be conducted individually.

The topic chosen must relate to the OPAL research reactor or the related technologies employed by or supported by this research reactor.

The topic must allow for the development and answer of one clear inquiry question related to the reactor and the supported technologies.

INVESTIGATION

1 What is OPAL? What general capabilities does it have?

2 Phrase your topic as a question. For example, 'How do the control plates control the fission reaction in OPAL?'. Some suitable starting points in the process of controlled fission in the OPAL research reactor include:

- the safety of the OPAL reactor, including structures and processes in place for protecting people and the environment from radiation produced by fission
- the composition of the reactor fuel and the benefits of using low-enriched uranium (LEU)
- the structure of the core of the OPAL reactor and of an individual fuel assembly with a discussion of how structure relates to function
- the role of the control plates in controlling the fission reaction in OPAL
- secondary-sourced data analysis of real data about control plates and neutron flux in the OPAL reactor
- the products of the fission reaction in the OPAL reactor
- neutron production in the fission reaction and the use of neutrons for different purposes in the OPAL reactor, such as production of radioisotopes, diffraction research, silicon doping or neutron activation analysis.

3 List three or four possible questions that would help answer your main question. For example, 'What do the control plates absorb?', 'What other structures assist in the control of the fission reaction?', or 'How are the control plates controlled?'

4 Do some background research to answer your initial questions. You may want to rephrase your questions to make them as clear and specific as possible. List your references and rephrased questions in the space provided.

ISBN 978 0 6557 0016 6

PRACTICAL ACTIVITY 9

5 Look back at your initial topic question. Construct a hypothesis that can be applied to answer your question. This becomes your working hypothesis and should summarise the answer to your main question. It may change after some further research.

6 ANSTO makes many resources available to the public, particularly for educational purposes. Start your research by visiting the ANSTO website and making appropriate contact with ANSTO. Identify the resources available for your topic through your own review—do not expect ANSTO to identify them for you. Confirm the steps you have taken to ensure the validity of the secondary-sourced data as it applies to your hypothesis.

7 Working in small groups, evaluate other students' topics. What are the strengths of their experimental investigations or research? How could you improve your own investigation or research question?

8 Carry out the remainder of your investigation, summarising key points as you proceed so that your topic has a clear focus and development. Use the tree diagram below to link your development back to your original hypothesis.

CONCLUSION

Evaluate your conclusions using the following questions.

1 Were you successful in answering your original hypothesis? Did you need to rephrase it?

2 Do your research and secondary data sources support your conclusions? How reliable is the data?

Communicate your findings in the form of a fact sheet. It should include explanations of the topic development, assumptions you have made, relevant calculations, data, graphs and diagrams along with suitable explanation for the intended audience.

3 Review other students' research. Are they presenting evidence-based arguments in a form readily understood by the intended general public audience?

 ISBN 978 0 6557 0016 6

EXAM-STYLE QUESTIONS

Multiple-choice questions

Question 1

Recall which of the following alternatives is beta-minus radiation.

A. an electron ejected from an atom

B. a helium nucleus emitted from an atom

C. an electron emitted from the nucleus of an atom

D. energy emitted from an electron of an atom

Question 2

Identify which of the following travels at the greatest speed.

A. gamma radiation

B. beta radiation

C. alpha radiation

D. They all have the same speed.

Question 3

The heaviest form of radiation from radioactive decay is:

A. gamma

B. alpha

C. beta-minus

D. none of the above

Question 4

The type of radiation that is most ionising is:

A. beta

B. alpha

C. gamma

D. none of the above

EXAM-STYLE QUESTIONS

Short-answer questions

Question 1 (1 mark)

Consider the following decay equation:

$^{238}_{92}U \rightarrow ^{x}_{90}Th + ^{4}_{2}\alpha + \gamma$

Find the value of x.

Strontium-90 is one of the radioisotopes that was released during the Fukushima nuclear disaster in Japan. Strontium-90 has a half-life of 28.8 years. Its atomic number is 38.

Question 2 (2 marks)

Determine the number of neutrons in each nucleus of strontium-90.

Question 3 (2 marks)

Determine how many of the original strontium-90 nuclides will still be in existence in 144 years if 1.8×10^{10} atoms of strontium-90 were released during the accident.

Question 4 (2 marks)

A radioactive sample of oxygen-15 has a half-life of 110 min. Calculate the mass of the original sample if the amount remaining after 5.5 h is 0.80 g.

Question 5 (3 marks)

Complete the following decay equations by replacing the ψ symbol in each.

a. $^{14}_{6}C \rightarrow ^{14}_{7}N + \psi$ 1 mark

b. $^{214}_{82}Pb \rightarrow ^{214}_{83}Bi + \psi$ 1 mark

c. $^{60}_{27}Co^{*} \rightarrow ^{60}_{27}Co + \psi$ 1 mark

ISBN 978 0 6557 0016 6

EXAM-STYLE QUESTIONS

Question 6 (5 marks)

The radioactive decay of a particular isotope is shown on the graph below. The initial mass of the radioisotope is 20 g.

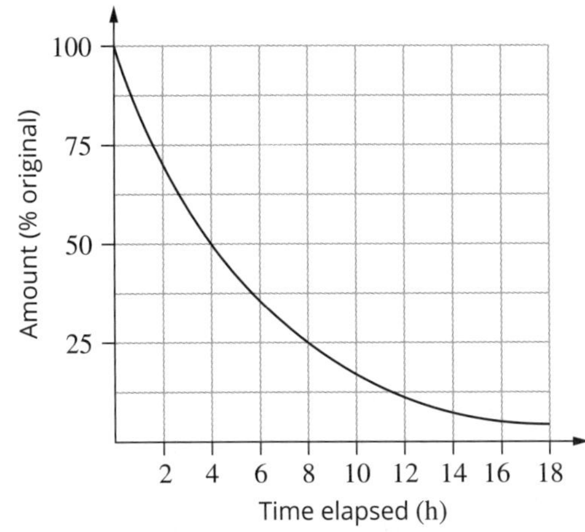

a. Determine the time it takes for a 20 g sample to decay to 5.0 g. 2 marks

b. Determine the half-life of the sample from the graph. 1 mark

c. Determine the amount of the original radioisotope (in grams) that remains after 20.0 h. 2 marks

ISBN 978 0 6557 0016 6

EXAM-STYLE QUESTIONS

Question 7 (10 marks)

The carbon–nitrogen–oxygen (CNO) cycle is a fusion reaction by which stars fuse hydrogen into helium. One of the stages of the CNO cycle is represented by the equation $^{12}C + {}^{1}p \rightarrow {}^{13}N + \gamma$.

Use the following table of data to answer the questions below ($1\ u = 1.660539040 \times 10^{-27}$ kg).

Particle	Mass (u)
$^{12}_{6}C$	12.00000
$^{13}_{7}N$	13.00573
$^{1}_{1}p$	1.00728
$^{1}_{1}n$	1.00866

a. Deduce the mass defect in this reaction (in u and kg). 2 marks

b. Use the mass defect to determine the amount of energy released (in both J and MeV). 3 marks

c. Determine the total mass of six neutrons and six protons (in u). 2 marks

d. Calculate the difference between this and the mass of a carbon-12 nucleus. 1 mark

e. Explain this difference and the energy represented by it. 2 marks

Question 8 (4 marks)

As a doctor, you prescribe a course of radiotherapy for a patient with breast cancer. The procedure involves inserting a radioactive source into the affected region. Explain which type of radiation source—alpha, beta-minus or gamma—you would prefer to use and why. Include in your explanation the reason why you wouldn't pick each of the other two types.

ISBN 978 0 6557 0016 6

UNIT 1

How is energy useful to society?

AREA OF STUDY 3

How can electricity be used to transfer energy?

Outcome 3

Investigate and apply a basic DC circuit model to simple battery-operated devices and household electrical systems, apply mathematical models to analyse circuits, and describe the safe and effective use of electricity by individuals and the community.

Key knowledge

Concepts used to model electricity

- apply concepts of charge (Q), electric current (I), potential difference (V), energy (E) and power (P), in electric circuits
- analyse and evaluate different analogies used to describe electric current and potential difference
- investigate and analyse theoretically and practically electric circuits using the relationships: $I = \frac{Q}{t}$, $V = \frac{E}{Q}$, $P = \frac{E}{t} = VI$
- justify the use of selected meters (ammeter, voltmeter, multimeter) in circuits
- apply the kilowatt-hour (kW h) as a unit of energy

Circuit electricity

- model resistance in series and parallel circuits using:
  - current versus potential difference (I–V) graphs
  - resistance as the potential difference to current ratio, including R = constant for ohmic devices
  - equivalent resistance in arrangements in
    - series: $R_{\text{equivalent}} = R_1 + R_2 + \ldots + R_n$ and
    - parallel: $\frac{1}{R_{\text{equivalent}}} = \frac{1}{R_1} + \frac{1}{R_2} + \ldots + \frac{1}{R_n}$
- calculate and analyse the equivalent resistance of circuits comprising parallel and series resistance
- analyse circuits comprising voltage dividers
- model household (AC) electrical systems as simple direct current (DC) circuits
- compare power transfers in series and parallel circuits
- explain why the circuits in homes are mostly parallel circuits

Using electricity

- investigate and apply theoretically and practically concepts of current, resistance, potential difference (voltage drop) and power to the operation of electronic circuits comprising resistors, light bulbs, diodes, thermistors, light dependent resistors (LDRs), light-emitting diodes (LEDs) and potentiometers (quantitative analysis restricted to use of $I = \frac{V}{R}$ and $P = VI$)
- investigate practically the operation of simple circuits containing resistors, variable resistors, diodes and other non-ohmic devices
- describe energy transfers and transformations with reference to resistors, light bulbs, diodes, thermistors, light dependent resistors (LDRs), light-emitting diodes (LEDs) and potentiometers in common devices

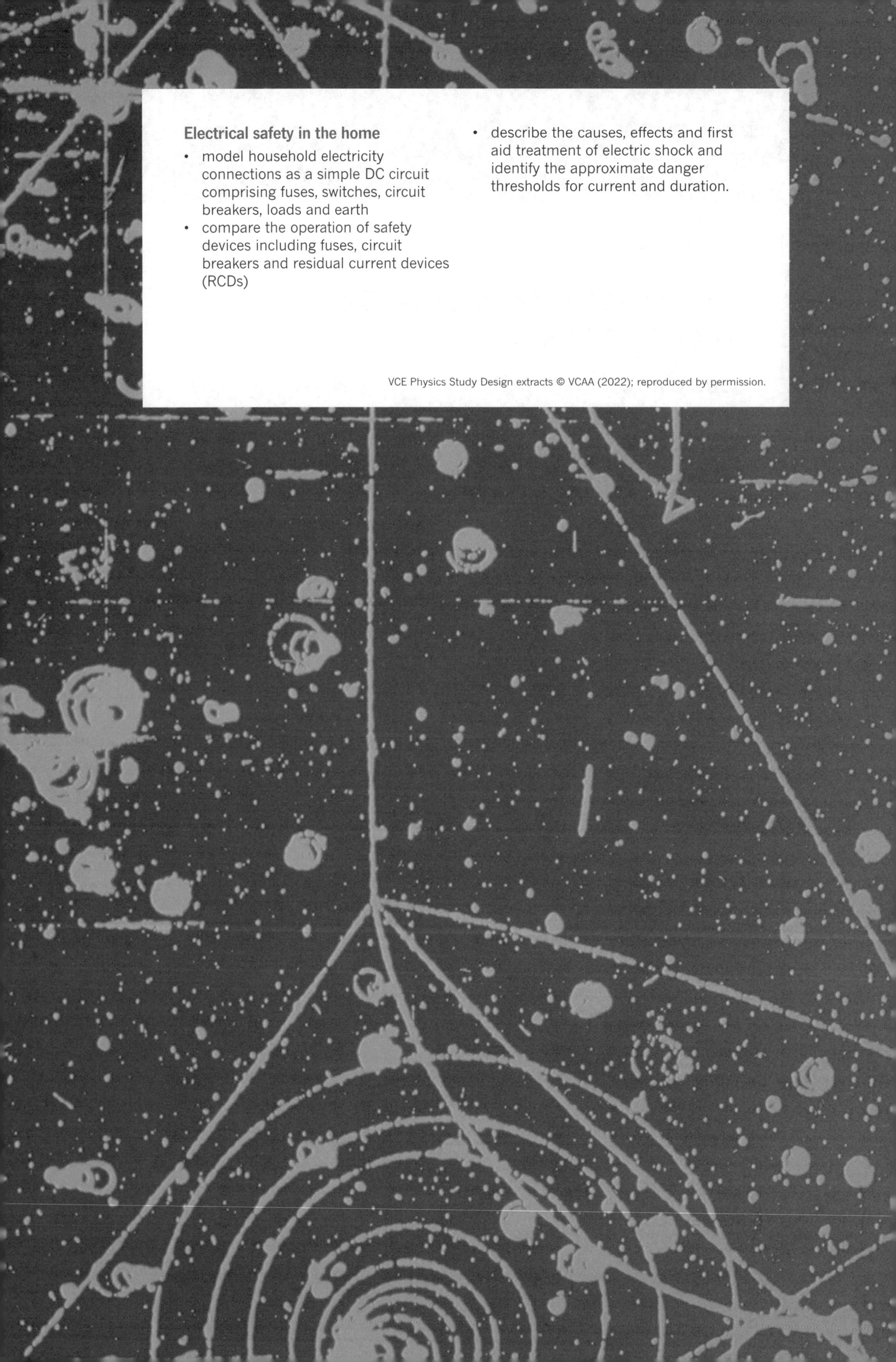

Electrical safety in the home

- model household electricity connections as a simple DC circuit comprising fuses, switches, circuit breakers, loads and earth
- compare the operation of safety devices including fuses, circuit breakers and residual current devices (RCDs)
- describe the causes, effects and first aid treatment of electric shock and identify the approximate danger thresholds for current and duration.

KEY KNOWLEDGE

- **You will now be able to complete Worksheet 17.**

Electricity

All matter in the universe is made of tiny particles called atoms. An atom contains a nucleus at its centre (Figure 1.3.1). The nucleus contains even smaller particles known as protons and neutrons, which are surrounded by particles called electrons.

Each particle has a property known as **charge**. Protons have a positive charge. Neutrons have no charge; they are described as neutral. Electrons have a negative charge.

When significant numbers of charged particles are separated, or move relative to each other, **electricity** results.

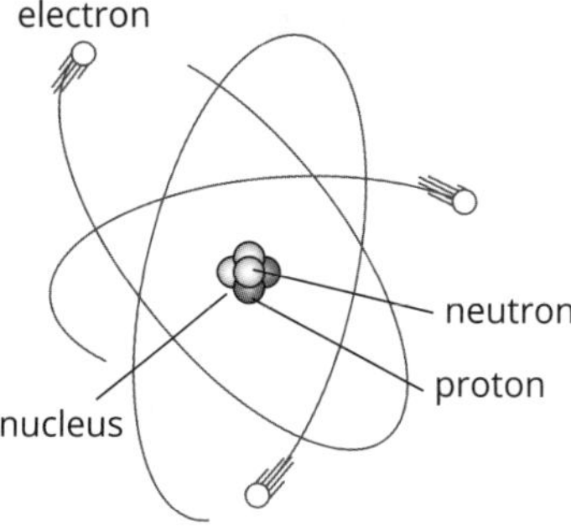

Figure 1.3.1 A simple model of an atom

The charge on a proton and an electron is equal and opposite. This charge is often called the **elementary charge** and given the symbol *e*. A proton has a charge of $+e$ and an electron has a charge of $-e$. The SI unit for charge is called the **coulomb**, C. One coulomb is equal to 6.2×10^{18} protons. And 6.2×10^{18} electrons is equal to −1 coulomb. Table 1.3.1 summarises the charge on a single proton or electron.

Table 1.3.1 The charge on a proton and an electron

	Charge in coulombs (C)
Electron ($-e$)	-1.6×10^{-19}
Proton ($+e$)	$+1.6 \times 10^{-19}$

Certain materials, known as **conductors**, conduct electricity better than others. These materials are known as **metals**. In metals, the electrons are only slightly attracted to the surrounding nuclei, so that electricity can flow more easily. In **non-metals**, the electrons are tightly bound so that they cannot easily move. Non-metals are known as **insulators**.

- **You will now be able to conduct Practical activity 10.**

ELECTRIC CURRENT AND CIRCUITS

An **electric circuit** is created when a conductive material, such as copper wire, is connected in a continuous closed loop so that charges can flow. The flow of charges is known as electric current. Originally, it was thought that the flow of charges in a circuit was positive; in other words, the charges travelled from the positive to the negative terminal of the circuit. This is known as **conventional current** and is given the symbol *I*. It can be measured using a device known as an **ammeter**.

Current is calculated as the amount of charge to pass through a given area per second. It can be expressed as:

$$I = \frac{Q}{t} = \frac{n_e q_e}{t}$$

where I is the current in amperes (A)
Q is the amount of charge in coulombs (C)
n_e is the number of electrons
q_e is the amount of charge of one electron ($q_e = 1.6 \times 10^{-19}$ C)
t is the number of seconds that have passed.

Current is measured in amperes, or amps (A). One ampere is equivalent to one coulomb per second ($C\,s^{-1}$).

It was later found that charge is due to the movement of electrons from the negative to the positive terminal. This is known as **electron flow**.

There are a few different analogies you can use to model the flow of charges in a circuit. One common model is to compare it to water being pumped through a pipe system (Figure 1.3.2). Table 1.3.2 describes elements of electric and water circuits that involve similar processes.

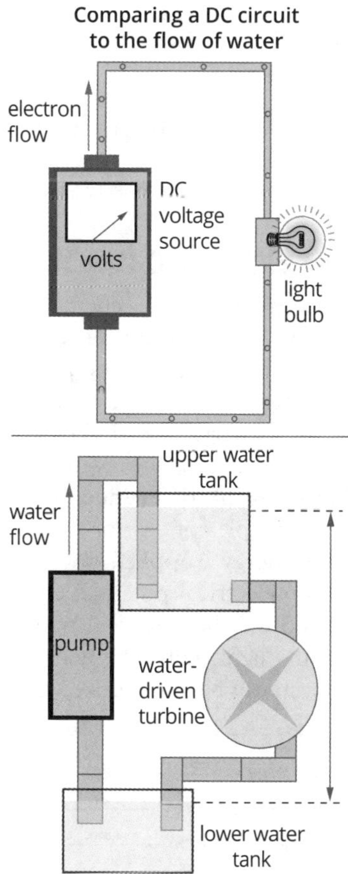

Figure 1.3.2 An electric current can be compared to water flowing through a pipe system.

KEY KNOWLEDGE

Table 1.3.2 Similarities between electric and water circuits	
Electric circuit	**Water circuit**
battery pushes electrons through the wires	pump pushes water through the pipes
current is the same in every part of the wire	water cannot be compressed—the same amount of water flows in every part of the pipe
circuit elements, such as light bulbs, convert electrical potential energy into heat and light	water turbine converts gravitational potential energy into kinetic energy

Figure 1.3.3 shows some of the most common symbols used to represent components in an electric circuit.

Device	Symbol	Device	Symbol
wires crossed not joined		cell (DC supply)	
wires joined, junction of conductor		battery of cells (DC supply)	
fixed resistor	or	AC supply	or
light bulb	or	ammeter	A
		voltmeter	V
diode		fuse	
		switch open	
earth or ground		switch closed	

Figure 1.3.3 Some commonly used electrical devices and their symbols

ENERGY IN ELECTRIC CIRCUITS

The battery in a circuit provides chemical energy, which is changed (**transformed**) into **electrical potential energy**. The electrical potential energy comes from the separation of charge between the positive and negative terminals of the battery. The difference in electrical potential energy between the battery's terminals is known as the **potential difference** (V).

Take the example of a torch (Figure 1.3.4). The chemical energy supplied by the batteries is transformed into electrical potential energy. When the torch is switched on, the electrical potential energy is transferred to the light bulb. The energy changes that occur in the torch can be summarised as:

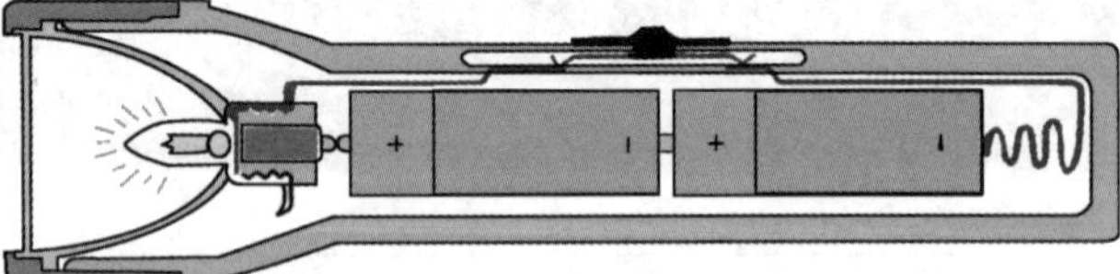

Figure 1.3.4 Energy is transformed and transferred when a torch is switched on

chemical energy $\xrightarrow{\text{transformed}}$ electrical potential energy
electrical potential energy $\xrightarrow{\text{transformed}}$ kinetic energy (electrons)
kinetic energy (electrons) $\xrightarrow{\text{transferred}}$ kinetic energy (filament atoms)
kinetic energy (filament atoms) $\xrightarrow{\text{transformed}}$ thermal energy + light

ISBN 978 0 6557 0016 6

KEY KNOWLEDGE

Potential difference is defined as the amount of electrical potential energy given to each coulomb of charge. As an equation, potential difference is:

> $V = \frac{E}{Q}$
>
> where V is potential difference (V)
> E is electric potential energy (J)
> Q is charge (C).

This means that the potential difference is measured in joules per coulomb (J C^{-1}). This quantity has been assigned a unit: the **volt** (V). The potential difference of $1\,\text{J C}^{-1}$ is equal to 1V.

Potential difference is also known as voltage. It is measured by devices such as voltmeters (Figure 1.3.5), multimeters and voltage sensors. These devices are connected in parallel with the component for which the voltage 'drop' is to be measured.

The potential difference produced by a battery or power source is also called the electromotive force (emf).

Figure 1.3.5 A voltmeter measures the voltage change (in this case, 6.23V) across a light globe.

Combining the equations for potential difference and current, and rearranging to make energy the subject of the equation, gives:

> $E = VIt$
>
> where E is the energy provided by the current, which is the same as the work done (J)
> V is the potential difference (V)
> I is the current (A)
> t is the time (s).

Power

Power is a measure of the rate energy is converted by an electrical appliance; in other words, it is the rate at which work is done. This can be written as:

> $P = \frac{\text{energy transformed}}{\text{time}} = \frac{E}{t} = VI$
>
> where P is the power in joules per second (J s^{-1}).
> One joule per second is 1 watt (W).

Resistance

Resistance (measured in ohms, Ω) is a measure of how hard it is for current to flow through a particular material. For example, conductors allow current to flow through easily, so they are said to have a low resistance.

Ohm's law

Georg Ohm was a German physicist. He discovered that if the temperature of an electrical conductor was kept constant, the current flowing through it was directly proportional to the potential difference across it. This is known as Ohm's law: $I \propto V$. Ohm's law is often written as:

> $\Delta V = IR$ (or just $V = IR$)
>
> where V is the potential difference in volts (V)
> I is current in amps (A)
> R is the constant of proportionality called resistance, in ohms (Ω).
>
> This equation can be transposed to give a quantitative (mathematical) definition for resistance:
>
> $R = \frac{V}{I}$

Conductors that obey Ohm's law are known as **ohmic** conductors. Figure 1.3.6 graphs an ohmic conductor. The relationship between current and potential difference produces a straight line.

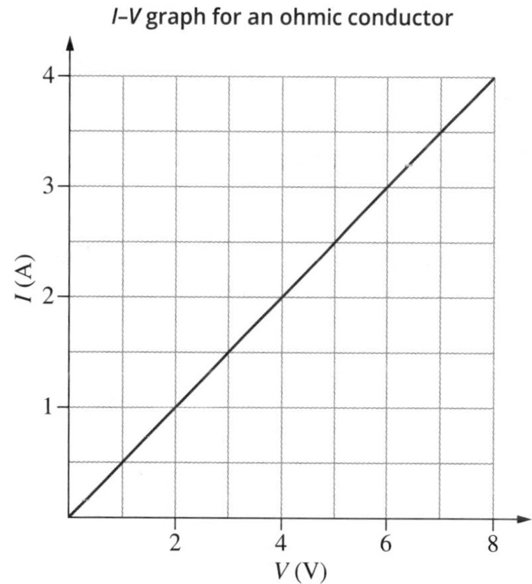

Figure 1.3.6 As the resistance of an ohmic conductor is constant, the *I–V* graph is a straight line.

- **You will now be able to complete Worksheet 18 and conduct Practical activities 11 and 12.**

Electric circuits

SERIES AND PARALLEL CIRCUITS

If components in a circuit are connected one after the other, it is called a **series circuit**. The circuit in Figure 1.3.7 shows three resistors connected in series with an electric cell. In a series circuit, all the components are in the same loop, and therefore each component has the same amount of current.

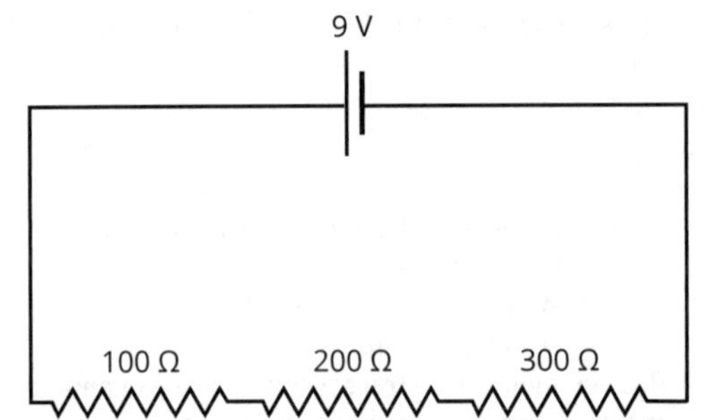

Figure 1.3.7 Three resistors connected in series to an electric cell

As every component in a series circuit is connected in a continuous loop, each component is dependent on each other. This means that if one element of the circuit is removed or stops working, then there is a break in the circuit. The whole circuit will no longer work.

It can be helpful to be able to turn devices on and off independently. For example, you wouldn't want the lights in your lounge room to turn off every time you turn off your TV. In this situation, we use **parallel circuits**. Each loop of a parallel circuit acts like an independent circuit with its own current. Most circuits in a home will be in parallel.

The circuit diagram in Figure 1.3.8 shows a simple parallel circuit. In this example, switch A is open, meaning that lamp A will be turned off. However, the current can still create a complete circuit through lamp B, which will stay on.

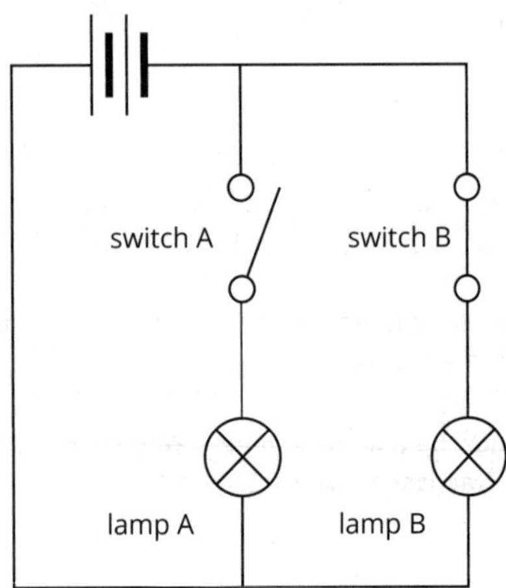

Figure 1.3.8 In this parallel circuit, lamp A will be off and lamp B will be on.

Kirchhoff's loop rule

Kirchhoff's loop rule says that the sum of the potential differences across all the elements around any closed circuit loop must be zero.

This means that the total potential drop around a closed circuit must be equal to the total potential gain in the circuit. For example, if a battery provides 9 V to a circuit, then the sum of all of the potential drops across the components must add up to 9 V.

Equivalent series resistance

In a series circuit, the total voltage drop across the components is summed together. As the current is the same at all parts of the circuit, you can write the following expression for a circuit with two resistors connected in series:

$$V_{Total} = V_1 + V_2 = IR_1 + IR_2 = I \times (R_1 + R_2)$$

In general, a number of individual resistors connected in series can be replaced by an **equivalent resistance** ($R_{equivalent}$) equal to the sum of the individual resistances.

Therefore, the effective resistance can be given as:

$R_{equivalent} = R_1 + R_2 + \ldots + R_n$

where $R_{equivalent}$ is the equivalent series resistance and $R_1, R_2, \ldots, R_n$ are the individual resistances.

Equivalent parallel resistance

In parallel circuits, the current is split at **junctions** where the circuit goes in different directions. The amount of current that flows into a junction is equal to the current flowing out of the junction.

This means that the current in each branch of the parallel circuit will sum to be the current in the main part of a circuit:

$I_T = I_1 + I_2 + \ldots I_n$

Consider two resistors connected in parallel. The total current is then:

$$I_T = I_1 + I_2$$

Using Ohm's law, this is equivalent to

$$\frac{V}{R_{total}} = \frac{V}{R_1} + \frac{V}{R_2}$$

This means that the equivalent resistance in a parallel circuit can be given by the expression:

$$\frac{1}{R_{equivalent}} = \frac{1}{R_1} + \frac{1}{R_2} + \ldots\ldots + \frac{1}{R_n}$$

where $R_{equivalent}$ is the equivalent resistance, and R_1, R_2, … R_n are the individual resistances.

- **You will now be able to complete Worksheets 19 and 20 and conduct Practical activities 13 and 14.**

 ISBN 978 0 6557 0016 6

KEY KNOWLEDGE

USING ELECTRICITY

To convert a signal into another form of energy, we use a **transducer**. Some examples of transducers and their functions are given in Table 1.3.3.

Table 1.3.3 Transducers

Transducer	Function
microphone	converts sound energy into an electrical signal
light dependent resistor (LDR)	the resistance is dependent on the amount of light falling on it
thermistor	the resistance is dependent on the temperature
diode	only allows current to flow in one direction
light-emitting diode (LED)	lights up as current passes through it

ELECTRICAL SAFETY

In Australia, power plugs have three pins (Figure 1.3.9). Each pin is connected to a different wire: an active wire, a neutral wire and an earth wire. The active and neutral wires carry the electrical current. The earth wire is a safety feature.

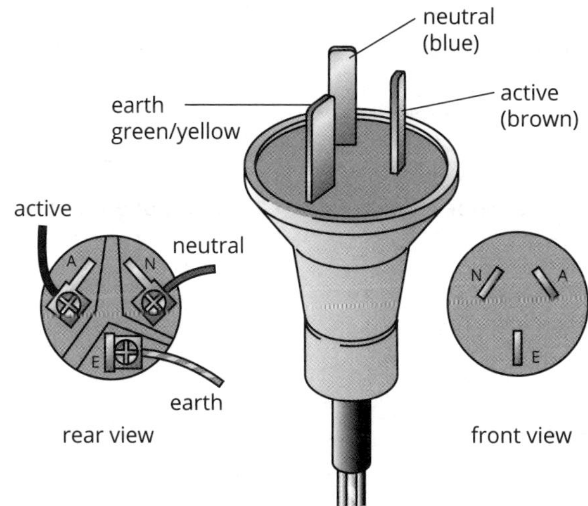

Figure 1.3.9 An Australian three-pin power plug

Fuses and circuit breakers

Household wiring systems are designed to prevent wires from becoming **overloaded**. Appliances that draw a lot of current are put on separate circuits to lights and power points. Despite these precautions, overloading can still occur, most often due to a **short circuit**.

Electric current will always follow the circuit along the path with the least resistance. In Figure 1.3.10, the globe is on when the switch is open, but turns off when the switch closes. This creates a zero-resistance alternative for the current; that is, a short circuit.

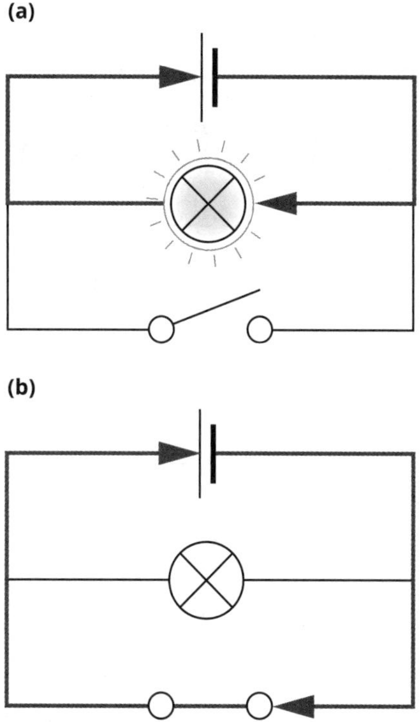

Figure 1.3.10 Short circuits

Short circuits can occur in household wiring, causing wires to heat. This can heat insulation in the walls and ceiling, making it melt or even catch alight.

Electric shock

Despite all the safety features of modern electrical systems and appliances, each year around 50 Australians are killed in electrical accidents. The effect of **electric shock** depends on factors such as:

- the amount of current passing through the body
- how long the current takes to pass through the body
- the path it takes through the body.

When attending to somebody who has been electrocuted, it is important to first check if they are still in contact with the electrical source. First aid should only be given when it is safe to approach the victim; otherwise the person giving first aid may also be electrocuted.

- **You will now be able to complete Worksheets 21, 22 and 23.**

WORKSHEET 17

Classification and identification

Knowledge review—electricity

1 Match the names of circuit components in the word list below with the symbols in the table.

AC supply ammeter battery of cells (DC supply) cell (DC supply) diode
earth or ground fixed resistor fuse light bulb switch open switch closed
voltmeter wires crossed not joined wires joined, junction of conductor

Device	Symbol	Device	Symbol	Device	Symbol
					A
					V
	or		+ −		
	or		+ −		
			or		

2 In the following table, identify which material is a conductor (C) and which is an insulator (I) by writing the corresponding letter alongside each material.

copper	graphite	rubber	plastic	steel	aluminium	glass	salt water

3 Consider the following circuit containing a cell and two identical globes. Recall what each component in the circuit is doing and complete the sentences below.

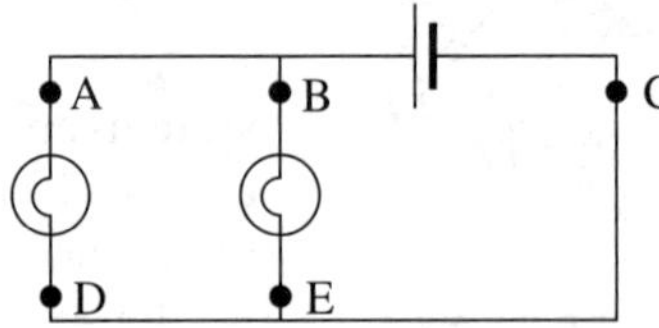

a This is a _______________ circuit.

b To measure the current in the cell, a _______________ needs to be inserted at point _______________.

c The current through the left globe is _______________ compared with the current in the right globe.

d Breaking the circuit at point/s _______________ would stop both globes working.

e Breaking the circuit at point/s _______________ would stop the right globe from working.

f The positive terminal of the cell is on the _______________ side.

4 Identify whether each of the following statements is true (T) or false (F).

a ________ The charge on an electron is equal to the negative of the charge on a proton.

b ________ In conventional current, the current is said to flow from the positive terminal to the negative terminal.

c ________ The total resistance in a series circuit equals the sum of the individual resistances in the circuit.

ISBN 978 0 6557 0016 6

WORKSHEET 18

Modelling

Resistance is variable—Ohm's law

A simple circuit has been constructed to test whether particular circuit loads are ohmic or non-ohmic. The circuit consists of some patch cords, a variable power supply, a resistor, and voltage and current sensors.

The voltage was varied through each of three loads load in turn and the following voltage versus current graph was drawn.

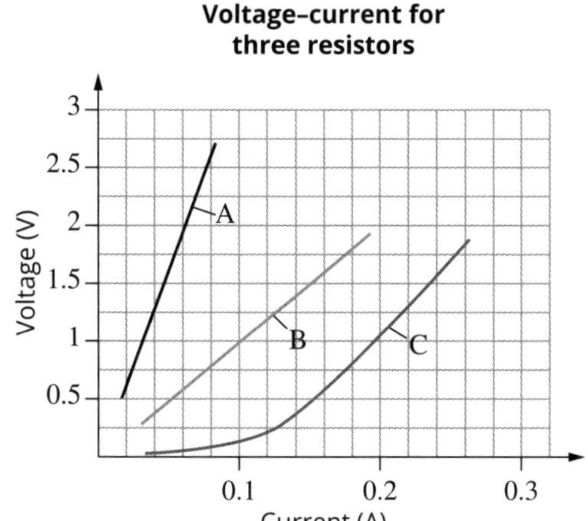

1 Using the *V–I* graph above, identify which of the resistors are ohmic and which are non-ohmic. Fill in your answers below.

ohmic _______________ non-ohmic _______________

2 Explain the reasoning behind your answer to question 1.

3 Using the *V–I* graph above, determine the resistance of resistors A and B.

4 Calculate the resistance of the non-ohmic conductor as the voltage is varied from 0.50 V through to 1.9 V.

5 Determine the conditions under which your answer to question 4 is valid for resistor C. Assess whether it applies to any voltage.

WORKSHEET 18

Complete the calculations for each of the ohmic resistors in questions 6–8.

6 The voltage across a 580 Ω resistor is 120 V. Determine the current through the resistor.

7 The current through a 100 Ω resistor is 0.150 A. Calculate the voltage being applied.

8 A circuit with a 3.0 V battery pack and a resistor has a current of 0.060 A. Determine the value of the resistor.

ISBN 978 0 6557 0016 6

WORKSHEET 19

Modelling

Series and parallel circuits

Determine the unknown quantities in each of the following circuits. Show your working in each case.

P = power, I = current, R = resistance and V = emf

1

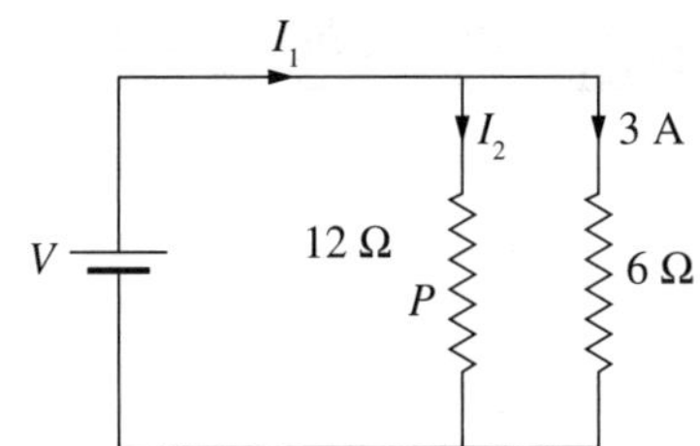

2

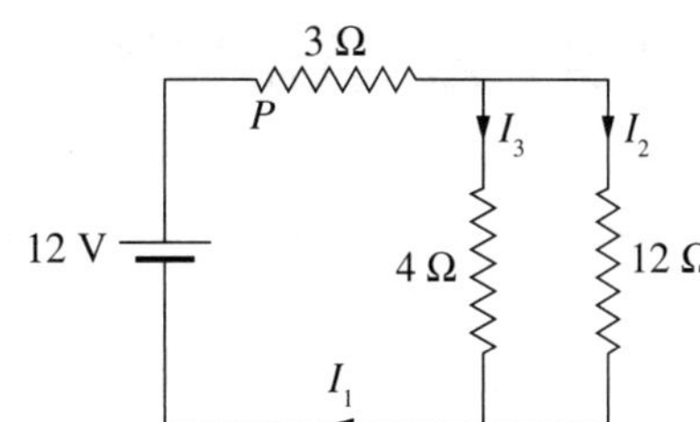

3

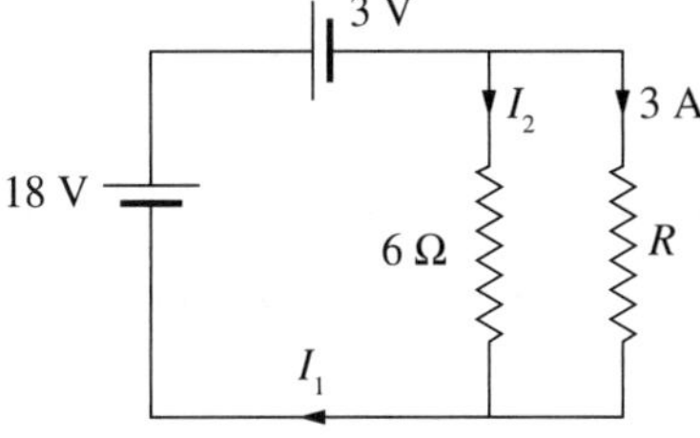

4

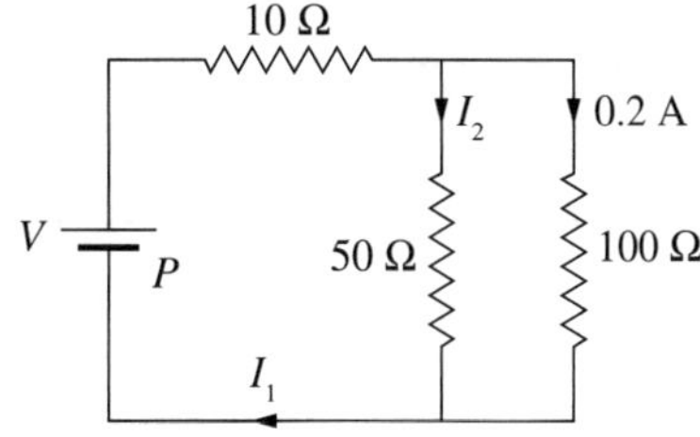

1 ....

....

....

....

2 ....

....

....

....

3 ....

....

....

....

4 ....

....

....

....

WORKSHEET 20

Modelling • Case study

Heating and power loss in electric circuits

1 Heat loss in electric circuits can be a positive effect in some circumstances and a negative effect in others. From your studies of energy and power loss in electric circuits, recall and list some examples where heating is a positive and desired outcome and others where it has a negative effect.

Positive	Negative

2 100 J of heat is produced each second in a 10 Ω resistor. Determine the potential difference across the resistor.

3 An electric iron has a resistance of 24 Ω and uses a current of 10 A. Calculate the total heat the iron transfers to its surrounds each minute.

4 An electric hotplate uses energy at a rate of 1500 W when it is at the maximum setting. At the minimum setting it uses energy at a rate of 350 W. If the voltage supplied is 240 V, determine the current and the resistance in each case.

5 A large electric room heater with a resistance of 16 Ω draws 15 A when heating at its maximum level. If it runs for 2 h, calculate how much energy, in kW h and in J, has been used.

 ISBN 978 0 6557 0016 6

6 Two resistance wires, each of $10\,\Omega$, are connected across a battery of $10\,\text{V}$.

a Calculate the power supplied through the wires when connected in series.

b Calculate the power supplied through the wires when connected in parallel.

c Determine the ratio of the power supplied via the series circuit to that supplied by the parallel circuit.

7 Two particular options are being considered as alternatives in the design of a new hair dryer. Both use the same length of the same resistive wire. One option is to connect the wire in series, but the designers think they could make a more compact design if the wires were connected in parallel. They wish to produce the highest power output possible. Calculate the ratio of the power supplied by the series option compared with the parallel option to advise the designers on which option they should choose.

ISBN 978 0 6557 0016 6

WORKSHEET 21

Classification and identification

Household circuits and electrical safety

1 Australian houses are supplied with 240 V AC. The 240 V rating is:

A the maximum value of the alternating current.

B the average value of the alternating current.

C the value of a DC voltage that would apply the same power.

D none of the above.

2 Explain why only an active and neutral wire come to a house from the street supply, even though Australian power points have three connections.

3 The function of a safety switch is to burn out and thus turn off the circuit in the event of a circuit overload. The safety switch is always placed on the active wire, yet it would still work if it was on the neutral wire. Explain why this is the case.

4 Describe the function of the 'earth stake' that will generally be found near a house's main switchboard.

5 A toaster cable with wires coloured red, black and green is to be joined to one with wires coloured blue, brown and green-yellow. State which colour wires match each other.

6 An appliance is mistakenly wired between the active and the earth wires, rather than active and neutral. Explain the danger of this arrangement despite the appliance still appearing to work.

7 Explain the main advantage of a 'double earthed' appliance over one with a standard earth wire.

 ISBN 978 0 6557 0016 6

8 Explain why the shock received if a person touches a live wire with the back of the hand will generally be less severe than that received by a person touching a live wire with uninsulated pliers.

9 Household circuits are wired in parallel. State why this is the case.

10 Calculate how much current would flow through a person with dry hands and a total contact resistance of 100 kΩ when they touch a live 240 V wire.

WORKSHEET 22

Classification and identification

Literacy review—electricity

1 The following is a list of units and other terms from the areas of electricity and magnetism. A significant proportion of these units are named after people. Categorise the quantities and units shown as being named after people or derived from a related term.

volt	current	ampere	resistance	ohm
solenoid	power	energy	watt	joule

Honouring a past scientist	Derived from a related term

2 For the terms listed in question 1, complete the table below, giving the meaning and the origin of each term.

Term	Meaning	Origin

3 The following statement is about series and parallel circuits. Recall what you know to fill in the blanks using the list of randomly ordered terms below. Some terms may be used more than once.

current	resistance	Ohm's law	inversely	directly

For a circuit with constant _______________, as voltage increases or decreases, _______________ increases or decreases respectively. They are said to be _______________ proportional. For the same circuit, when resistance increases, _______________ decreases, and vice versa. They are said to be _______________ proportional. This relationship is called _______________.

ISBN 978 0 6557 0016 6

WORKSHEET 23

Reflection—How can electricity be used to transfer energy?

The following table lists the key knowledge covered in this area of study.

1 Reflect on how well you understand the concepts listed. Rate your learning by shading the circle that corresponds to your current level of understanding for each one.

Key knowledge	Not confident ⟵				⟶ Very confident
concepts of charge (Q), electric current (I), potential difference (V), energy (E) and power (P) in electric circuits	○	○	○	○	○
electric circuits using the relationships: $I = \frac{Q}{t}, V = \frac{E}{Q}, P = \frac{E}{t} = VI$	○	○	○	○	○
equivalent resistance of circuits comprising parallel and series resistance	○	○	○	○	○
circuits comprising voltage dividers	○	○	○	○	○
power transfers in series and parallel circuits	○	○	○	○	○
concepts of current, resistance, potential difference (voltage drop) and power to the operation of electronic circuits	○	○	○	○	○
operation of simple circuits containing resistors, variable resistors, diodes and other non-ohmic devices	○	○	○	○	○
operation of safety devices including fuses, circuit breakers and residual current devices (RCDs)	○	○	○	○	○

2 Consider the points you have shaded from Not confident to Very confident. List specific ideas you can identify that were challenging.

3 Write down two different strategies that you will apply to help further your understanding of these ideas.

PRACTICAL ACTIVITY 10

Experiment

Electrostatics with a Van de Graaff generator

SUGGESTED DURATION

- 50 minutes

MATERIALS

- Van de Graaff generator
- plain balloons
- metal-coated balloons (available from novelty shops and supermarkets)
- woollen cloth
- cotton string
- foil pie plates
- discharging sphere
- insulating rod
- galvanometer or charge sensor and data logger
- rubber mat to stand on

INTRODUCTION

Normally, atoms have a neutral charge, meaning that the number of electrons equals the number of protons. If the number of protons is greater than the number of electrons (or the number of electrons is greater than the number of protons), then the atom is said to have a positive charge or negative charge, respectively.

Objects with like charge will repel one another, and objects with unlike charge will attract one another.

In the right conditions, an object can acquire an electric charge by rubbing it with another object: for example, rubbing your shoes on a carpet, sliding across a car seat, or rubbing a balloon against your hair. In the last case, the charged balloon and hair will have the same amount of charge, but the charges will be opposite, and therefore they will attract one another. In this experiment, a Van de Graaff generator is used to examine the transfer of electric charges from one material to another.

AIM

To investigate and describe processes by which materials become electrically charged.

To investigate variables that affect how charged objects interact at a distance.

 **Safety**

Even though a Van de Graaff generator creates a very high voltage, the amount of actual charge is relatively low, making it safe when used responsibly.

Use with care and avoid touching the sphere!

METHOD

1 ▪ Examine the construction of the Van de Graaff generator. Explain the method by which charge is transferred to the sphere. (The top of the sphere can generally be carefully removed to view the internal operation while unplugged.) You may like to use an illustration.

2 ▪ Describe the distribution of charge on the sphere.

ISBN 978 0 6557 0016 6

BALLOON TEST 1

3 ▪ Charge a standard rubber balloon suspended by a string by rubbing it with a woollen cloth (or woollen jumper). Start the Van de Graaf generator and bring a metal-coated balloon, held by an insulating rod, near the sphere. Carry the coated balloon to the suspended, charged rubber balloon. Observe and describe the action between them.

BALLOON TEST 2

4 ▪ Fix two coated balloons to the side of the sphere of the Van de Graaff generator with damp cotton strings. Start the generator. Observe and describe the action between the balloons.

5 ▪ Develop a hypothesis to explain why the cotton strings holding the balloons need to be damp. Explain why they couldn't be nylon fishing line.

GALVANOMETER OR CHARGE SENSOR

6 ▪ Follow the instructions that come with the school's Van de Graaff generator, and connect a galvanometer or charge sensor capable of registering small currents in series with a Van de Graaff generator and an earth. If you have access to a data logger, set the sample rate to between 200 Hz and 500 Hz. Hold the discharge sphere about 1–2 cm from the generator's sphere. Turn the galvanometer to its highest range and start the generator. Observe the discharge and the reading on the galvanometer. If no reading is observed, turn to a slightly more sensitive range and repeat. Describe your observations.

PIE PLATES

7 ▪ Make sure the sphere of the generator is fully discharged. Stack a group of foil pie plates upside down, and loosely, on top of the sphere. Start the generator. Observe and describe what happens to the pie plates.

8 ▪ Check with your teacher as to whether the school has accessories for the Van de Graaff generator that would make other tests possible. Record your observations of these tests in the following space.

DISCUSSION

1 Explain the processes by which objects become electrically charged. Summarise your findings from this practical investigation.

2 The brush and belt of the generator charge the belt by friction. The sphere at the top collects the charge. Explain the function of the moving belt and the reason why it needs to be insulated.

3 Compare the charge from friction from, for example, rubbing a balloon with a woollen cloth with that from a Van de Graaff generator. Describe any differences and/or similarities.

4 Discuss whether charges obtained from friction (for example, the electrostatic charge from a Van de Graaff generator) are able to form a current.

CONCLUSION

 ISBN 978 0 6557 0016 6

PRACTICAL ACTIVITY 11

Experiment • Simulation

Ohmic and non-ohmic conductors

SUGGESTED DURATION

- 50 minutes

INTRODUCTION

An ohmic conductor is said to have a resistance that obeys Ohm's law. That is, its resistance does not vary but is a constant where $V \propto I$. Non-ohmic conductors have a resistance that varies with changing current or potential difference.

AIM

To investigate the properties of an ohmic and a non-ohmic conductor.

Safety

Most current sensors have a 1 A range and are suitable for this experiment. They are generally current protected, but check the manufacturer's specifications and use with care. Exceeding the maximum current rating for an ammeter or sensor can permanently damage the meter.

Exercise caution when using the power supply: use only low voltages (10 V DC or less) and only make changes to the circuit when the circuit switch is open.

To reduce chances of spills and subsequent electrical shock, do not allow food or drinks near the equipment.

Be sure resistor ratings and power supplies settings are appropriate for your voltage and current sensors or meters.

Complete a risk assessment before starting the activity.

MATERIALS

- power supply 10 V DC, 1 A (preferably fully filtered and rectified. A DC battery pack is one option.)
- connecting wires
- DC ammeter (0–1 A and 0–5 A) or current sensor
- DC voltmeter (0–15 V) or voltage sensor
- data logger (if using current and/or voltage sensors)
- rheostat or variable resistor
- approximately 50 cm of nichrome wire laid out straight or taped to a ruler
- light globe (6 V) and holder

METHOD

Before starting, if you are using a data logger, connect the voltage and current sensors following the manufacturer's instructions.

1 ▪ Connect the non-variable terminals of the rheostat to the DC terminals of the power supply. Connect the rest of the circuit as shown in the diagram below. The positive terminal of the ammeter should be connected to the positive side of the rheostat.

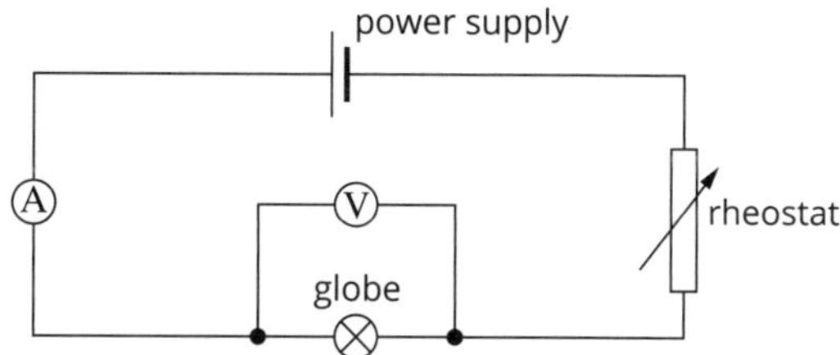

2 ▪ Connect the voltmeter initially across the globe. Set the sliding contact of the rheostat near the positive end to produce the rheostat's lowest resistance value. Turn the power supply on to 6 V and watch the meters. Describe the change you observe with the circuit connected correctly.

....

....

3 ▪ Adjust the rheostat until a current of 0.20 A is recorded through the globe. Record the corresponding potential difference across the globe in the table in the Results section. Record the uncertainty in the measurement of voltage and current based on the meters or sensors you are using.

4 ▪ Using the rheostat, increase the current by steps of 0.2 A. Note and record the potential difference and current each time in the table.

5 ▪ Switch off the power supply and replace the globe in the circuit with a 50 cm length of nichrome wire stretched out reasonably straight. You may find it best to tape it to a ruler, but make sure it is not in contact with any other conductor.

6 ▪ Turn the power supply back on and repeat steps 3 and 4 for the nichrome wire, recording your results in the table.

RESULTS

1 Record your results in the table below.

Type of resistance (load)	Current (A) ±	Voltage (V) ±
globe	0.20	
	0.40	
	0.60	
	0.80	
	1.00	
nichrome wire	0.20	
	0.40	
	0.60	
	0.80	
	1.00	

2 Plot a graph of potential difference versus current for the nichrome wire (a) and globe (b) on the same set of axes below. If you have used a data logger, print and paste your graph over the space provided.

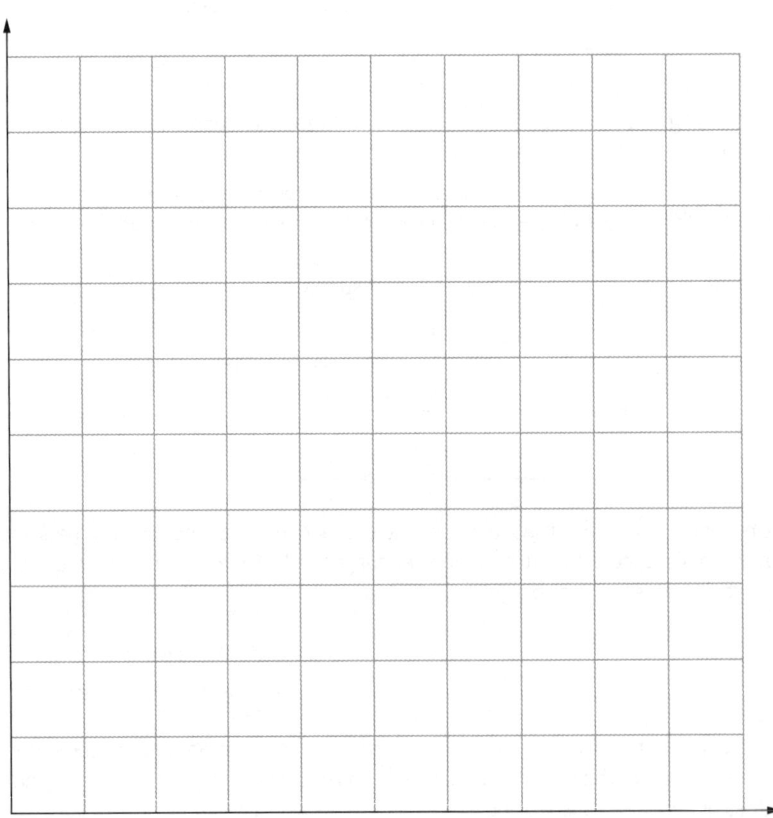

 ISBN 978 0 6557 0016 6

3 Recall why the potential difference is plotted on the vertical axis.

4 Determine the value of the resistance of the nichrome wire.

DISCUSSION

1 Based upon your results, categorise the nichrome wire and the globe as ohmic or non-ohmic conductors. Make reference to your graph in justifying your conclusion.

2 Identify potential improvements to the methodology in this experiment.

Your teacher may have additional conductors for you to test. Repeat the investigation for the additional conductors if available.

CONCLUSION

PRACTICAL ACTIVITY 12

Experiment • Simulation

Finding the resistance of an ohmic resistor

SUGGESTED DURATION

- 50 minutes

INTRODUCTION

The voltage, V, across an ohmic resistor and the current, I, through it are related to its resistance by the linear relationship of Ohm's law: $V = IR$. The resistance is the inverse of the gradient of the line in a graph of the current drawn by a resistor when the potential difference is varied.

This experiment requires correct use of a voltmeter and ammeter.

AIM

To find the resistance of an ohmic resistor by measuring the current that flows through it when the potential difference across it is varied.

Safety

The voltmeter and ammeter must be connected correctly. To avoid damaging the equipment, make sure that the ammeter is connected in series and that the voltmeter is connected in parallel across the resistor.

An appropriately sized resistor should be chosen to keep the current in the circuit small. Otherwise, the current will burn out the resistor and might cause a short circuit.

Complete a risk assessment before starting this activity.

MATERIALS

- variable DC power supply (preferably fully filtered and rectified. A DC battery pack is one option.)
- connecting wires
- switch
- ohmic resistors (various values between 33 Ω and 2 kΩ)
- DC voltmeter (0–10 V) or voltage sensor
- data logger (if using current and/or voltage sensors)
- DC ammeter (0–1 A) or current sensor

METHOD

If using voltage and current sensors, connect these to your data logger following the manufacturer's directions and set to view a standard meter in digital form. Sample rates are not important, as only spot readings will be taken in this practical activity.

1 ▪ Connect the circuit as shown in the diagram below. Make a note of the uncertainty in the readings from the voltmeter and ammeter in the spaces provided in the table in the Results section.

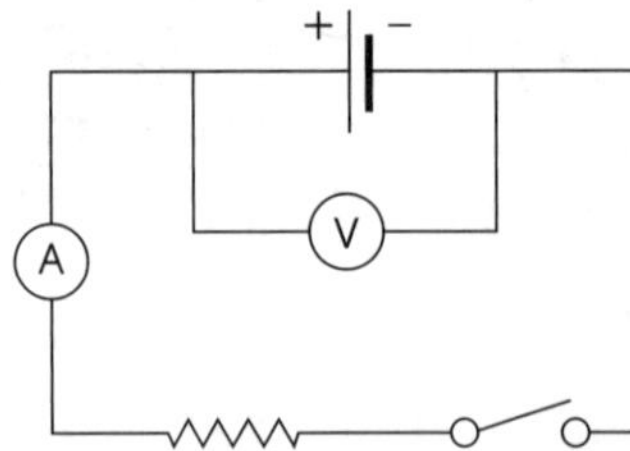

2 ▪ Set the variable power supply to 0 V and turn it on. Explain why it is essential to first zero the power source.

3 ▪ Adjust the power supply until the voltmeter or sensor reads 2 V. If you're using a stepped power supply with set values, set the power supply to 2 V and record the corresponding reading on the voltmeter or sensor. Close the switch and record the ammeter or current sensor reading. Note the values in the table.

4 ▪ Increase the voltage from the variable power supply to 4 V and record the results in the table. Repeat for steps of 2 V through to 10 V. Record the corresponding voltmeter and ammeter readings.

5 ▪ Set the power supply back to 0 V and repeat the measurements twice more to allow an average to be calculated across three trials.

 ISBN 978 0 6557 0016 6

RESULTS

1 List the variables in this experiment:

Independent: ______________________

Dependent: ______________________

Controlled: ______________________

Measured voltage (V) ±	Measured current (A) ±			
	Trial 1	Trial 2	Trial 3	Average ±

2 Plot your results, including error bars, on the axes below. Plot the independent variable, *V*, on the horizontal axis and the dependent variable, *I*, on the vertical axis. Take care with units and check that the units of current are in A, not mA.

If using a data logger, print out a graph and paste it over the graph template below.

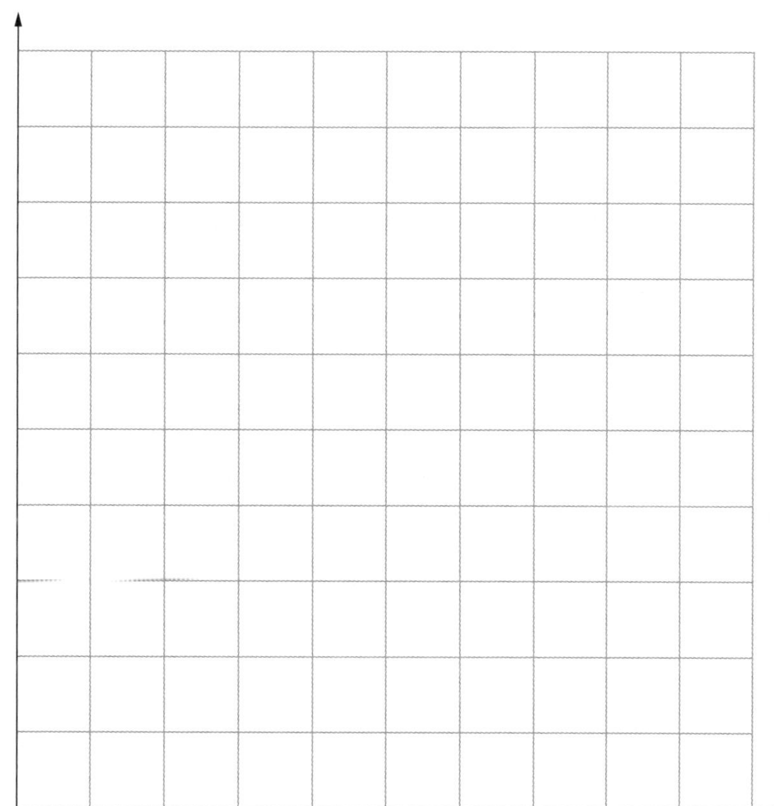

3 Draw a line of best fit, including minimum and maximum gradient lines.

4 Calculate the gradient of the line of best fit. Use this to find the resistance of the resistor.
Recall that the gradient of an *I–V* graph = $\frac{I}{R}$.

5 Look for any points on your graph that do not fit the trend. Explain why this may have been the case.

6 Compare your value for resistance with the values obtained by other groups who used the same resistor. Describe the similarities and differences.

7 Compare your graph to the graphs drawn by other groups who used different resistors. Describe what you notice about the shape of the graphs.

DISCUSSION

1 Use the coloured bands on the resistor to identify its resistance. Compare your experimental value for the resistance with the theoretical value.

2 Considering your results and conclusion, discuss whether the experiment provided an effective method of finding the resistance of the resistor.

 ISBN 978 0 6557 0016 6

3 Constructively critique whether there was a reasonable level of uncertainty in your calculations for the resistors.

4 Many other components have a resistance. Discuss the suitability of this method for finding the resistance of other circuit components.

CONCLUSION

PRACTICAL ACTIVITY 13

Experiment • Simulation

Series and parallel circuits

SUGGESTED DURATION

- 60 minutes

MATERIALS

- data logger and current and voltage sensors or ammeter and voltmeter
- resistors (3–6), at least three different known values
- DC power supply, 10 V, 1 A minimum. A DC battery pack can make a good option.
- switch (single-pole, single-throw)
- 4 mm patch cords
- alligator-clip adapters for the patch cords

INTRODUCTION

Ohm's law states that the voltage drop across an electrical resistor is mathematically equal to the magnitude of the current through the resistor multiplied by the resistance:

$V = IR$

When circuits have multiple resistors connected in either series or parallel, each resistor will have a voltage and a current associated with it. By measuring the current and voltage associated with individual components and comparing them to the behaviour of the whole circuit, it is possible to experimentally determine if there is an equivalent resistance for a set of resistors.

AIM

To investigate combinations of resistors in series and parallel circuits, and determine the overall resistance of each particular combination.

Safety

Exercise caution when using the power supply: use only low voltages (10 V DC or less) and only make changes to the circuit when the circuit switch is open.

To reduce chances of spills and subsequent electrical shock, do not allow food or drinks near the equipment. Be sure that resistor ratings and power-supply settings are appropriate for your voltage and current sensors or meters. Complete a risk assessment before starting the activity.

METHOD

RESISTORS IN SERIES

1. If you are using a data logger, connect the voltage and current sensors and set up a display that enables both readings to be monitored simultaneously. Record the uncertainties inherent in your meters in Table 1 in the Results section.
2. With the power off, connect the first resistor and the open switch in series to the power supply using the patch cords.

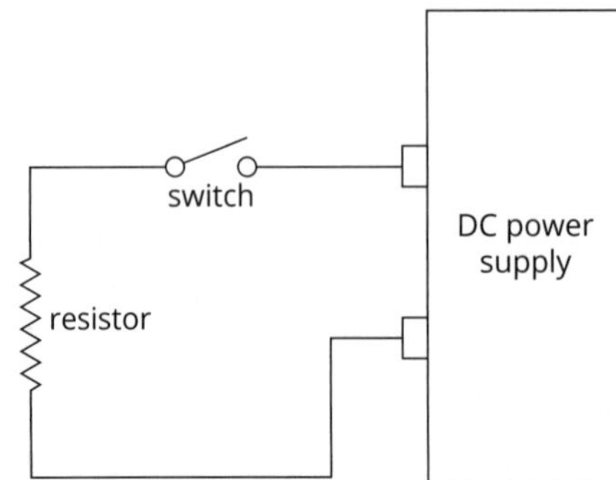

 ISBN 978 0 6557 0016 6

3 ▪ Connect the voltage meter across the resistor, and then connect the current meter in series with the resistor and switch. Make sure the switch is left open.

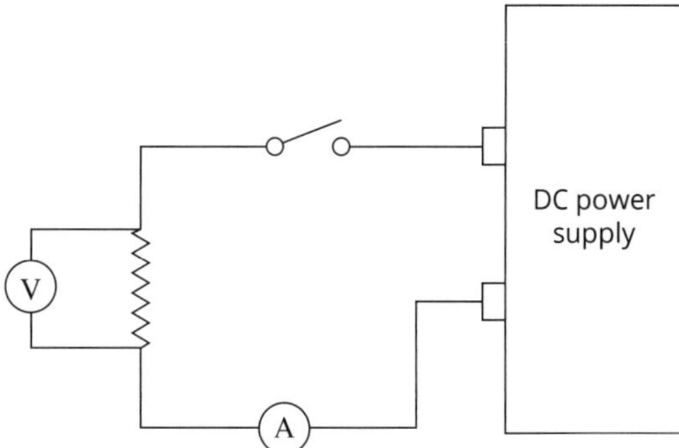

4 ▪ Set the output voltage from the power supply to 5.0 V and turn on your power supply. Record this value in Table 1.

5 ▪ Close the switch, and then record the voltage and current readings in Table 1. After recording the values, open the switch.

6 ▪ Add the second resistor in series with the first, and then move the voltage sensor leads to measure the total voltage across both resistors. Close the switch, and record the voltage and current reading in Table 1.

7 ▪ Move the voltage-meter leads to measure the voltage across the first resistor by itself, and record the voltage in Table 1.

8 ▪ Move the voltage-meter leads to measure the voltage across the second resistor by itself, and record the voltage in Table 1. After recording the values, open the switch.

9 ▪ The voltage has been measured for each component. Explain why the current isn't being measured for each component as well.

10 ▪ Add the third resistor in series with the first, and then repeat the previous steps, recording the voltage and current across all three resistors together, and then the voltage for each individual resistor in the circuit. Record the values in Table 1.

11 ▪ Open the switch before moving on to the next section.

12 ▪ If time allows, repeat these steps at least twice to give three independent trials.

RESISTORS IN PARALLEL

13 ▪ With the power supply off, connect the first resistor and the switch (open) in series to the power supply using the patch cords.

14 ▪ Connect the voltage meter across the resistor, and then connect the current meter in series with the resistor and switch. Make sure the switch is open.

15 ▪ Set the output voltage to 5 V and turn the power supply on.

16 ▪ Close the switch, and then record the voltage and current reading in Table 2. After recording the values, open the switch.

17 ▪ Add the second resistor in parallel with the first as shown in the diagram below.

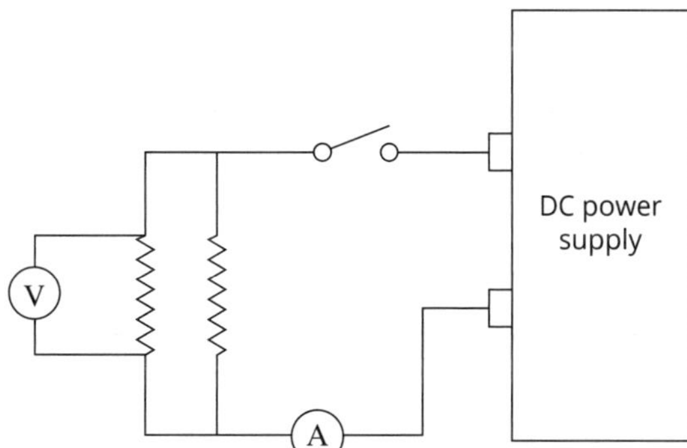

18 ▪ Close the switch and record the voltage and current readings in Table 2. After recording the values, open the switch.

19 ▪ Move the current meter leads to measure the current through the first resistor by itself.

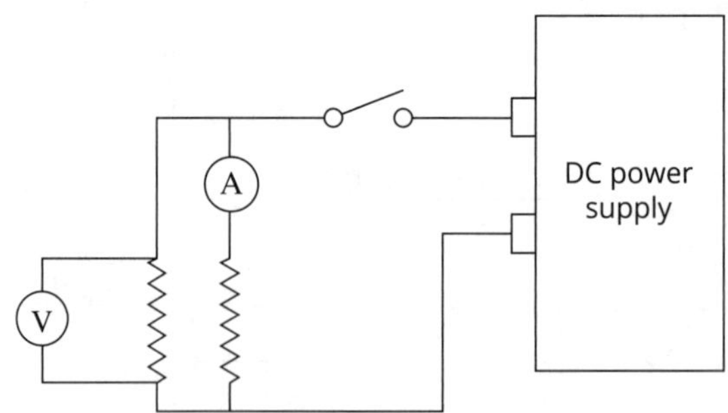

20 ▪ Close the switch, and record the current in Table 2. After recording the value, open the switch.

21 ▪ Move the current meter leads to measure the current through the second resistor, close the switch, and record the current reading in Table 2. After recording the value, open the switch.

22 ▪ The current has been measured for each component. Explain why the voltage isn't being measured as well.

23 ▪ Add the third resistor in parallel with the first two, and repeat the previous steps, recording the voltage and current across all three resistors together, then the current for each individual resistor in the circuit. Record the values in Table 2.

24 ▪ Open the switch after you have made the final measurement.

25 ▪ If time allows, repeat these steps at least twice to give three independent trials.

RESULTS

1 Using the coloured bands on the resistors, determine and record the theoretical rating for each of the resistors used in Tables 1 and 2. Include an estimate of the uncertainty from the tolerance given on the resistor.

2 Calculate the measured value for resistance for each circuit using $R = \frac{V}{I}$ and enter the values into the corresponding columns in Tables 1 and 2.

Potential difference from power supply: __________ V ± __________.

Table 1 Series circuit

Number of resistors	Resistor	Voltage ± ______(V)	Current ± ______(A)	$R = \frac{V}{I}$ (Ω)	Theoretical resistance (Ω)
1	first				
2	first				
	second				
total potential difference for two resistors: __________ V ± __________					
3	first				
	second				
	third				
total potential difference for three resistors: __________ V ± __________					

 ISBN 978 0 6557 0016 6

Table 2 Parallel circuit

Number of resistors	Resistor	Voltage ± ______ (V)	Current ± ______ (A)	$R = \frac{V}{I}$ (Ω)	Theoretical resistance (Ω)
1	first				
2	first				
	second				
total current for two resistors: __________ A ± __________					
3	first				
	second				
	third				
total current for three resistors: __________ A ± __________					

DISCUSSION

1 Comment on how the measured resistances compare with the theoretical resistances for each circuit.

2 Discuss how the methodology of this experiment could be improved.

CONCLUSION

PRACTICAL ACTIVITY 14

Experiment

Electrical equivalent of heat

SUGGESTED DURATION

- 50 minutes

INTRODUCTION

The purpose of this experiment is to determine the amount of electrical energy that is equivalent to a certain amount of thermal energy. This is accomplished by measuring the amount of electrical energy dissipated by a heating resistor to heat water, and the resulting thermal energy added to the water.

From the study of thermodynamics, we know that when heat is added to a solid or a liquid, that energy goes into increasing the material's internal energy, thus increasing its temperature. The relationship between the heat and the resulting change in temperature is given by:

$Q = mc\Delta T$

where:

Q is the energy transferred (J)

m is the mass (kg)

c is the specific heat capacity of the material ($c = 4200\ \text{J kg}^{-1}\text{K}^{-1}$ for water)

ΔT is the change in temperature (K).

In this experiment, heat is added to the calorimeter using a heating resistor or heating coil. Electrical energy is converted into heat in the resistor, increasing the temperature of the water and the cup. Historically, this has been referred to as the electrical equivalent of heat. Electrical power is determined by the energy supplied by the power source:

$P = VI$

where:

P is the power (W)

V is the voltage across the resistor (V)

I is the current through the resistor (A).

Power is the rate at which energy is generated or used (i.e. power = energy/time)

Thus energy can be calculated by:

$E = Pt$

where:

E is the energy supplied or generated (J)

P is the power (W)

t is the time (s).

The efficiency of the energy conversion is: $\text{efficiency (\%)} = \frac{\text{useful energy out}}{\text{total energy in}} \times 100\% = \frac{\text{power used}}{\text{power input}} \times 100\%$

MATERIALS

- DC power supply
- DC ammeter (0–1 A) or current sensor
- DC voltmeter (0–5 V) or voltage sensor
- digital thermometer or temperature sensor
- data logger
- heating resistor, heating coil or low-voltage immersion heater
- leads to connect the resistor to the power supply
- calorimeter (A suitable calorimeter can be constructed from an insulating coffee cup for the inner and a beaker with an insulated cover.)
- electronic balance (at least one per class)
- cool water (around 5°C below room temperature)
- stopwatch (not necessary when using electronic measure)

AIM

To determine the amount of electrical energy that is equivalent to a certain amount of thermal energy.

ISBN 978 0 6557 0016 6

PRACTICAL ACTIVITY 14

Safety

Never apply power to the heating resistor unless the resistor is immersed in water. Never touch the resistor. It gets hot! Do not apply over 10 V.

Do not exceed the maximum power rating of the heating resistor. For best results, do not exceed 80% of the rating. Exceeding the maximum current rating will permanently damage an ammeter or sensor.

Most current sensors have a 1 A range and are suitable for this experiment. They are generally current protected, but take care to check the manufacturer's specifications and use with care.

METHOD

Before starting to take measurements, connect the voltage, current and temperature sensors following the manufacturer's directions. Set up the software so that all three quantities can be monitored simultaneously.

1. Connect the power supply to the heating resistor, with the current sensor connected in series and the voltage sensor connected in parallel to the heating resistor, as shown in the circuit diagram below.

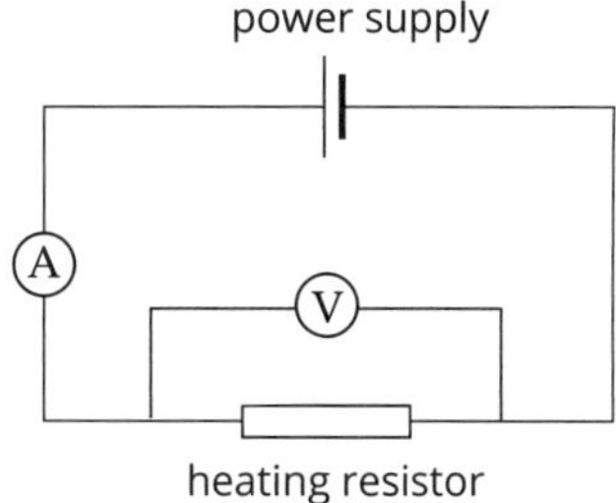

2. Measure the mass of the calorimeter with the electronic balance while it is dry, and record this measurement together with the uncertainty in the Results section.
3. Fill the calorimeter around three-quarters full of cold tap water and measure the mass of the calorimeter and the water combined. Record this mass in the Results section.
4. Place the heating resistor and thermometer in the water, being careful to avoid the resistor touching the walls of the calorimeter or the thermometer. Place an insulating cover over the top of the calorimeter, leaving only room for the thermometer and leads to extend out. Explain why this is an important consideration in this activity.

5. Start monitoring temperature using the thermometer or sensor, and wait until the temperature of the water in the calorimeter and the heating resistor equalises. Ideally, the temperature should remain around 3°C below that of room temperature. Explain why a lower temperature is a significant factor in reducing overall error in this activity.

6. Start recording time, temperature, voltage and current. Note the uncertainty in each measurement in the Results section.
7. Turn on the power supply and monitor voltage and current. Always stay below 10 W (lower still depending on the rating of the heating resistor). Record the values for temperature, voltage and current in the table 1 in the Results section every 20 s (if using electronic measure, record continuously at 2 Hz).
8. Gently swirl the calorimeter cup to mix the water during the entire recording time.
9. Watch the temperature graph until the water is above room temperature by about the same amount as it started below room temperature. Then turn off the power supply but do not stop recording.
10. Continue to record data until the temperature has reached equilibrium or is very slightly decreasing. Do not forget to continuously (and gently) swirl the water.
11. Stop recording data.
12. If time permits, repeat the experiment using a fresh sample of water at least twice more. Dry the calorimeter cup between each trial.

PRACTICAL ACTIVITY 14

RESULTS

Mass of calorimeter cup: _________ kg ± ______

Mass of calorimeter cup & water: _________ kg ± ______

Mass of water: _________ kg ± ______

Uncertainty in mass: ± ______ kg

Time (s) ±	Voltage (V) ±	Current (A) ±	Power, $P = VI$ (W)	Temperature (°C) ±

1 Calculate the power supplied at each time, and enter it in the table.

2 Plot a graph of power against time for your results on the axes below. If your data logger allows, print a graph of power against time, and paste it over the axes below. Label the graph appropriately, including the choice of horizontal and vertical axes.

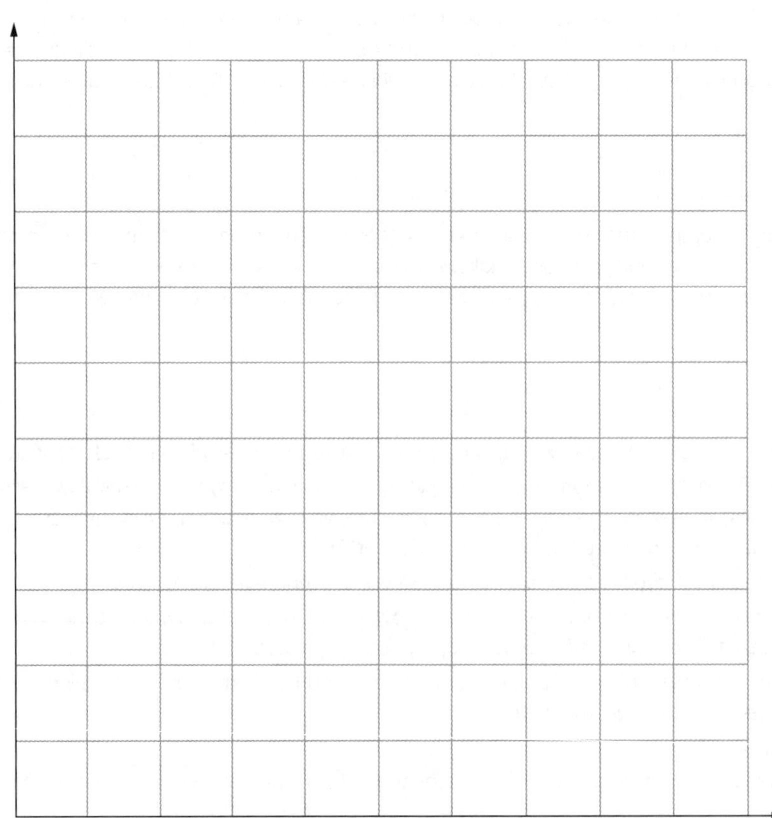

ISBN 978 0 6557 0016 6

3 Based on the temperature data, calculate the total amount of energy added to the water.

4 From the graph of P–t, find the area under the graph.

DISCUSSION

1 Compare the value found for the energy delivered to the water with that supplied by the heating resistor. Evaluate the effectiveness of the experiment in determining the electrical equivalent of heat.

2 Assess the methodology and evaluate aspects of the experiment that could be improved.

3 The experiment was started below room temperature and stopped above room temperature by about the same temperature difference. Explain the significance of this aspect of the experimental technique.

CONCLUSION

 ISBN 978 0 6557 0016 6

EXAM-STYLE QUESTIONS

Multiple-choice questions

Question 1

Recall which one or more of the following terms are equivalent to the energy gained or lost by charge in a circuit.

A. emf

B. voltage

C. amperage

D. resistivity

Question 2

Identify which of the following options corresponds to the amount of current drawn by a 6.0 W torch globe powered by two 1.5 V batteries placed in series.

A. 0.5 A

B. 4.0 A

C. 9.0 A

D. 2.0 A

Question 3

To correctly measure the current in a simple series circuit, an ammeter must be placed

A. in series anywhere in the circuit.

B. in parallel anywhere in the circuit.

C. in series just after the power supply.

D. in parallel just after the power supply.

Question 4

Electricity passing through a copper wire primarily relates to the movement of

A. atoms.

B. protons.

C. neutrons.

D. electrons.

EXAM-STYLE QUESTIONS

Short-answer questions

Question 1

1 mark

The *I–V* graph for a light bulb is shown below. Using the graph, determine the resistance of the bulb when a current of 4.0 A passes through it.

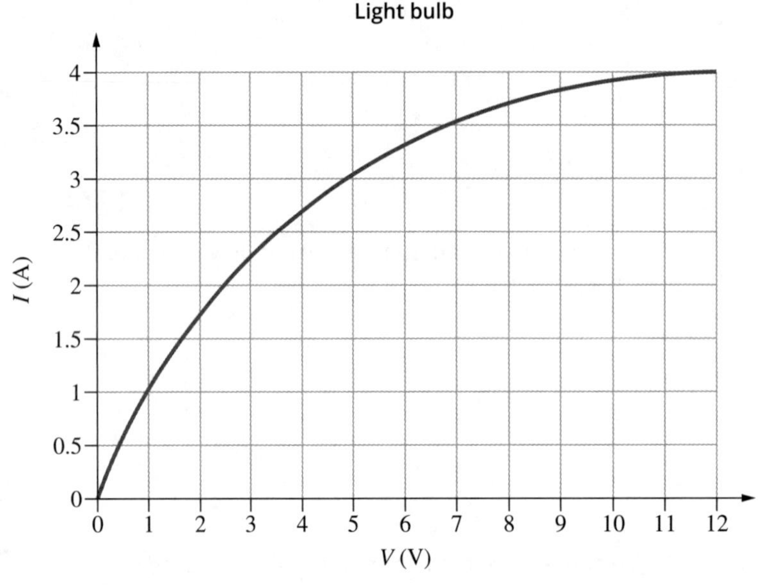

Question 2

3 marks

In an experiment, the resistance of an unknown ohmic resistor was found. Draw a suitable circuit diagram, using standard symbols that would allow the resistance to be determined.

 ISBN 978 0 6557 0016 6

EXAM-STYLE QUESTIONS

Question 3 3 marks

Sketch the shape of the *I–V* graph that would be found for the ohmic resistor using the above circuit.

Question 4 2 marks

Calculate how much charge must have flowed to recharge a mobile phone if a constant current of 1.2 A was recorded for 2 h 20 min.

Question 5 (8 marks)

A kettle rated at 2 kW is plugged into the mains supply (230 V).

a. Determine the size of the current when the kettle is being used. 2 marks

b. Determine how many joules of energy the kettle uses if it takes 3 min for it to boil some water. 2 marks

c. Calculate the number of coulombs of charge that flows in the 3 min. 2 marks

d. Based on your calculation of the amount of charge that flowed in 3 min, determine the number of electrons that would have passed through the power cord to the kettle in that same time period. 2 marks

Question 6

6 marks

Analogies are commonly used to describe a new concept by likening it to something that is already known. You will have already read that electricity is like water flowing through a pipe. Using a means of major transport, such as Melbourne's City Loop underground train system or a local road system, create your own analogy for electricity and describe it in the space below. Ensure you include references to voltage, current, resistance, electrons and coulombs.

 ISBN 978 0 6557 0016 6

UNIT

2 How does physics help us to understand the world?

AREA OF STUDY 1

How is motion understood?

Outcome 1

Investigate, analyse, mathematically model and apply force, energy and motion.

Key knowledge

Concepts used to model motion

- identify parameters of motion as vectors or scalars
- analyse graphically, numerically and algebraically, straight-line motion under constant acceleration:

  $v = u + at$, $v^2 = u^2 + 2as$, $s = \frac{1}{2}(u+v)t$,

  $s = ut + \frac{1}{2}at^2$, $s = vt - \frac{1}{2}at^2$
- analyse, graphically, non-uniform motion in a straight line
- apply concepts of momentum to linear motion: $p = mv$

Forces and motion

- explain changes in momentum as being caused by a net force: $\Delta p = F_{net}\Delta t$
- model the force due to gravity, F_g, as the force of gravity acting at the centre of mass of a body, $F_{\text{on body by Earth}} = mg$, where g is the gravitational field strength ($9.8\,\text{N kg}^{-1}$ near the surface of Earth)
- model forces as vectors acting at the point of application (with magnitude and direction), labelling these forces using the convention 'force on A by B' or $F_{\text{on A by B}} = -F_{\text{on B by A}}$
- apply Newton's three laws of motion to a body on which forces act: $a = \frac{F_{net}}{m}$, $F_{\text{on A by B}} = -F_{\text{on B by A}}$
- apply the vector model of forces, including vector addition and components of forces, to readily observable forces including the force due to gravity, friction and normal forces

Energy and motion

- apply the concept of work done by a constant force using:
  - work done = force × displacement: $W = Fs\cos\theta$ where force is constant
  - work done = area under force vs distance graph
- investigate and analyse theoretically and practically Hooke's Law for an ideal spring: $F = -kx$ where x is extension
- analyse and model mechanical energy transfers and transformations using energy conservation:
  - changes in gravitational potential energy near Earth's surface: $E_g = mg\Delta h$
  - strain potential energy in ideal springs: $E_s = \frac{1}{2}kx^2$
  - kinetic energy: $E_k = \frac{1}{2}mv^2$
- analyse rate of energy transfer using power: $P = \frac{E}{t}$
- calculate the efficiency of an energy transfer system: $\eta = \frac{\text{useful energy out}}{\text{total energy in}}$
- analyse impulse in an isolated system (for collisions between objects moving in a straight line): $F\Delta t = m\Delta v$
- investigate and analyse theoretically and practically momentum conservation in one dimension

Equilibrium

- calculate torque: $\tau = r_{\perp}F$
- analyse translational and rotational forces (torques) in simple structures in translational and rotational equilibrium

Application of motion

- investigate the application of motion concepts through a case study, for example, through motion in sport, vehicle safety, a device or a structure.

KEY KNOWLEDGE

- **You will now be able to complete Worksheet 24.**

Scalars and vectors

Scalars are variables that have **magnitude** (size) and **units** but no direction. For example, a car speed of $50\,\text{km}\,\text{h}^{-1}$ is a scalar.

Vectors are variables that have magnitude as well as direction. For example, the velocity of the same car is $50\,\text{km}\,\text{h}^{-1}$ north.

Some examples of vector and scalar quantities are given in Table 2.1.1.

Table 2.1.1 Scalar and vector quantities

Scalar	Vector
• distance	• displacement
• speed	• velocity
• time	• acceleration
• mass	• force

Vectors can be represented using a **vector diagram**, like the one in Figure 2.1.1. The length of the arrow describes the magnitude and the arrowhead points in the direction of the vector.

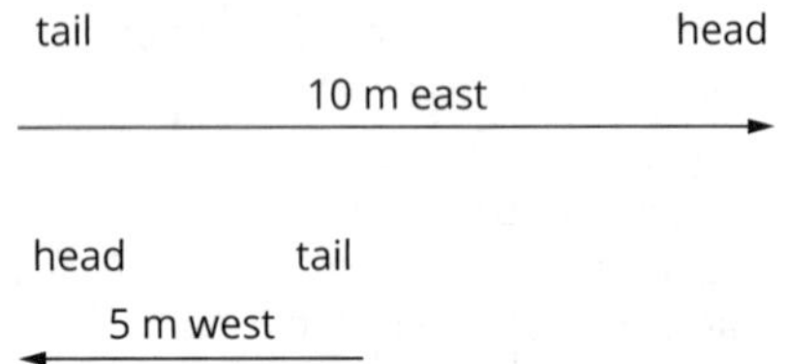

Figure 2.1.1 Two vector diagrams

Several conventions are used to describe vectors in one **dimension**, such as forwards or backwards, up or down, north or south. Two or more vectors that are in the same dimension are said to be **collinear** (in line with each other).

For vectors in two dimensions, the two common methods for describing direction are:

- full circle (or true) bearing. A ‘full circle bearing’ describes north as zero degrees true. In this convention, all directions are given as a clockwise angle from north.
- quadrant bearing. An alternative method is to provide a ‘quadrant bearing’, in which all angles are referenced from either north or south and are between 0° and 90° towards east or west.

ADDING VECTORS IN ONE AND TWO DIMENSIONS

To add collinear vectors, first draw them head to tail as in Figure 2.1.2. The resultant vector (the sum of all the vectors) is then drawn from the tail of the first vector to the head of the last vector. By drawing the original vectors to scale, it is possible to use a ruler to find the magnitude of the resultant vector. For example, when adding the two displacement vectors together from Figure 2.1.2, assuming they are to scale with 1 cm = 5 m, the resultant vector would be 3 cm long, i.e. 15 m.

To add collinear vectors algebraically, it is helpful to assign a sign convention to represent the direction of the vectors (Figure 2.1.3).

For example, say you needed to find the resultant displacement of a student who walks 25 m west, 16 m east and then 44 m west. By applying the sign convention given in Figure 2.1.3, the final displacement would be: $-25 + 16 - 44 = -53$ = 53 m west.

To add together vectors in two dimensions (Figure 2.1.4), a couple of key properties of right-angled triangles are needed.

s_1 = 15 m east + s_2 = 5 m east = s_1 = 15 m east s_2 = 5 m east

s_R = 20 m east

Figure 2.1.2 Adding vectors head to tail

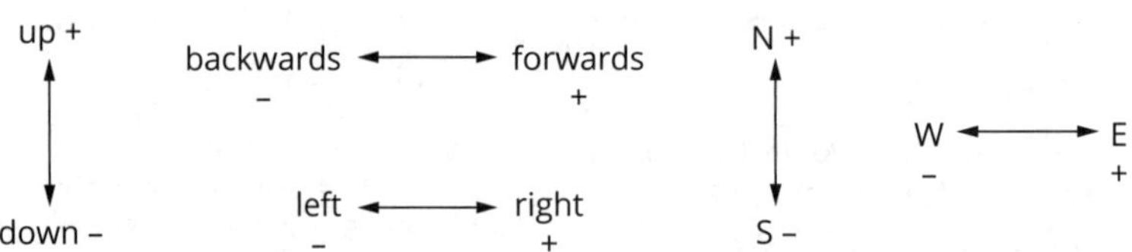

Figure 2.1.3 Common sign and direction conventions

Pythagoras’ theorem is used to find the magnitude of the resultant vector.

$$a^2 + b^2 = c^2$$

Trigonometric ratios of sin, cos and tan can be used to find the direction of the resultant vector.

$$\sin\theta = \frac{\text{opposite}}{\text{hypotenuse}},\ \cos\theta = \frac{\text{adjacent}}{\text{hypotenuse}},\ \tan\theta = \frac{\text{opposite}}{\text{adjacent}}$$

 ISBN 978 0 6557 0016 6

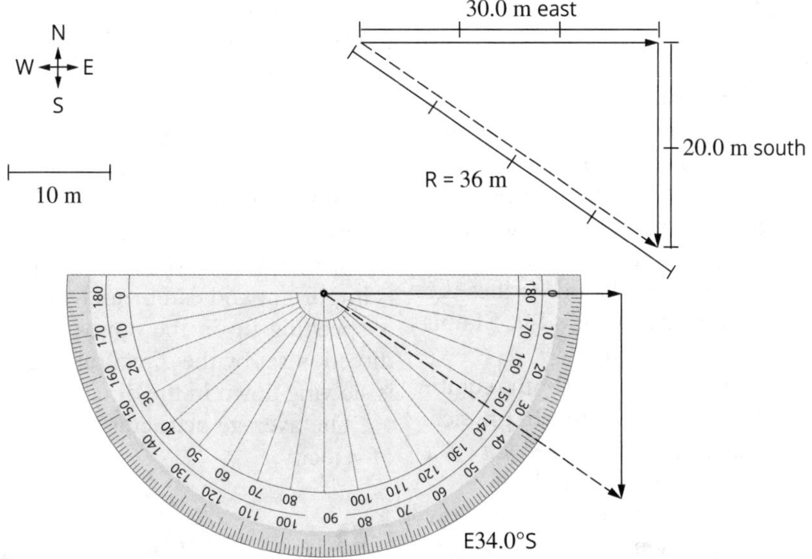

Figure 2.1.4 Adding two vectors at right angles, using the graphical method

SUBTRACTING VECTORS IN ONE AND TWO DIMENSIONS

When subtracting vectors, a similar approach is used. It can be helpful to think of this process algebraically at first.

Imagine you need to find the difference between two vectors: v_1 and v_2. The resultant vector Δv will be equal to:

$$\begin{aligned}\Delta v &= v_2 - v_1\\ &= v_2 + (-v_1)\end{aligned}$$

This means that to subtract v_1 from v_2, you are actually adding together v_2 with the opposite of v_1.

For example, say you are initially travelling with a velocity of $9\,\mathrm{m\,s^{-1}}$ east before then travelling at $3\,\mathrm{m\,s^{-1}}$ east. The change in velocity is the difference between these vectors and can be found graphically as shown in Figure 2.1.5. The final vector is added to the opposite of the initial vector.

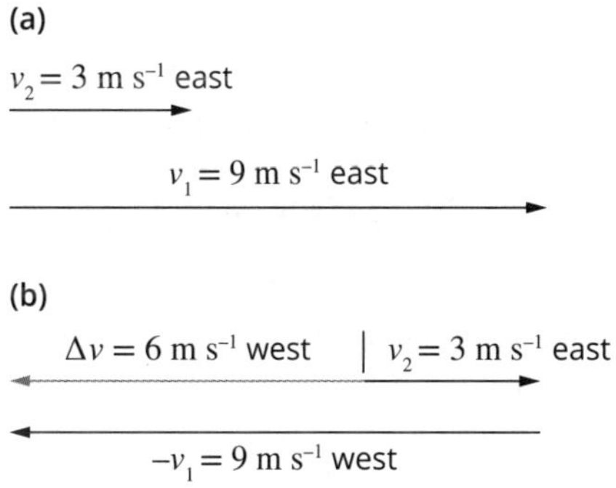

(a)

$v_2 = 3\ \mathrm{m\ s^{-1}}$ east

$v_1 = 9\ \mathrm{m\ s^{-1}}$ east

(b)

$\Delta v = 6\ \mathrm{m\ s^{-1}}$ west | $v_2 = 3\ \mathrm{m\ s^{-1}}$ east

$-v_1 = 9\ \mathrm{m\ s^{-1}}$ west

Figure 2.1.5 (a) Two velocity vectors; (b) subtracting vectors using the graphical method

Change in velocity =
final velocity + opposite of initial velocity.

VECTOR COMPONENTS

A vector can be broken down into its perpendicular components. For example, in Figure 2.1.6, the force vector of 45 N at 20° from the horizontal can be broken down into its horizontal and vertical components by creating a right-angled triangle.

Recall Pythagoras' theorem and the trigonometric ratios for sin, cos and tan that were introduced earlier.

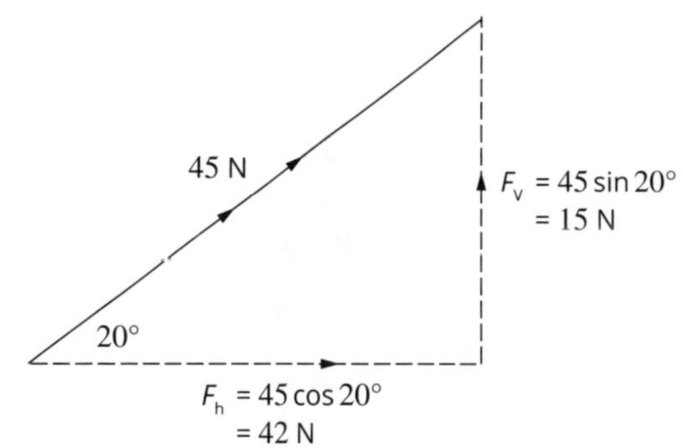

Figure 2.1.6 The perpendicular components of the original vector

- **You will now be able to complete Worksheet 25.**

Linear motion

During this course, the motion of objects is simplified by treating the objects as a single point known as the **centre of mass**. The centre of mass is the balance point of an object. For a person, the centre of mass is located near the waist.

KEY KNOWLEDGE

DISPLACEMENT, SPEED AND VELOCITY

The term 'position' in physics describes where an object is in reference to the origin. Position is a vector quantity, so it requires a magnitude and a direction.

Displacement, s, describes the change in position of an object. It is also a vector quantity, and is calculated by s = final position − initial position.

The scalar quantity distance travelled describes the total distance a body travels over its journey. The SI unit for each of these variables is metres (m).

The definitions for **speed** and **velocity** both require a description of how fast an object is moving. In physics, however, speed is a scalar quantity whereas velocity is a vector. The SI unit for both quantities is $m\,s^{-1}$.

The instantaneous speed and velocity describe how fast the object is moving at a specific point in time (as shown on the speedometer on a car). You may need to calculate the average speed or velocity. To do so, use the following formulas:

$$\text{average speed } v_{av} = \frac{\text{distance travelled}}{\text{time taken}} = \frac{d}{\Delta t}$$

$$\text{average velocity } v_{av} = \frac{\text{displacement}}{\text{time taken}} = \frac{s}{\Delta t}$$

If a body is moving at a constant speed (known as uniform motion), then its average speed will be equal to its instantaneous speed.

Take the example of an athlete slowing to a stop at the end of a race (Figure 2.1.7). The athlete takes 3 s to come to a stop. Each second, the change in velocity is $-2\,m\,s^{-1}$.

The acceleration of an object is defined as the change in velocity over time. This means that in the example of the athlete, the acceleration is −2 metres per second per second. This is usually expressed as $-2\,m\,s^{-2}$.

As **acceleration** is a vector quantity, a negative sign is important and can mean two things: either the object is speeding up in the opposite direction (the negative direction set by the direction convention), or the object is slowing down in the direction of travel.

The average acceleration, a_{av}, is the rate of change of velocity:

$$a_{av} = \frac{\text{change in velocity}}{\text{time taken}} = \frac{\Delta v}{\Delta t} = \frac{v-u}{\Delta t}$$

where v is the final velocity ($m\,s^{-1}$)
u is the initial velocity ($m\,s^{-1}$)
Δt is the time interval (s).

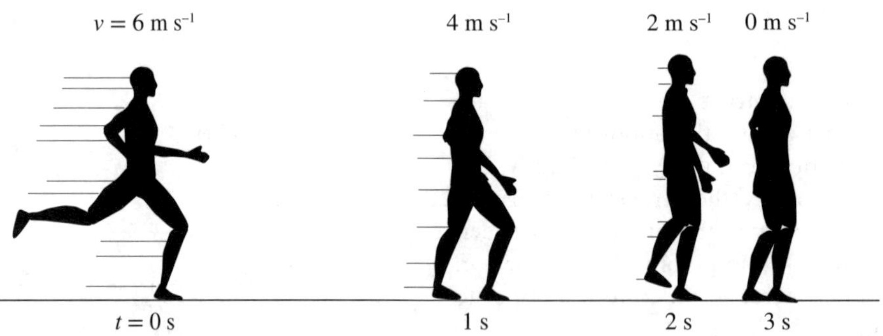

Figure 2.1.7 The velocity of the athlete changes by $-2\,m\,s^{-1}$ each second.

ACCELERATION

The symbol Δ (Greek letter delta) is used to describe the change in a variable. For instance, Δv means the change in velocity or speed. It is given by:

$$\Delta v = v - u$$

where u is the initial speed or velocity (in $m\,s^{-1}$)
v is the final speed or velocity (in $m\,s^{-1}$).

Speed is a scalar quantity, so when calculating the change in speed no direction is required. Velocity, however, is a vector quantity, so the change in velocity should be calculated by performing a vector subtraction. As for all vectors, direction is required.

- **You will now be able to complete Worksheet 26.**

GRAPHING POSITION, VELOCITY AND ACCELERATION OVER TIME

This section examines position–time, velocity–time and acceleration–time graphs.

Position–time (x–t) graphs

A position–time graph indicates the position, x, of an object at any time, t, for motion that occurs over an extended time interval.

Consider Ellisa swimming laps of a 50 m pool. Her position–time data are shown in Table 2.1.2 and in the graph in Figure 2.1.8. The starting point is treated as the origin for this motion (i.e. where the position is zero).

ISBN 978 0 6557 0016 6

Table 2.1.2 Positions and times of a swimmer completing 1.5 lengths of a pool

Time (s)	0	5	10	15	20	25	30	35	40	45	50	55	60
Position (m)	0	10	20	30	40	50	50	50	45	40	35	30	25

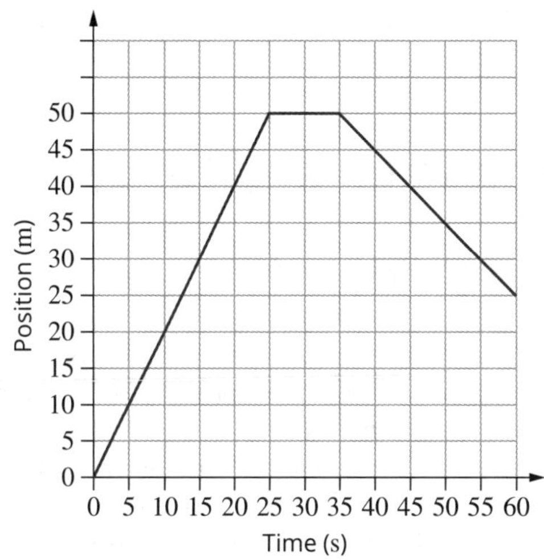

Figure 2.1.8 This position–time graph represents the motion of a swimmer travelling 50 m along a pool, then resting and swimming back towards the starting position. The swimmer finishes halfway along the pool.

As you can read the initial and final positions of the swimmer directly from the graph, you can then calculate the displacement, s. To calculate the average velocity, where velocity is equal to the rate of change of position, first look at the first 25 seconds of motion. Ellisa travels +50 m in this time, so that her average velocity is:

$$v_{av} = \frac{s}{\Delta t} = \frac{+50}{25} = \frac{\text{rise}}{\text{run}} = \text{gradient of the graph}$$

This is for uniform (constant) velocity. If the velocity is non-uniform, the graph will be curved (Figure 2.1.9). In this case, the instantaneous velocity will be the gradient of the tangent to the line at the point of interest and the average velocity will be the gradient of the chord between two points.

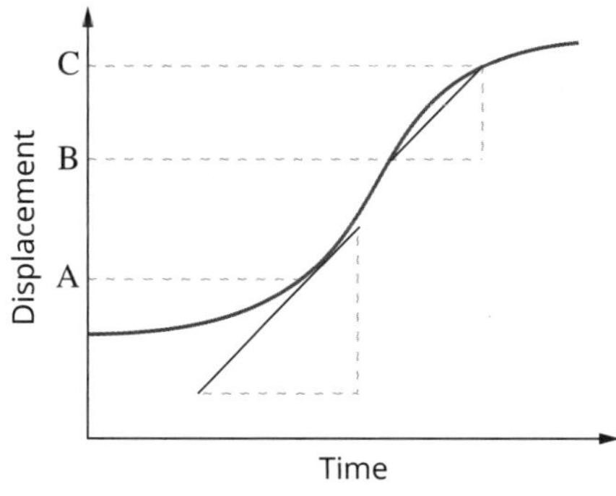

Figure 2.1.9 For non-uniform velocity, you can calculate the instantaneous velocity as the gradient of the tangent at that particular time, or the average velocity as the gradient of a chord between two points.

Velocity–time (*v–t*) graphs

Now consider Figure 2.1.10, which shows a velocity–time graph. In the same way as you calculated the velocity from a position–time graph, the acceleration can now be calculated.

Look at the time between 4 s and 6 s. The average acceleration can be calculated from the gradient of the slope, as this is equal to the rate of change of velocity.

$$a_{av} = \frac{\text{rise}}{\text{run}} = \frac{\Delta v}{\Delta t} = \frac{v-u}{\Delta t} = \frac{0-3}{2} = -3\,\text{m}\,\text{s}^{-2}$$

Figure 2.1.10 A velocity–time graph

To calculate the displacement from a v–t graph, you need to find the total area under the curve. For the 10 s journey in Figure 2.1.10, you will need to break the area down into sections.

$$0\text{–}4\,\text{s: area} = b \times h = 4 \times 3 = +12\,\text{m}$$

$$4\text{–}6\,\text{s: area} = \frac{1}{2}(b \times h) = \frac{1}{2}(2 \times 3) = +3\,\text{m}$$

$$7\text{–}8\,\text{s: area} = \frac{1}{2}(b \times h) = \frac{1}{2}(1 \times -1) = -0.5\,\text{m}$$

$$8\text{–}9\,\text{s: area} = b \times h = 1 \times -1 = -1\,\text{m}$$

$$9\text{–}10\,\text{s: area} = \frac{1}{2}(b \times h) = \frac{1}{2}(1 \times -1) = -0.5\,\text{m}$$

The total displacement is then:

$$s = +12 + 3 - 0.5 - 1 - 0.5 = 13\,\text{m}$$

The total distance travelled, however, increases throughout the journey no matter in which direction you are travelling. This is equal to:

$$d = +12 + 3 + 0.5 + 1 + 0.5 = 17\,\text{m}$$

Acceleration–time (*a–t*) graphs

A similar approach is taken with an acceleration–time graph. The area under an a–t graph gives the change in velocity, Δv:

$$\text{area} = a \times \Delta t = \Delta v$$

- **You will now be able to complete Worksheets 27, 28 and 29 and conduct Practical activity 15.**

KEY KNOWLEDGE

EQUATIONS FOR UNIFORM ACCELERATION

In situations involving uniform acceleration, a set of equations can be used to calculate unknown variables. These equations are listed below. When selecting which equation to use, first identify all known variables. When you use the equations of uniform acceleration, make sure to always choose a direction convention before you begin.

> $v = u + at$
>
> $s = \frac{1}{2}(u + v)t$
>
> $s = ut + \frac{1}{2}at^2$
>
> $s = vt - \frac{1}{2}at^2$
>
> $v^2 = u^2 + 2as$
>
> where s is the displacement (m)
> u is the initial velocity ($m\,s^{-1}$)
> v is the final velocity ($m\,s^{-1}$)
> a is the acceleration ($m\,s^{-2}$)
> t is the time taken (s).

VERTICAL MOTION

Mass (the amount of matter) is a scalar quantity. In scientific contexts, mass is measured in kilograms (kg). In the late 1500s, Galileo was able to show that all objects that are dropped near the surface of Earth accelerate at the same rate, g, towards the centre of Earth. The force that produces this acceleration is the force due to gravity. The force due to gravity is an attractive force that exists between all masses. In other words, it is a 'pulling' force that exists between everything that has a mass.

The force on a body due to gravity, F_g is a vector quantity. Like other forces, it is measured in newtons (N).

> $F_g = mg$
>
> where F_g is the force of gravity acting at the centre of mass of a body (in N)
> m is the mass of the body (in kg)
> g is the gravitational field strength, which is $9.8\,N\,kg^{-1}$ near the surface of Earth.

The term 'acceleration due to gravity' is equivalent to the term 'gravitational field strength'. The units for gravitational field strength ($N\,kg^{-1}$) are also equivalent to the units for acceleration ($m\,s^{-2}$).

If you throw an object upwards, it will eventually fall back to the ground because of Earth's gravity. If air resistance is ignored, all objects falling freely near Earth's surface will move with the same constant acceleration. This is represented by g and is equal to $9.8\,m\,s^{-2}$ down at the surface (towards the centre) of Earth.

As the acceleration of a free-falling body is constant, the equations of motion can be used to solve vertical motion problems, where $a = g$.

Three other pieces of information are useful in solving problems about projectile motion:

- time taken to go up = time taken to come down
- final velocity = –initial velocity
- at the highest point, $v = 0\,m\,s^{-1}$.

- **You will now be able to conduct Practical activities 16, 17 and 20.**

Momentum and force

NEWTON'S FIRST LAW

A force can be thought of as a push or a pull. Some forces act only on contact, such as when balls collide; others are known as non-contact forces, such as gravitation and magnetism.

Force is a vector quantity and its SI unit is the newton (N). If more than one force acts on a body at the same time, the body behaves as if only one force is acting: the vector sum of all the forces.

The net force acting on a body experiencing a number of forces acting simultaneously is given by the vector sum of all the individual forces:

$$F_{net} = F_1 + F_2 + \ldots + F_n$$

Inertia is the tendency of an object to maintain its velocity. This tendency is related to the mass of an object, so that the greater the mass, the harder it is to get it moving or to stop it from moving.

Newton's first law (also known as the law of inertia) can be written in many ways, but two main ways are:

1. An object will continue moving with a constant velocity unless an unbalanced force acts upon it.
2. A non-zero net force causes acceleration.

NEWTON'S SECOND LAW

Newton's second law of motion states that the acceleration of an object is directly proportional to the net force and inversely proportional to the mass of the object.

> $a = \frac{F_{net}}{m}$
>
> where a is the acceleration of an object ($m\,s^{-2}$)
> F_{net} is the force applied to the object (N)
> m is the mass of the object (kg).

- **You will now be able to conduct Practical activity 19.**

NEWTON'S THIRD LAW

For every action (force), there is an equal and opposite reaction (force). This is known as **Newton's third law**.

Newton's third law basically means that in every interaction, a pair of forces is acting on two interacting objects. The action force and the reaction force always act on different objects, so you cannot add them together.

ISBN 978 0 6557 0016 6

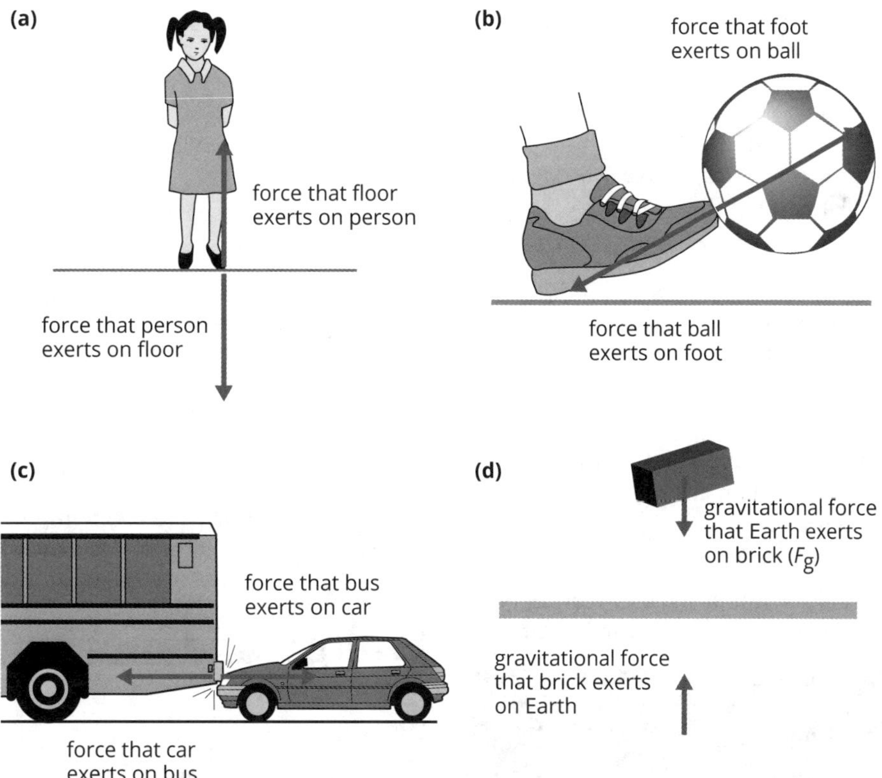

Figure 2.1.11 Some action–reaction pairs

A few action–reaction pairs are shown in Figure 2.1.11. The action and reaction forces are equal and opposite even when the masses of the objects are different. The individual forces making up a Newton's-third-law pair act on different masses, causing different accelerations (as from Newton's second law).

When labelling force vectors, you can use the following technique. Use the capital letter F to represent the force. Then include a subscript consisting of the word 'on' and the object on which the force is acting. Lastly, use the word 'by' and the object that is applying the force, i.e. $F_{\text{on A by B}}$. See Table 2.1.3 for some examples.

A common misconception around Newton's third law is in reference to the **normal force**, F_N. This upwards force is provided by the surface an object sits on, and is perpendicular to the surface. Although it is equal and opposite to the force due to gravity on the object, these two forces *do not* make an action–reaction pair.

Table 2.1.3 Labels of action and reaction force vectors

Action vector	Reaction vector
$F_{\text{on floor by person}}$	$F_{\text{on person by floor}}$
$F_{\text{on ball by foot}}$	$F_{\text{on foot by ball}}$
$F_{\text{on bus by car}}$	$F_{\text{on car by bus}}$
$F_{\text{on Earth by brick}}$	$F_{\text{on brick by Earth}}$

Figure 2.1.12 describes the action–reaction pairs for a bin sitting on a table. It highlights that the third-law pair for the normal force (equal to the force on bin by the table) is actually the force on the table by the bin.

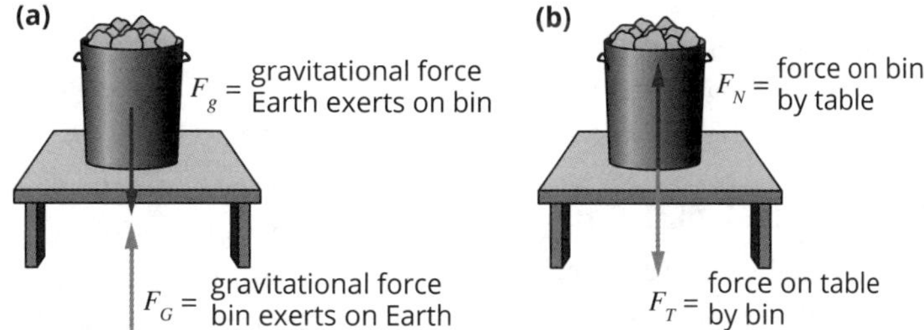

Figure 2.1.12 (a) The force due to gravity F_g is in an action–reaction pair with the gravitational force the bin exerts on Earth. (b) The normal force F_N is in a separate third-law pair.

- **You will now be able to complete Worksheets 30 and 31 and conduct Practical activity 18.**

ISBN 978 0 6557 0016 6

KEY KNOWLEDGE

MOMENTUM AND CONSERVATION OF MOMENTUM

The **momentum** of an object is a vector quantity that is the product of its mass and velocity.

Any object in motion will have momentum. Momentum is calculated using the equation:

> $p = mv$
>
> where p is momentum (m s^{-1})
> m is the mass of the object (kg)
> v is the velocity of the object (m s^{-1}).

The momentum of a system will be **conserved** in any interaction or collision. The law of conservation of momentum can be represented by:

$$\Sigma p_{before} = \Sigma p_{after}$$

where Σp is the sum of the momentum of objects in a system. Table 2.1.4 shows how this law can be applied.

Table 2.1.4 The law of conservation of momentum applied to different situations

Situation	Change in momentum
two objects collide and remain separate	$\Sigma p_{before} = \Sigma p_{after}$ $m_1u_1 + m_2u_2 = m_1v_1 + m_2v_2$
two objects combine when they collide	$\Sigma p_{before} = \Sigma p_{after}$ $m_1u_1 + m_2u_2 = m_3v_3$
an explosive collision—one object breaks into two	$\Sigma p_{before} = \Sigma p_{after}$ $m_1u_1 = m_2v_2 + m_3v_3$

MOMENTUM TRANSFER

If an object's velocity changes, its momentum will also change. A change in momentum, Δp, is also called **impulse**. The impulse is a vector quantity.

> $\Delta p = p_{final} - p_{initial}$
> $= mv - mu$
> $= m(v - u)$
> $= m\Delta v$
>
> where Δp is the impulse or change in momentum (kg m s^{-1})
> m is the mass (kg)
> v is the final velocity (m s^{-1})
> u is the initial velocity (m s^{-1})
> Δv is the change in velocity (m s^{-1}).

MOMENTUM AND NET FORCE

Newton's second law describes the relationship between impulse, force and period of time during which the force acts:

$$F_{net} = ma = m \times \frac{\Delta v}{\Delta t} = \frac{m\Delta v}{\Delta t}$$

Since $\Delta p = m\Delta v$, therefore:

$$F_{net} = \frac{\Delta p}{\Delta t}$$

Alternatively:

$$F_{net}\,\Delta t = \Delta p$$

or

> $\Delta p = F_{net}\,\Delta t$
>
> where Δp is the impulse or change in momentum (kg m s^{-1})
> F_{net} is the net force causing the change in momentum (N)
> Δt is the time taken for the change in momentum (s).

This means that for a given impulse, the product of force and period of time is constant.

Energy and motion

WORK

Energy and work have many meanings in everyday life, but in physics they have precise meanings. It is important to understand what these terms mean and how they are achieved.

Energy is the capacity to cause change. There are many different forms of energy. **Mechanical energy** is defined as the energy that a body possesses due to its position or motion. This category of energy can be broadly classified into two groups: kinetic energy and potential energy.

In physics, work cannot be done without energy, and vice versa. Work is equal to the change in energy ($W = \Delta E$), and therefore its unit is also the joule. Work is done when:

- energy is transferred or transformed
- a force causes an object to be displaced.

Work is the product of the net force and the displacement.

> $W = Fs$
>
> where W is work (J)
> F is force (N)
> s is the displacement in the direction of the force (m).

You can calculate the work done in a situation by finding the area under a force–displacement graph.

Sometimes, when a force is applied, the object does not move in the same direction as the force. For example, in Figure 2.1.13, when a person pulls a suitcase, the direction of the force is at an angle upwards, although the suitcase moves horizontally forwards.

ISBN 978 0 6557 0016 6

KEY KNOWLEDGE

Figure 2.1.13 When a person pulls a suitcase, the force is applied at an angle to the displacement of the suitcase.

In this case, only the horizontal component of the pull contributes to the work being done on the suitcase. The vertical component of this force pulls the suitcase upwards and is balanced by the downwards force due to gravity.

In situations where the force applied is not parallel to the object's displacement, work can be calculated using the general equation:

> $W = Fs\cos\theta$
>
> where θ is the angle between the force, F, and the displacement, s.

MECHANICAL ENERGY

As work is equal to a change in energy (ΔE), this can be written as the change in **kinetic energy** of an object. Kinetic energy is the energy of motion. Mathematically, this becomes:

> $W = \frac{1}{2}mv^2 - \frac{1}{2}mu^2$
>
> where W is work (J)
> m is mass (kg)
> u is initial velocity (m s^{-1})
> v is final velocity (m s^{-1}).
>
> This equation is known as the '**work–energy theorem**'.

The work–energy theorem can be seen as a definition for the change in kinetic energy produced by a force:

$$W = \frac{1}{2}mv^2 - \frac{1}{2}mu^2 = (E_k)_{\text{final}} - (E_k)_{\text{initial}} = \Delta E_k$$

Similarly, the amount of work can be related to the change in gravitational potential energy. **Gravitational potential energy** is a measure of the amount of energy available to an object due to its position in a gravitational field.

> $W = \Delta E_g = mg\Delta h$
>
> where E_g is the gravitational potential energy (J)
> m is the mass of the object (kg)
> g is the gravitational field strength ($9.8\ \text{N kg}^{-1}$ on Earth)
> Δh is the change in height of the object (m).

ELASTIC POTENTIAL ENERGY

Elastic potential energy occurs in situations where energy can be considered to be stored temporarily. When this energy is released, work may be done on an object.

Elastic potential energy is stored when a spring is stretched, a rubber ball is squeezed, air is compressed in a tyre or a bungee-jumper's rope is extended during a jump.

Materials that have the ability to store elastic potential energy when work is done on them, and then release this energy, are called **elastic** materials.

Consider the situation in which a spring is stretched by the application of a steadily increasing force. As the force increases, the extension of the spring, x, can be graphed against the applied force, F (Figure 2.1.14).

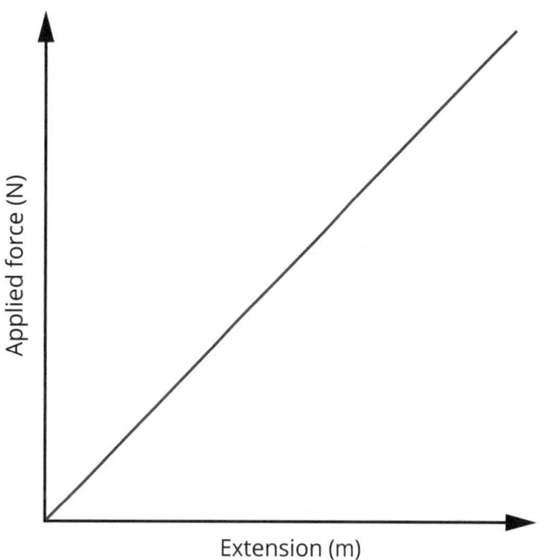

Figure 2.1.14 Ideal springs obey Hooke's law, so they produce a linear graph.

The gradient of a force–extension graph tells us the force, in newtons, required to produce each unit of extension in metres.

The gradient of the graph is called the **spring constant**, k, and is measured in N m^{-1}. The gradient indicates the stiffness of the spring. For an ideal spring, this gradient has a set value (as the force–extension graph has a constant slope). A very stiff spring that is difficult to stretch would have a steep gradient: that is, a large value of k.

The relationship between the applied force and the subsequent extension or compression of an ideal spring is known as **Hooke's law**.

Hooke's law states that the force applied by a spring is directly proportional, but opposite in direction, to the spring's extension or compression. That is:

> $F = -kx$
>
> where F is the force applied by the ideal spring (in N)
> k is the spring constant (force constant or stiffness constant) (in N m^{-1})
> x is the amount of extension or compression of the ideal spring (in m).

Note: the negative sign in Hooke's law indicates that the restorative force inside the spring and the extension are in opposite directions.

The elastic (or spring) potential energy, E_s, stored in an object is given by the area under the force–extension graph for the object. For objects that obey Hooke's law, the spring potential energy is given by:

$$E_s = \frac{1}{2}kx^2$$

where E_s is the elastic potential energy stored during the extension/compression (in J)
k is the spring constant (force constant or stiffness constant) (in $N\,m^{-1}$)
x is the amount of extension or compression of the ideal spring (in m).

In a system of bodies, it is assumed that no other forms of energy are present except kinetic energy and potential energy. Since the total energy must be conserved (principle of **conservation of mechanical energy**), this means that the total mechanical energy of the system is constant.

- **You will now be able to complete Worksheets 32 and 33 and conduct Practical activities 22 and 23.**

EFFICIENCY

In the real world, energy transformations are never perfect—there is always some energy 'lost' when energy is transformed from one form into another. However, it is not truly lost, since it cannot be created or destroyed; rather, the energy becomes a form that is not necessarily useful (e.g. heat or sound). The percentage of energy that is effectively transformed by a device is called its **efficiency**.

The efficiency of a transformation from one energy form to another, as a decimal, is:

$$\text{Efficiency } (\eta) = \frac{\text{useful energy out}}{\text{useful energy in}}$$

To express the efficiency as a percentage, multiply this by 100.

POWER

Power is a measure of the rate at which work is done:

$$P = \frac{W}{\Delta t}$$

Recall that when work is done, energy is transferred or transformed. So the equation can also be written as:

$$P = \frac{E}{t}$$

where P is the power (in W)
E is the energy transferred or transformed (in J)
t is the time taken (in s).

The unit of power is the watt (W). A watt (W) is defined as the rate of work of one joule per second; in other words:

$$1\,\text{W} = \frac{1\,\text{J}}{1\,\text{s}} = 1\,\text{J}\,\text{s}^{-1}$$

- **You will now be able to complete Worksheets 34 and 35 and conduct Practical activity 21.**

Forces and equilibrium

TORQUE

When an object rotates, it does so around a **pivot point**. For the object to turn, a force must be applied. The force vector is aligned along an imaginary line known as the **line of action of the force**.

The **torque** (τ) on an object is a measure of the tendency of a force to cause the object to rotate. The applied force, F, must be some distance, r, from the pivot point, so that the torque can be calculated by:

$$\tau = r_\perp F$$

where τ is the torque (N m)
$r_\perp$ is the force arm (m)
F is the force (N).

The force arm is the perpendicular distance from the pivot point to where the force is applied. Maximum torque occurs when the acting force is applied perpendicular to the force arm. The larger the force, the larger the torque will be; or, the longer the force arm, the greater the torque will be (Figure 2.1.15).

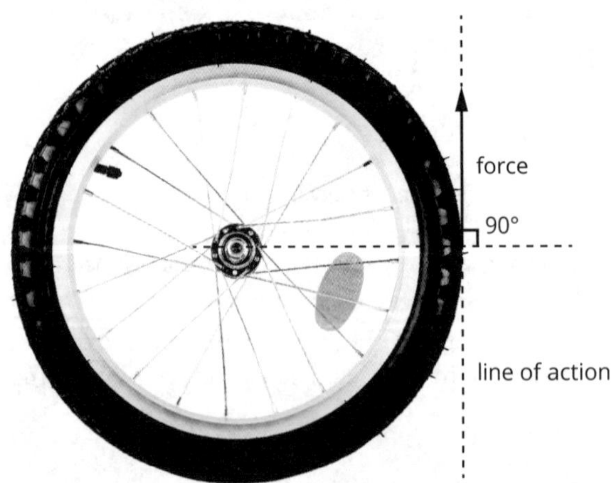

Figure 2.1.15 Maximum torque occurs when the force applied is perpendicular (at 90°) to a line drawn from the pivot point to the point of application.

TRANSLATIONAL EQUILIBRIUM

Translational equilibrium occurs when the sum of forces acting on an object gives zero net translational force, i.e. $F_{net} = 0$. The object will then be travelling at constant velocity. An object in translational equilibrium

 ISBN 978 0 6557 0016 6

may still have some net torque. For example, when turning a bolt, the bolt will not accelerate in any translational direction, but will still have some net torque applied that keeps it rotating.

STATIC EQUILIBRIUM

Rotational equilibrium occurs when the sum of all torques acting in the clockwise direction on the object is equal to the sum of all torques acting in the anticlockwise direction, i.e. $\tau_{net} = 0$. The object will then be rotating at a constant rate. An object in rotational equilibrium may still have some net force applied to it. For example, if you push a table along the floor, it will have a net translational force to keep it moving, but it will still be in rotational equilibrium.

Static equilibrium occurs when an object is in both rotational and translational equilibrium. That is, the sum of the net forces and the net torques is zero. It is both travelling and rotating at a constant velocity.

For example, when a body or a system is not accelerating or rotating, it is in both translational and rotational equilibrium. This can be represented by:

$$F_{net} = 0 \text{ and } \tau_{net} = 0$$

which can also be represented as:

$$F_{net} = 0 \text{ and } \Sigma\tau_{clockwise} = \Sigma\tau_{anticlockwise}$$

Centre of mass

The centre of mass is an important concept when considering an object's stability. There is as much mass above the centre of mass as there is below, as much mass to the left as there is to the right, and as much mass in front as there is behind.

If the positions of the two objects are marked relative to an origin, as indicated in Figure 2.1.16, the position of the centre of mass is defined as: $x_{cm} = \dfrac{m_1x_1 + m_2x_2}{m_1 + m_2}$

Stability and equilibrium

Equilibrium refers to a state in which an object is balanced, so that as long as no external factors are changed, the object will not accelerate. Stability refers to the tendency of the system to maintain, or return to, the equilibrium state if external factors are changed. There are three types of equilibrium related to the stability of an object:

- **neutral equilibrium**—The object will remain stationary no matter where it is placed (e.g. placing a ball anywhere on a large, flat surface).
- **stable equilibrium**—If the object is moved away from its equilibrium position, forces will act to return it to its equilibrium position. For example, if you place a ball in a large bowl, the equilibrium position is at the bottom of the bowl, and if the ball is moved to any other position, gravity will act to return it to the bottom of the bowl.
- **unstable equilibrium**—If the object is moved away from its equilibrium position, forces will act to push it further from the equilibrium position. For example, if you place a ball on top of a large dome, the equilibrium position is at the top of the dome, but if the ball is moved in any direction, gravity will pull it further from the top of the dome.

● **You will now be able to complete Worksheets 36, 37 and 38.**

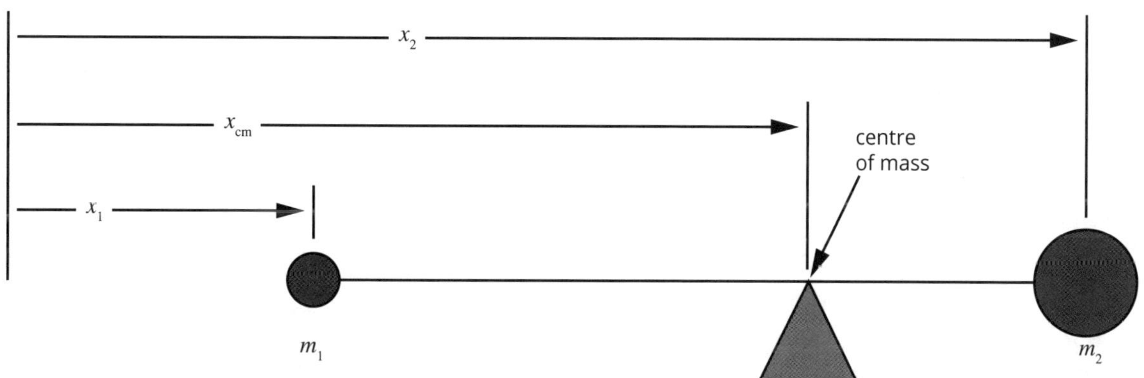

Figure 2.1.16 Calculation of the centre of mass: the product of mass and distance is equal for each side of the fulcrum.

ISBN 978 0 6557 0016 6

WORKSHEET 24

Classification and identification • Modelling

Knowledge review—understanding motion

1 A girl on a skateboard travels 16 m down the street in 2 s. What is her speed? In general, speed is found by dividing distance by the time taken.

2 The following diagram shows the journey of an ant from start to end.

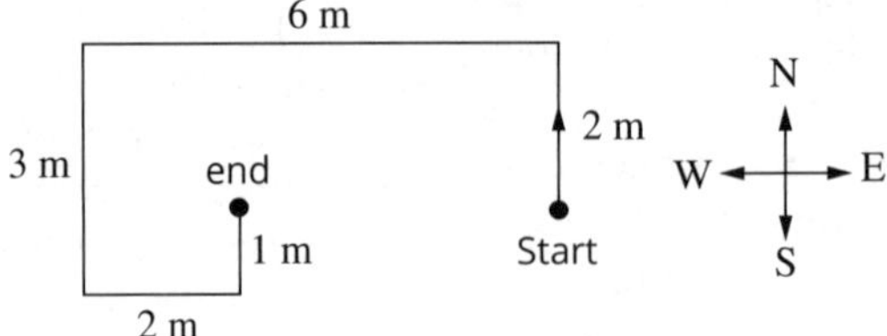

a What distance did the ant travel?

b If the journey took 56 s altogether, what was the ant's average speed?

c What was the total displacement of the ant? (Remember that displacement is the difference between the final position and the starting position, and it is a vector quantity.)

3 When you are standing up on a moving bus, it is a good idea to make sure you are hanging onto something. Using Newton's first law, explain why this is the case.

4 When a ball bounces on a hard floor, the 'action' is the force of the ball downwards on the floor. What is the 'reaction'?

 ISBN 978 0 6557 0016 6

WORKSHEET 24

In the following statements, fill in the blanks from the list of words below. You can use a word more than once.

first	second	third	force due to gravity	acceleration	displacement	energy
force	kinetic energy	mass	potential energy	work–energy theorem	conserved	momentum
vector	collision	velocity	half	double	proportional	

5 Newton's _______________ law predicts the following relationship between _______________, force and mass. The acceleration of an object is directly _______________ to the net force and will always be in the same direction as the net _______________. Acceleration is inversely proportional to the _______________ of the object, meaning that more massive objects have less acceleration if subjected to the same net force.

6 An object subject to an unbalanced force will experience a displacement. The work done by that unbalanced force is equal to the component of the _______________ in the direction of the object's displacement multiplied by the magnitude of the displacement. If the _______________ imparted to the object by the force is converted entirely into kinetic energy, the work done by the unbalanced force is equal to the change in the object's _______________. This concept is known as the _______________.

ISBN 978 0 6557 0016 6

WORKSHEET 25

Modelling

Vectors in the classroom

Any motion between two points can be described in terms of scalar and vector quantities. Describing a journey purely in terms of scalar quantities makes it very difficult, if not impossible, to determine the final destination. By adding direction and knowing the starting point, the final destination can be found.

Below is a 1 cm grid representing your classroom. The front and back of the classroom are shown, as is a 'classroom compass', which uses forwards (F), backwards (B), left (L) and right (R) to indicate direction. Your task is to plot a path on the grid that would allow you to navigate from your current seat to the teacher's desk, wherever that might be in the room. There are some rules that apply:

- Determine a scale that would work for your classroom. 1 cm = _____ m
- Use only straight lines. Show these as displacement vectors, labelled with the distance in metres and the direction based on the classroom compass directions.
- You may only travel left, right, forwards or backwards: no diagonals!
- Add your displacement vectors head to tail.
- Estimate your distance travelled; your teacher may allow you to measure directly, but ask before moving around. The nearest half metre or metre will do.
- You must avoid any desks, students and other obstacles in the room. (You might like to draw these in to assist your plot.) Plot a path that you could really walk.
- Your path must use a minimum of five displacement vectors, and a maximum of ten.

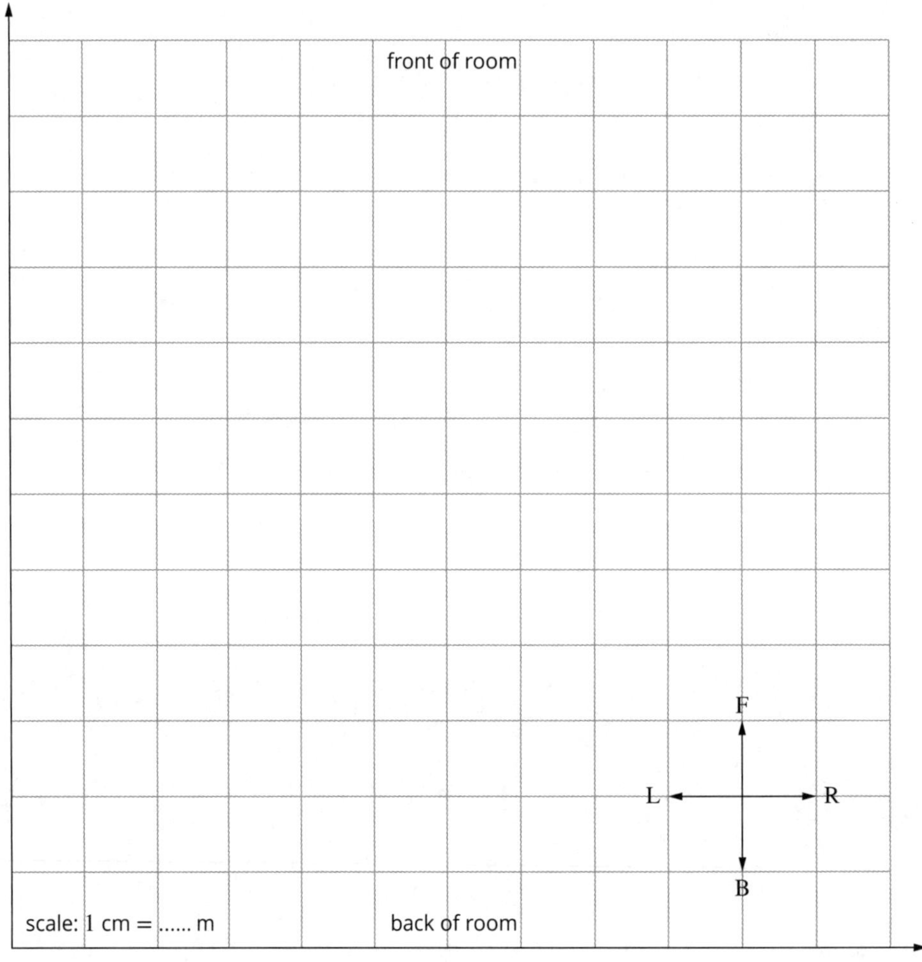

 ISBN 978 0 6557 0016 6

WORKSHEET 25

1 Tabulate your displacement vectors in the table below. Treat the directions of forwards and right as positive, and left and backwards as negative.

Step	Displacement	Forwards/backwards component	Right/left component
(Example)	3 m left	0	−3
1			
2			
3			
4			
5			
6			
7			
8			
9			
10			
Total			

2 Calculate the total resultant forwards/backwards and right/left components.

3 Draw the displacement vector from your position to that of your teacher on the classroom grid. Use a protractor and ruler to determine the distance and direction of this vector, and label the vector.

4 Calculate the total displacement (resultant vector) from your desk to your teacher's desk.

5 Compare your calculated resultant vector with that measured from your diagram.

WORKSHEET 26

Speed versus velocity

In everyday language, speed and velocity are often used interchangeably. In physics there is an important distinction between the two terms.

1 Speed is a ______________ quantity. It is completely described by its ______________.

Velocity is a ______________ quantity. It is completely described by its______________ and ______________.

2 A GPS offers a teacher three potential paths to travel by car between a Shepparton school and a local takeaway restaurant for lunch. To arrive at the same time, on which route (A, B or C in the diagram) would the:

a average speed be highest? ______________

b average velocity be highest? ______________

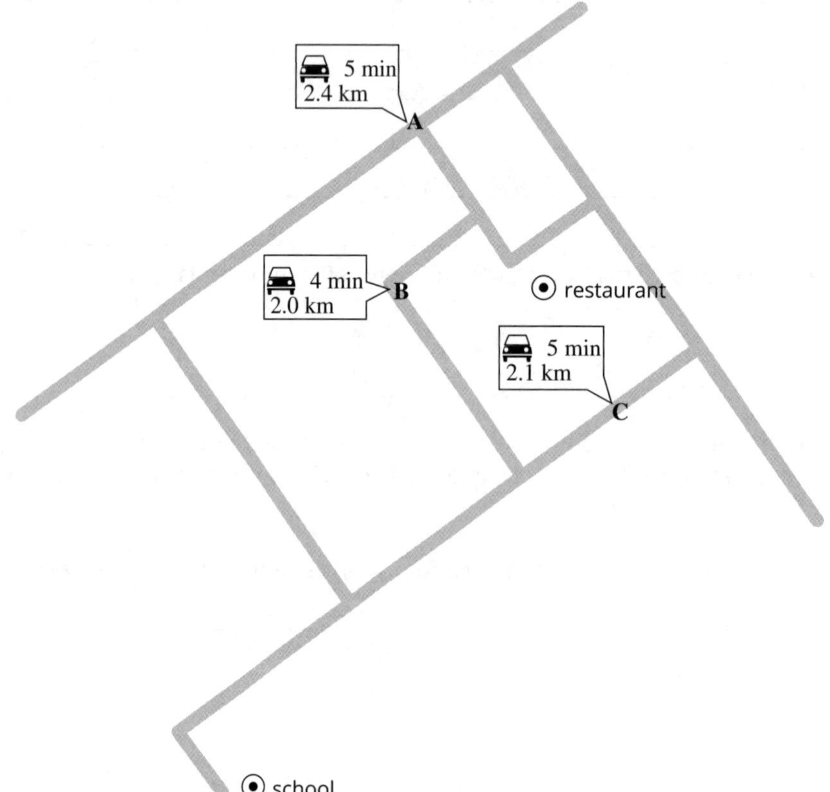

3 After buying lunch, the teacher in question 2 returns along the route that has the highest average speed, taking the same time. Based on the full trip to and from the restaurant, what would be the teacher's:

a average speed in $m\,s^{-1}$ and $km\,h^{-1}$?

____

____

b average velocity in $m\,s^{-1}$ and $km\,h^{-1}$?

____

____

 ISBN 978 0 6557 0016 6

4 An athlete is completing a set of high-intensity shuttle runs of increasing distance, as shown in the figure below.

The lines are 10 m apart.

She completes each run from the origin in the time shown in the table.

The total test is completed when each run, from O to A and back, O to B and back, and O to C and back, is completed.

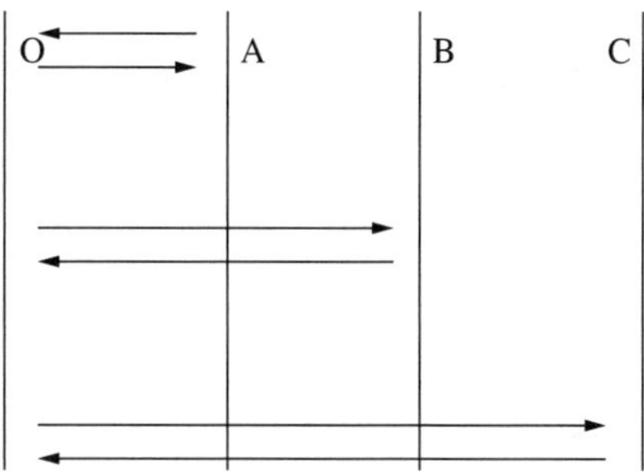

Complete the table below for the missing quantities. Give your answers to one decimal place.

Step	Distance (m)	Time (s)	Average speed ($m\,s^{-1}$)	Average velocity ($m\,s^{-1}$)
O–A	10	1.6		
O–A–O		3.5		
O–B		3.4		
O–B–O		7.2		
O–C		5.2		
O–C–O		10.7		
Total time				

5 On the grid below, draw a distance–time graph and a displacement–time graph showing the athlete's total test.

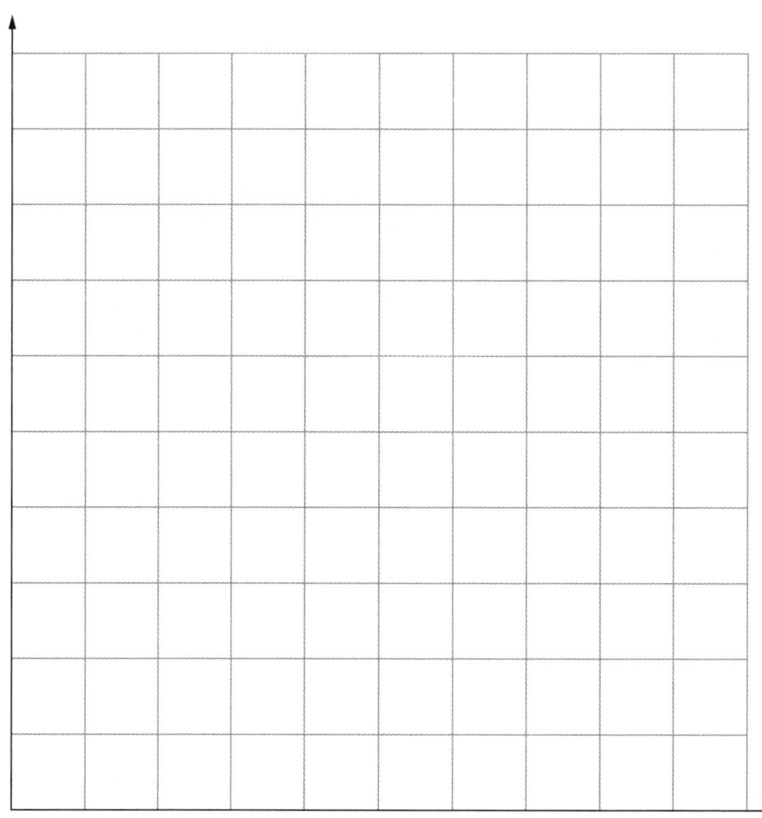

ISBN 978 0 6557 0016 6

WORKSHEET 27

Classification and identification

Position–time and velocity–time graphs

The left-hand side of this worksheet has five position–time graphs (1–5). On the right-hand side are five velocity–time graphs (a–e).

Some of the velocity–time graphs correspond to the position–time graphs.

1 Match each position–time graph with its corresponding velocity–time graph.

Position–time graphs

1

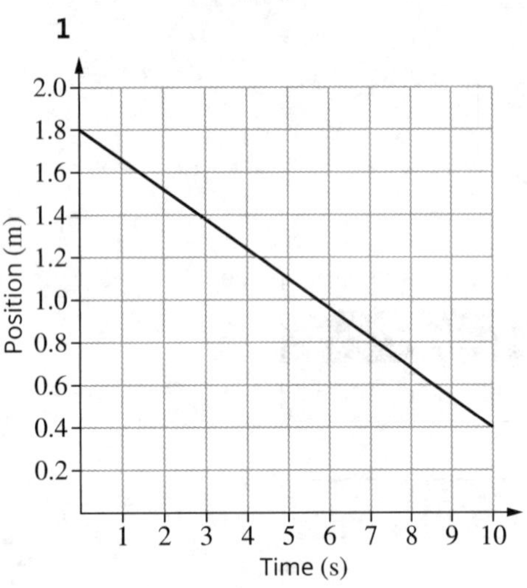

2

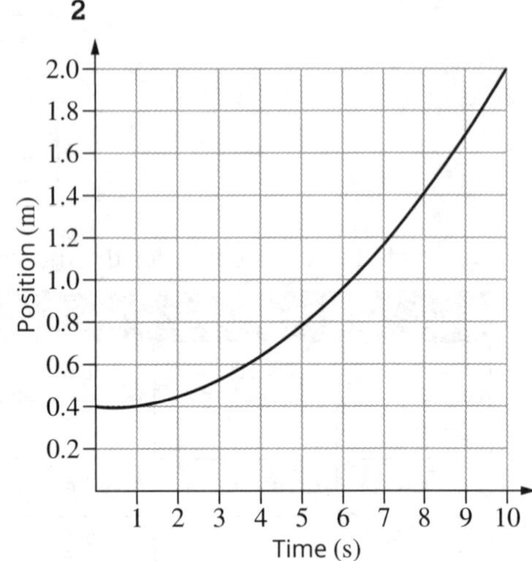

3

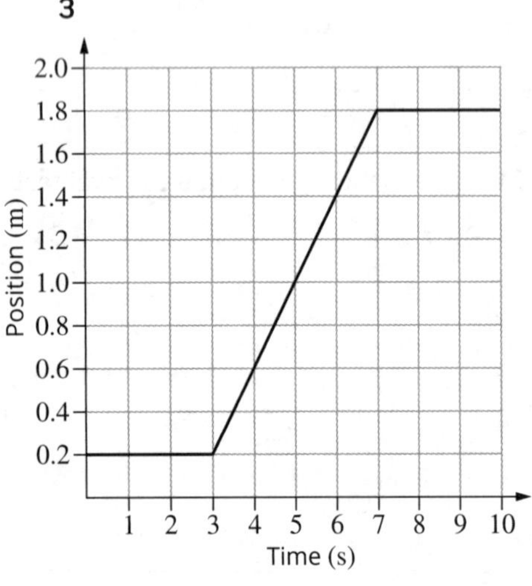

4

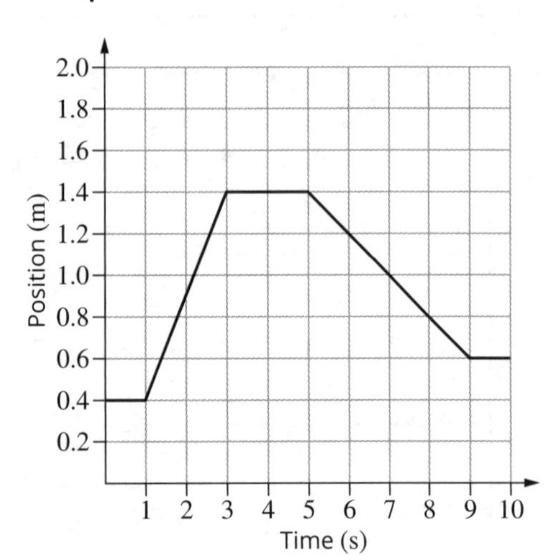

5

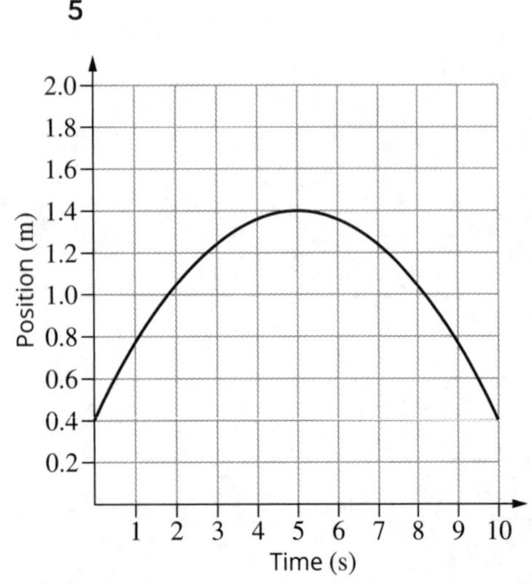

ISBN 978 0 6557 0016 6

Velocity–time graphs

a

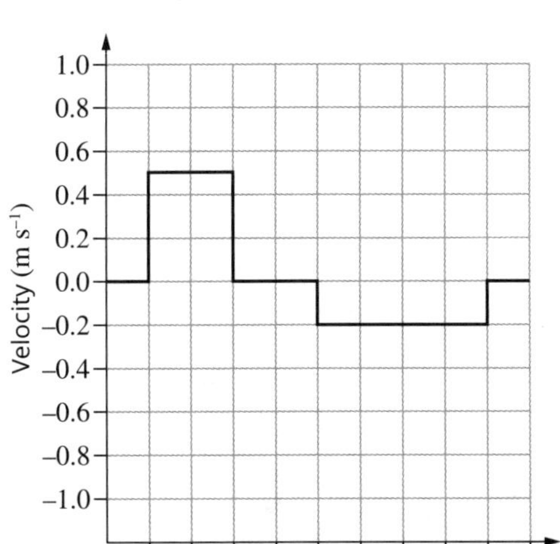

b

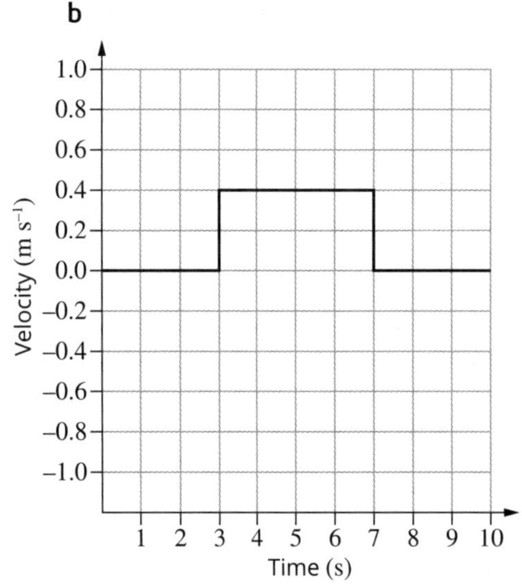

c

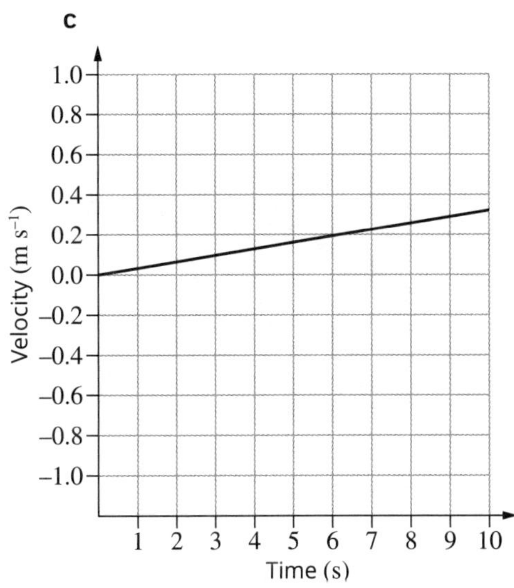

d

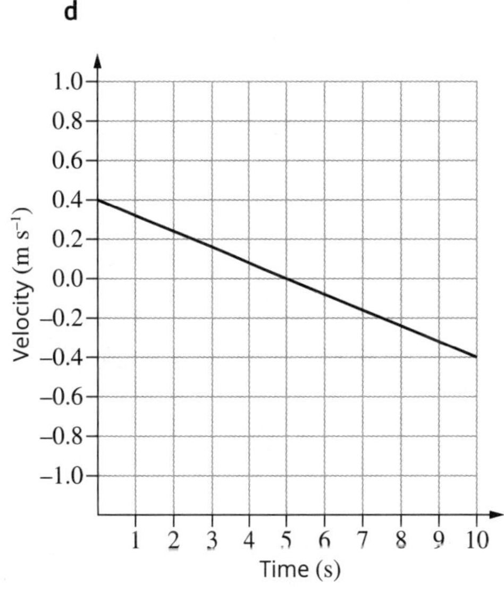

e

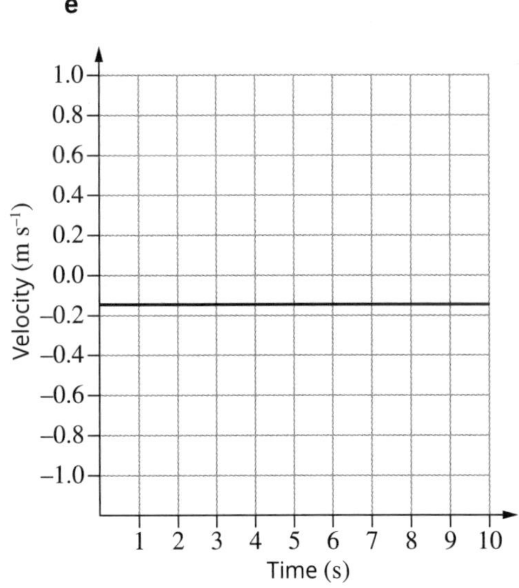

WORKSHEET 27

2 Describe the motion of each position–time graph shown in question 1 in your own words. Make reference to starting and finishing positions, any other key times and the velocity of the object being graphed.

1

2

3

4

5

 ISBN 978 0 6557 0016 6

WORKSHEET 28

Modelling

Race analysis—a study of relative motion

Australia was represented by two competitors for the 200 m women's freestyle final in the 2016 Olympic Games. Emma McKeon led the field for the first two laps, turning under world-record pace at the 100 m mark. She faded on the third 50 m lap to finally place 3rd for the bronze medal. Bronte Barratt placed a very creditable 5th, finishing only 0.33 s outside the medal positions.

Their split times are shown in the table below.

Competitor	50 m split (m:ss.ss)	100 m split (m:ss.ss)	150 m split (m:ss.ss)	200 m split (m:ss.ss)
Emma McKeon	0:26.64	0:55.37	1:25.37	1:54.92
Bronte Barratt	0:27.35	0:56.40	1:26.02	1:55.25

1 Draw a position–time graph for the split times of both competitors on the one set of axes below.

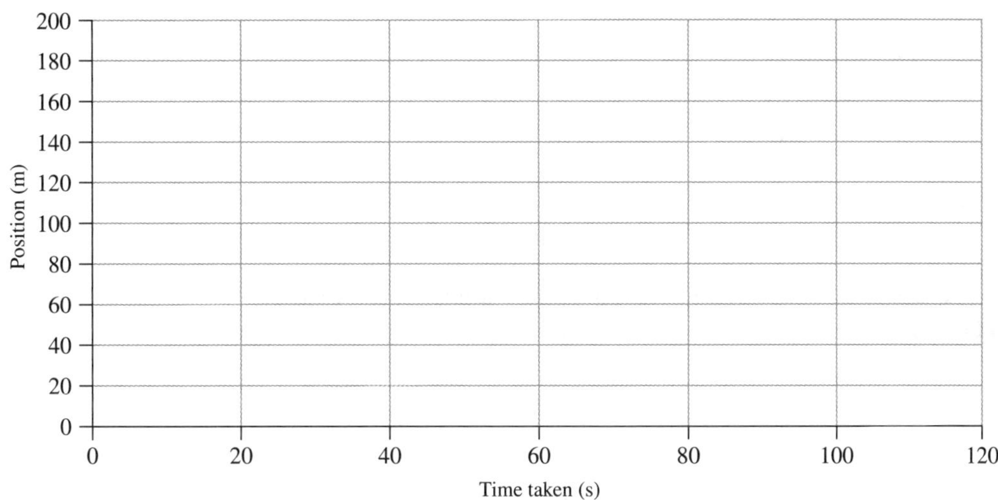

2 Calculate the average speed for each lap for each competitor. Record your answers in the table below.

Competitor	Lap 1 ($m s^{-1}$)	Lap 2 ($m s^{-1}$)	Lap 3 ($m s^{-1}$)	Lap 4 ($m s^{-1}$)
Emma McKeon				
Bronte Barratt				

3 Using a vector diagram and relevant calculations, find the difference in relative velocity between McKeon and Barratt during Lap 1. Adopt a suitable direction as positive to show your answer.

4 Barratt has a faster speed than McKeon in Lap 3 and Lap 4. Using a vector diagram and appropriate calculations, find the velocity of Barratt relative to McKeon for these laps.

5 Based on the average speed for each lap, what was the greatest difference in the magnitude of the relative velocity between McKeon and Barratt during the race? Use a vector diagram and appropriate calculations to show your working.

 ISBN 978 0 6557 0016 6

WORKSHEET 29

Case study

Analysing motion in two dimensions

A soccer team uses GPS trackers as part of their pre-season player assessment. Each player wears a special vest fitted with a tracker that records time, position, speed and direction during game play, as shown in the figure below. Analysis of the data provides key metrics for player performance and positioning during play.

The data for one of the players during a short period of play is shown in the table below.

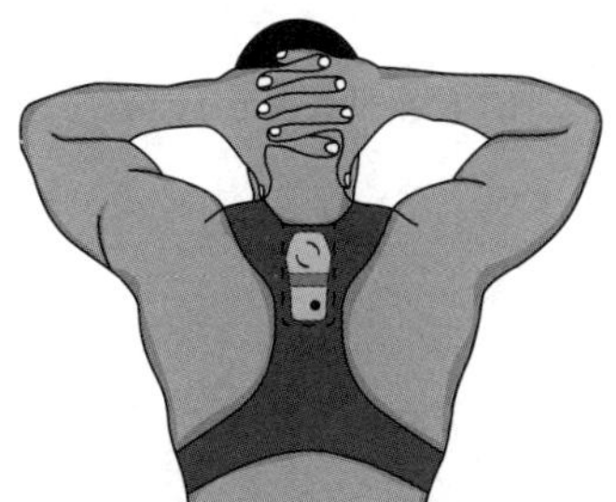

- The player has taken the kick-off at the start of play and then moved off around the playing field.
- The table shows the player's speed, full circle bearing and the time travelled for each individual move (not the total running time).
- A new entry is made for each change of direction. Each entry can be assumed to be in a straight line.
- Complete the table. Give your answers to two decimal places.

Position	Time, t (s)	Speed, v (m s^{-1})	Full circle bearing (°T)	Angle (°) from north or south	Distance travelled, d (m)	North–south component (m)	East–west component (m)
1	1.2	5.0	270				
2	0.8	2.4	322				
3	2.5	4.3	180				
4	1.1	3.2	95				
5	2.3	0.0	0				
6	4.6	3.4	42				
7	1.3	3.1	132				
Totals		–	–	–			

1 The diagram below shows the playing field and the player's starting position. Plot each entry at a suitable scale, and draw vectors to illustrate the player's motion.

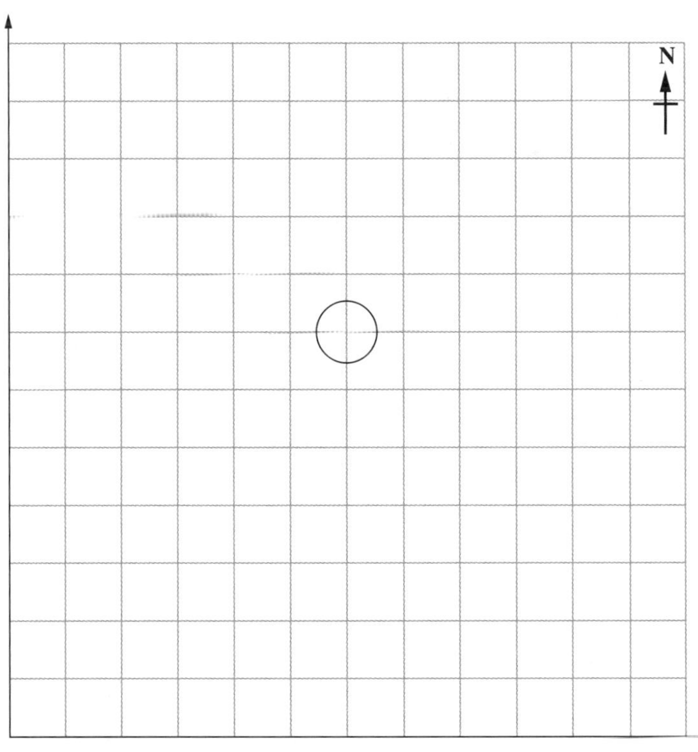

2 Draw the resultant vector for the player's displacement from his starting position to his finishing position. Measure this displacement from the vector diagram and record it on the diagram.

3 Using the data provided, calculate the following.

a the total distance travelled

b the player's average speed

c the player's final displacement from his initial position

d the player's average velocity

4 Compare the calculated displacement with the measured displacement.

 ISBN 978 0 6557 0016 6

WORKSHEET 30

Which Newton is that?

In each of the following questions, identify the relevant law of motion that applies, and explain your answer.

1 What happens to the velocity of an object if it never experiences an unbalanced force?

Newton's law: ☐ 1st ☐ 2nd ☐ 3rd

2 A horse that is hitched to a stationary carriage begins to pull on the carriage. If the force exerted by the carriage on the horse is always equal in size and opposite in direction to the force exerted by the horse on the carriage, how can the horse move the carriage?

Newton's law: ☐ 1st ☐ 2nd ☐ 3rd

3 We know from experience that the harder we throw a ball (apply more force), the faster it will move (greater initial velocity resulting from acceleration). If you throw a 1 kg ball as hard as you can, and it leaves your hand at $20\,m\,s^{-1}$, how fast do you think a 5 kg ball would leave your hand when you throw it as hard as you can?

Newton's law: ☐ 1st ☐ 2nd ☐ 3rd

4 An object's resistance to change in motion is called inertia. Give an example of something with a relatively large amount of inertia, and something else with a relatively small amount of inertia.

Newton's law: ☐ 1st ☐ 2nd ☐ 3rd

5 If a rocket's engine produces a constant force, will the rocket's acceleration when it is launched be the same as the acceleration just before the fuel is completely used up?

Newton's law: ☐ 1st ☐ 2nd ☐ 3rd

6 An astronaut is about 20 m from her space station when the small rocket thrusters she uses to move around run out of fuel. If she is carrying a few tools and can also remove the rocket thruster, what should she do to get back to the space station?

Newton's law: ☐ 1st ☐ 2nd ☐ 3rd

7 A force sensor is used to measure the force applied to drag a 1.5 kg brick across a table while a motion sensor is used to measure the brick's acceleration. Several trials are conducted, and the slope of the force versus acceleration graph is about 2.0 kg in each trial.

Newton's law: ☐ 1st ☐ 2nd ☐ 3rd

8 What would happen to a ball thrown into deep space where there were no forces acting on it? Describe its motion during the time you are in contact with it and then after release.

Newton's law: ☐ 1st ☐ 2nd ☐ 3rd

WORKSHEET 31

Modelling

Understanding Newton's third law

The following is a snippet from an article covering some of the misconceptions of Newton's third law. Imagine someone is holding a ball, as shown in the figure.

'What is the force that is equal and opposite the gravitational field force exerted by Earth on the ball?' said the physics teacher.

'The force exerted by the hand on the ball,' said the class.

The physics teacher replied, 'Let's say this ball is in free fall; what forces are on it?'

Now only the gravitational field force exerted by Earth on the ball is left, so what is the force that is equal and opposite of this?

Turns out that the force that is equal and opposite to the gravitational field force exerted by Earth on the ball is the gravitational field force exerted by the ball on Earth.

The ball accelerates toward Earth, and Earth accelerates toward the ball. However, because of Earth's mass compared to the ball's mass, the ball accelerates at a much larger rate. The forces are always directly toward each other, and are always equal and opposite in direction. The equal and opposite forces are acting on different objects altogether.

(Source: Hughes, M.J, 2002. How I misunderstood Newton's Third Law. *The Physics Teacher*, *40*(6) 381–382.)

1 Explain one misconception associated with Newton's third law.

2 From the below diagram, identify the paired forces acting on the bucket and explain which forces can be disregarded and why.

ISBN 978 0 6557 0016 6

3 Compare Newton's third law to Newton's first and second laws and explain how each of them is connected.

4 Describe a situation that includes all three laws.

5 For your situation in question 4, use reasonable estimates of the mass, starting velocities, and acceleration to estimate the forces involved in the interaction between the objects.

WORKSHEET 32

Modelling

Working against the force

Circle the best option in each of the following multiple-choice questions.

1 Mechanical work is related to which pair of variables?

A distance and time

B distance and force

C distance and velocity

D distance and acceleration

2 A raven carries a stick from the ground to its nest in a tree. Complete this statement: 'The work done on the stick is directly related to the stick's ...?'

A gravitational potential energy

B elastic potential energy

C kinetic energy

D none of the above

3 A ball is thrown straight up into the air and returns to be caught by the thrower. Describe the energy changes that occur during this process.

4 A 1000 kg rocket is launched vertically upwards at a constant acceleration. When it reaches an altitude of 15 km it is travelling at 900 m s^{-1}.

a How much work was done by the rocket?

b Using the work done by the rocket, what is the magnitude of its acceleration?

c How long did the rocket take to reach an altitude of 15 km?

5 A seal with a mass of 120 kg slides straight down a 35° slope of ice for 70 m. At the end of the slope it is travelling at 30 m s^{-1}. Assuming the slope is frictionless, what was the seal's initial velocity?

ISBN 978 0 6557 0016 6

WORKSHEET 33

Modelling

Data analysis—determining the spring constant

The relationship between a load force and a light spring ($F = -kx$) was first determined by Robert Hooke in the seventeenth century. Hooke's law states that when an elastic material is subjected to a force (F), the amount of extension or compression, x, is proportional to the applied force. The constant k describes the stiffness for a particular spring.

In a simple experiment, a spring is anchored at one end, and a force sensor is used to extend the spring as shown below.

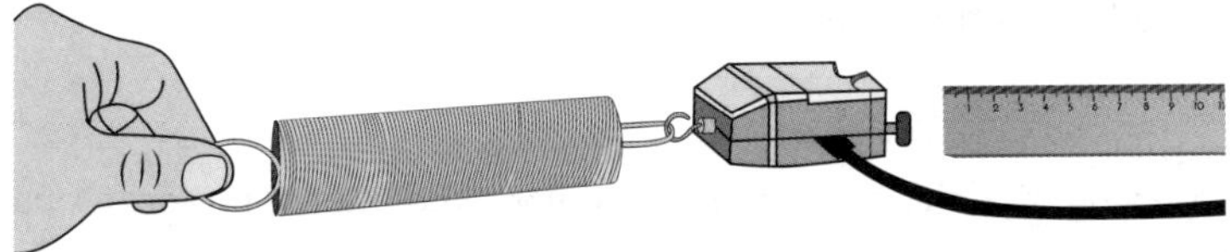

A ruler marked in millimetre minimum segments is used to measure the initial length of the spring and the extended length as the force sensor is pulled to extend the spring. The force sensor is slowly pulled until the spring comfortably (without deforming) reaches its maximum extension. The average force for each 2 cm increment across three such tests for the same spring was recorded in the following table.

Extension (m)	Applied force (N)
0.04	0.61
0.08	0.75
0.12	0.87
0.16	0.98
0.20	1.13
0.24	1.27
0.28	1.45
0.32	1.56
0.36	1.74
0.40	1.85

1 Plot a force–extension graph for the data provided and draw an appropriate line of best fit.

2 Determine the equation for the line of best fit for your graph.

3 State the physical meaning of the gradient.

4 State the units for the gradient of the graph.

5 Explain the physical meaning of the vertical intercept. If your line of best fit doesn't have a vertical intercept, explain why.

6 Assuming that the force sensor is pulling in the positive direction, state the direction that the spring is pulling.

7 If this experiment was an observation of a compression spring such that we measure displacement as positive in the direction of compression, and force as push positive, state the direction the spring is pushing and explain your answer.

8 Given your answers to the above questions, write an equation that generally describes the force exerted by an ideal spring as it is extended or compressed using k to represent the spring constant.

9 For an ideal spring like the one used in this data analysis, determine the spring constant if a force of –5.0 N is measured when pulling it 4 cm.

10 The same spring (as in question 9) is stretched to 7 cm. Determine the force required to do so.

 ISBN 978 0 6557 0016 6

Engine power

Most internal combustion engines have a well-defined 'power band'. The power band is defined as the range of engine speeds (in terms of engine rpm, or revolutions per minute) over which the engine delivers its greatest power.

Typically, a power band for a four-stroke engine would range from 3500 rpm to 4500 rpm. It is possible for an engine to operate at speeds below or above the power band, but such operation will seriously affect fuel economy and might even damage the engine. Other types of internal combustion engines, such as two-stroke, diesel or rotary engines, may have quite different characteristics.

The graph below depicts the relationship between the traction force a car can apply and the speed at which it can travel.

Notice that there are five curves, each for a different gear in a five-speed car. Having a range of different gears allows the engine to operate optimally at many different speeds.

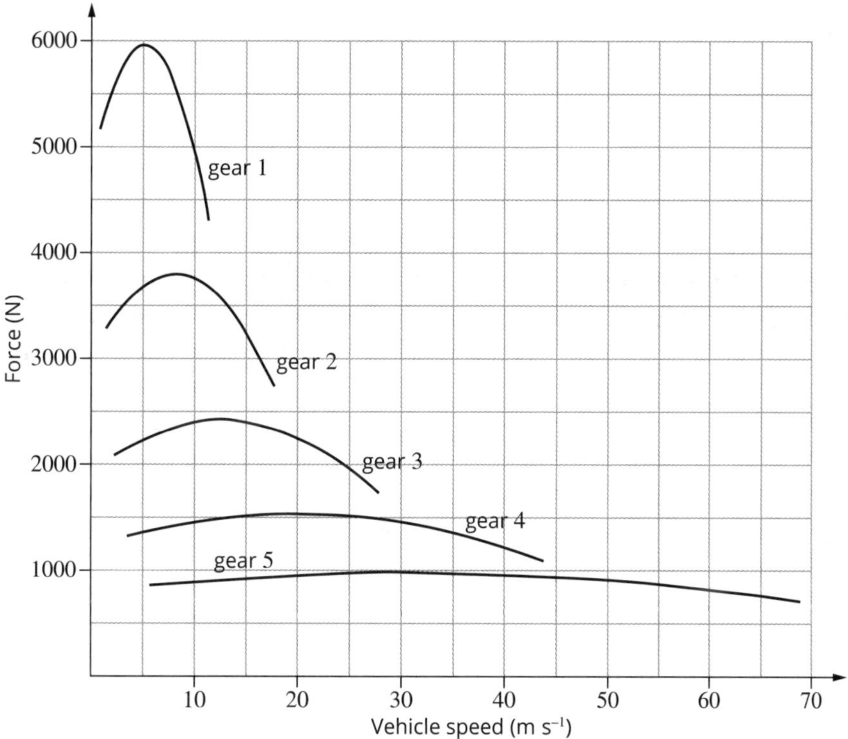

1 Using the data in the graph, complete the table below for each gear for peak force (F_{peak}), peak velocity (v_{peak}), minimum velocity (v_{min}) and maximum velocity (v_{max}).

Gear	F_{peak} (N)	v_{peak} (m s^{-1})	v_{min} (m s^{-1})	v_{max} (m s^{-1})	P (W)
1st					
2nd					
3rd					
4th					
5th					

2 Plot a graph of F_{peak} versus v_{peak}. What relationship is suggested by the graph?

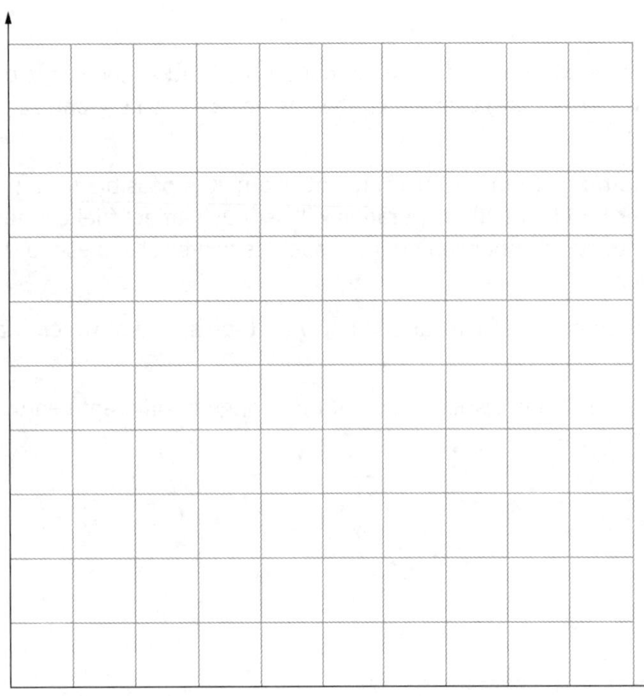

3 Recall that power is the rate of doing work, and can be written as $P = \frac{E}{t}$. For a constant force moving an object at constant velocity, this relationship can also be expressed as $P = Fv$. Calculate the optimum power for each of the five gears, assuming that the optimum power is given by F_{peak}. Add this data to the table above. What do you notice?

4 Assuming that the car in this example has a mass of 1200 kg, how much traction can the car apply at 5 m s^{-1} in first gear?

5 What is the car's maximum acceleration at that point?

6 When this car tows an 800 kg caravan, its performance changes markedly. The additional mass will reduce the possible acceleration. Ignoring air resistance, what acceleration is now possible at 5 m s^{-1} in first gear?

7 How will the caravan affect the maximum acceleration at 30 m s^{-1} in fourth gear? What will it do to the maximum speed attainable?

 ISBN 978 0 6557 0016 6

WORKSHEET 35

Modelling

Human earthquake

From time to time it has been suggested that, if millions of people in the same country (e.g. China) all jumped down from a height at exactly the same time, an earthquake could occur. The idea is that their combined gravitational potential energy would be converted to kinetic energy, which would then be transferred to Earth.

Your task is to determine whether this idea has any merit. Use reasonable estimates of the quantities involved, including the impact time for people landing on the ground, to determine:

1 the initial gravitational potential if the whole population of China was standing 2.0 metres above the ground

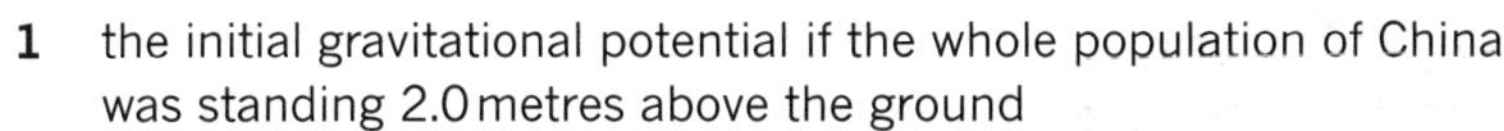

2 the total kinetic energy at the time of impact if everyone landed at the same time

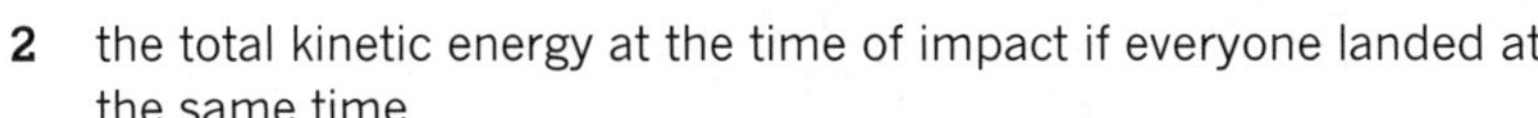

3 the impulse generated on impact, and hence the force, based on a reasonable estimate of stopping time

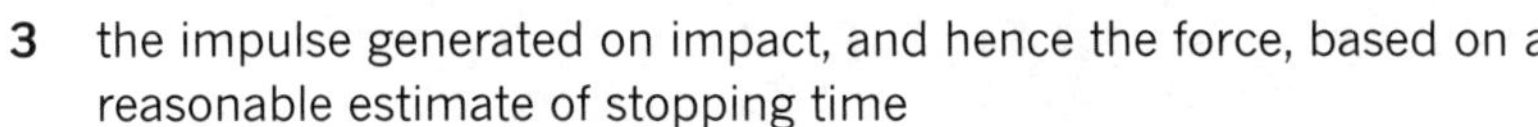

4 the average mechanical power during this impact. (Recall that power is the rate of doing work: $P = \frac{E}{t} = Fv$.)

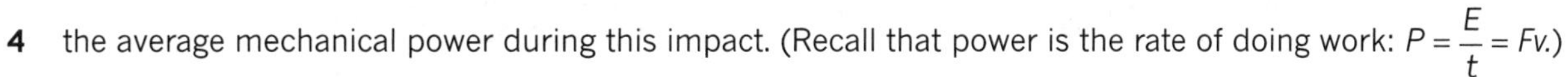

5 the velocity at which Earth would move after the impact, assuming all of the energy from the jump is transferred to Earth.

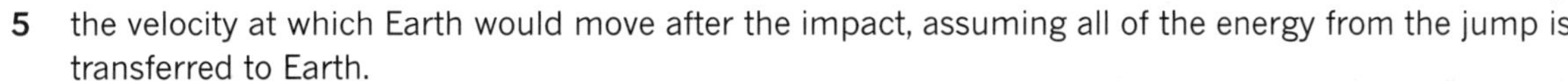

The following figures will assist in determining your estimate.

Mass of Earth: 5.97×10^{24} kg

Population of China: 1400 million

6 1 tonne of TNT releases approximately 4.2×10^{9} J of energy. Based on your estimates, how much TNT would be needed to match the energy generated by the whole population of China jumping down at the same time from a height of 2.0 metres?

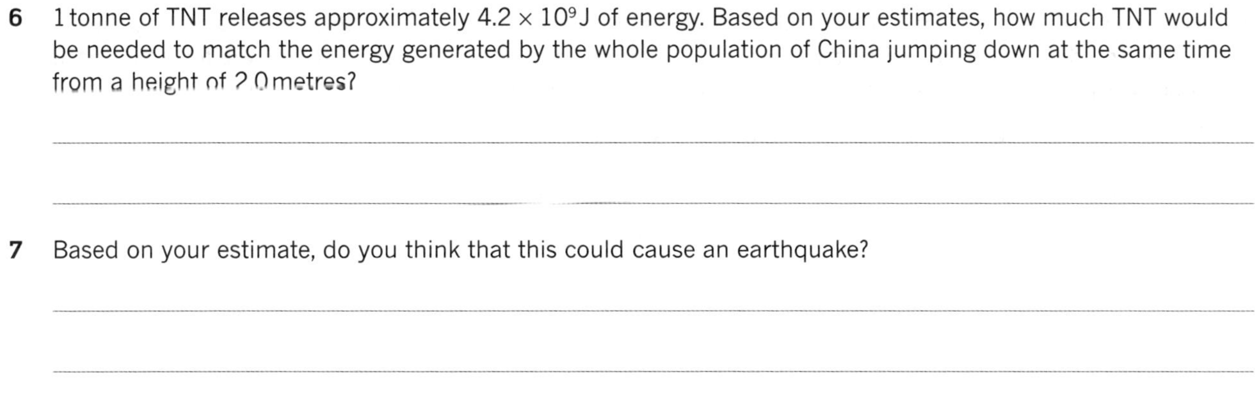

7 Based on your estimate, do you think that this could cause an earthquake?

ISBN 978 0 6557 0016 6

WORKSHEET 36

Modelling

Calculating torque

Torque is the rotational equivalent of force. Torque must be applied to an object to start an object rotating. For calculations involving torque, the entire force due to gravity on an object can be considered to act at a single point: the centre of gravity or centre of mass of the object. Torque is a vector quantity with a direction parallel to the axis of rotation. A torque is positive when it is applied in the anticlockwise direction and negative when it is applied in the clockwise direction.

In an experiment to investigate torque and the rotation of mechanical systems, the following system was set up.

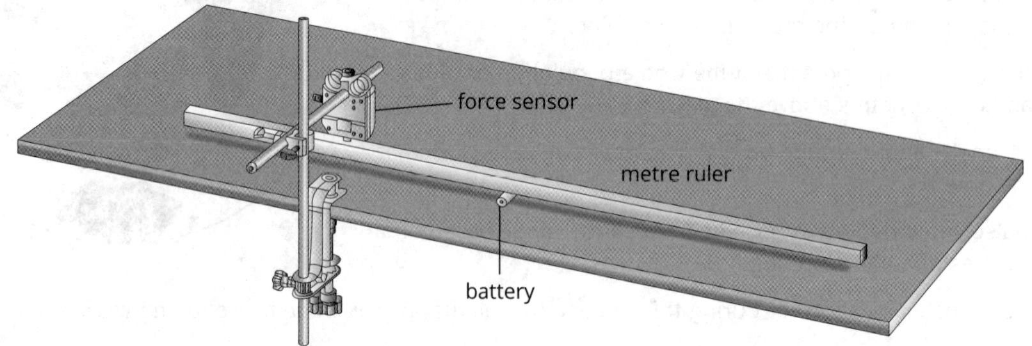

The battery acts as the pivot point or point of rotation about which the metre ruler will rotate. The force sensor measures the force at a fixed point, when a mass is placed at varying distances along the ruler on the opposite side of the pivot point.

The following data was collected in a series of trials in which the horizontal distance from the force sensor to the pivot point was 0.350 m.

Trial	Horizontal distance of mass to pivot point (m)	Force measured by sensor (N)	Torque measured by sensor (N m)	Torque applied by mass (N m)
1	0.100	0.280		
2	0.200	0.560		
3	0.300	0.840		
4	0.400	1.12		
5	0.500	1.40		

1 Assuming the ruler is in rotational equilibrium, complete the table to show the torque measured by the sensor and the torque applied by the mass. Treat the direction of the torque applied by the force sensor as anticlockwise (i.e. imagine you are looking at the apparatus from across the table).

2 Based on the test results, what is the size of the mass being applied?

 ISBN 978 0 6557 0016 6

3 Draw a force diagram of the experimental setup when the net torque acting on the object is zero. Indicate the direction and magnitude of the forces involved.

4 The equipment is rearranged so that the force sensor is now applied at an angle of 30° to the perpendicular. What would be the force measured by the force sensor with the mass at a distance of 0.500 m from the pivot point? Assume that the force sensor is still applied at a distance of 0.350 m from the pivot point.

5 What is the relationship between static equilibrium and net torque?

6 Can you assume that a larger force always produces a greater torque? Why? Justify your answer with an example.

7 A log has been placed on two supporting concrete blocks to allow a river to be crossed. Assuming the log is in static equilibrium and has a mass of 52 kg when positioned as shown below, find the normal force acting on each of the concrete blocks.

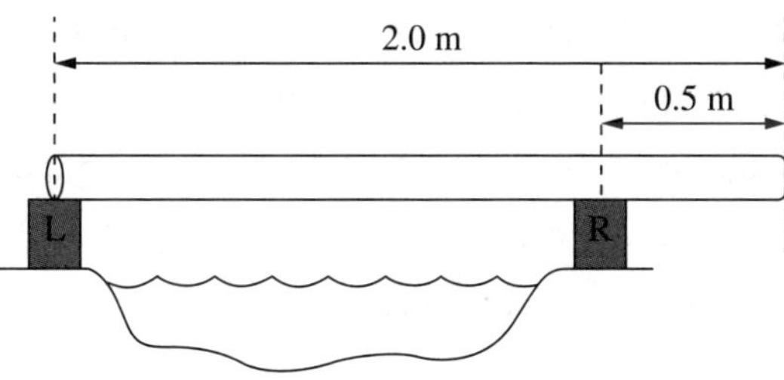

ISBN 978 0 6557 0016 6

WORKSHEET 37

Classification and identification

Literacy review—motion

In the following statements, fill in the blanks from the list of randomly ordered words in the list below. You may use some words more than once.

acceleration	during	greater	potential energy
after	elastic	half	proportional
before	energy	inelastic	second
collisions	explosion	internal forces	the same
conservation of energy	external forces	kinetic energy	total
conservation of mass	first	less	vectors
conservation of momentum	force	mass	velocity
conserved	force due to gravity	mechanical work	work
displacement	friction	momentum	work–energy theorem
double	gravitational potential	partial	

1 Newton's _______________ law predicts the following relationship between _______________, force, and mass: The acceleration of an object is directly _______________ to the net force and will always be in the same direction as the net _______________. Acceleration will be inversely proportional to the _______________ of the object, meaning that more massive objects will have less acceleration if subjected to the same net force.

2 An object subject to an unbalanced force will experience a _______________. The work done by that unbalanced force is equal to the component of the _______________ in the direction of the object's displacement multiplied by the magnitude of the displacement. If the _______________ imparted to the object by the force is converted entirely into kinetic energy, the work done by the unbalanced force will equal the change in the object's _______________. This concept is known as the _______________.

3 The momentum of an object equals its _______________ multiplied by its _______________. When two objects collide, the total momentum of the system is _______________ as long as there are no outside forces acting on the system. This concept is known as the law of _______________, which states the total momentum of the system _______________ an event (like a collision) is the same as the momentum _______________ the event.

4 If momentum is conserved during a collision or an explosion, this means that the total momentum of the objects will be _______________ both _______________ and _______________ the event. Consider an inelastic collision with two identical cars, one that is initially moving, and the other stationary. Because the _______________ of each object is the same, the _______________ of the two carts together after collision must be _______________ the initial velocity of the cart that was moving before the collision.

5 In an ideal frictionless environment, a trolley poised at the top of a hill has _______________ energy. As the trolley begins to roll down the hill, this _______________ energy is transformed into _______________energy. When the trolley reaches the bottom of the hill, the _______________ energy of the system consists entirely of _______________ energy. In the real world, some of this energy would be lost to the environment in the form of heat.

ISBN 978 0 6557 0016 6

WORKSHEET 38

Reflection—How is motion understood?

The following table lists the key knowledge covered in this area of study.

1 Reflect on how well you understand the concepts listed. Rate your learning by shading the circle that corresponds to your current level of understanding for each one.

Key knowledge	Not confident ◄				► Very confident
Scalars and vectors	○	○	○	○	○
Equations of motion, graphs	○	○	○	○	○
Newton's three laws	○	○	○	○	○
Momentum and net force	○	○	○	○	○
Work and mechanical energy; power and efficiency	○	○	○	○	○
Torque; translational, rotational and static equilibrium	○	○	○	○	○

2 Consider the points you have shaded from Not confident to Very confident. List specific ideas you can identify that were challenging.

3 Write down two different strategies that you will apply to help further your understanding of these ideas.

PRACTICAL ACTIVITY 15

Experiment

Analysing motion with a motion sensor

SUGGESTED DURATION

- 45 minutes

MATERIALS

- data logger and data analysis software
- base and support rod
- motion sensor

INTRODUCTION

When describing the motion of an object, it is essential to know where the object is relative to a reference point, how fast and in what direction it is moving, and how it is accelerating (changing its rate of motion).

An ultrasonic motion sensor sonar uses pulses of ultrasound that reflect from an object to determine the position of that object. As the object moves, the change in its position is measured many times each second. The change in position from moment to moment is expressed as a velocity ($m\,s^{-1}$). The change in velocity from moment to moment is expressed as an acceleration ($m\,s^{-2}$). The position of an object at a particular time can be plotted on a graph. You can also graph the velocity and acceleration of the object versus time.

A graph is a mathematical picture of the motion of an object. For this reason, it is important to understand how to interpret a graph of position, velocity or acceleration versus time. In this activity, you will plot a graph of position in real time: that is, as the motion is happening.

AIM

To investigate the relationships between the motion of an object and a position–time graph for the object.

METHOD

For this activity, you will be the object in motion. The motion sensor will measure your position as you move in a straight line at different speeds. The software and/or data logger that supports your sensor will plot your motion on a graph of position and time. Your lab partner will try to recreate your motion from your position–time data.

Setting up the motion sensor

Graph: position–time

Sampling rate: 10 samples per second (10 Hz). Stop condition at 10 s if available.

You do not need to calibrate ultrasonic motion sensors for temperatures around 20°C.

Consult the manuals for your electronic equipment or see your teacher for the options to set these values with your equipment and software.

1. Mount the motion sensor on a support rod so that it is aimed at your midsection when you are standing in front of the sensor. Make sure that you can move at least 2 m away from the motion sensor.
2. Position the device screen so you can see the screen while you move away from the motion sensor. Make sure the graph of position–time is visible and active.
3. When you are ready, stand in front of the motion sensor and click the RECORD button to begin recording data. Data recording will begin almost immediately. The motion sensor will make a faint clicking noise. Your partner should not be able to see you while you are moving.
4. Watch the plot of your motion on the graph, and try to move backwards and forwards so that the plot of your motion creates a relatively simple position versus time plot. Click the STOP button to finish measuring after about 10 s. Run #1 will appear in your Data list in the Experiment Setup window.
5. Now invite your partner to try to precisely match your graph. Your partner's trace can be set to appear directly over your own.
6. Try a more complex motion or ask your partner to leave the room while you create the initial graph. Invite them back to try to match the graph of your movement without the opportunity of having witnessed your movement first hand.

 ISBN 978 0 6557 0016 6

RESULTS

1 Use your software, or the position versus time data, to draw a velocity–time graph. You may want to print and insert copies of your graphs here.

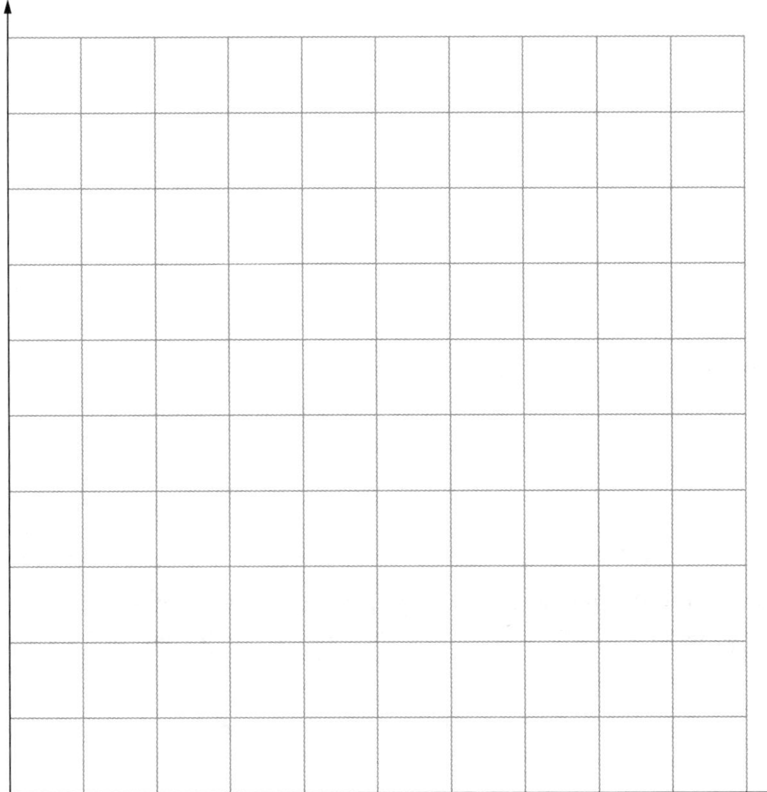

2 Use your software, or the velocity versus time data from step 1, to draw an acceleration–time graph. Insert a copy of your graph here.

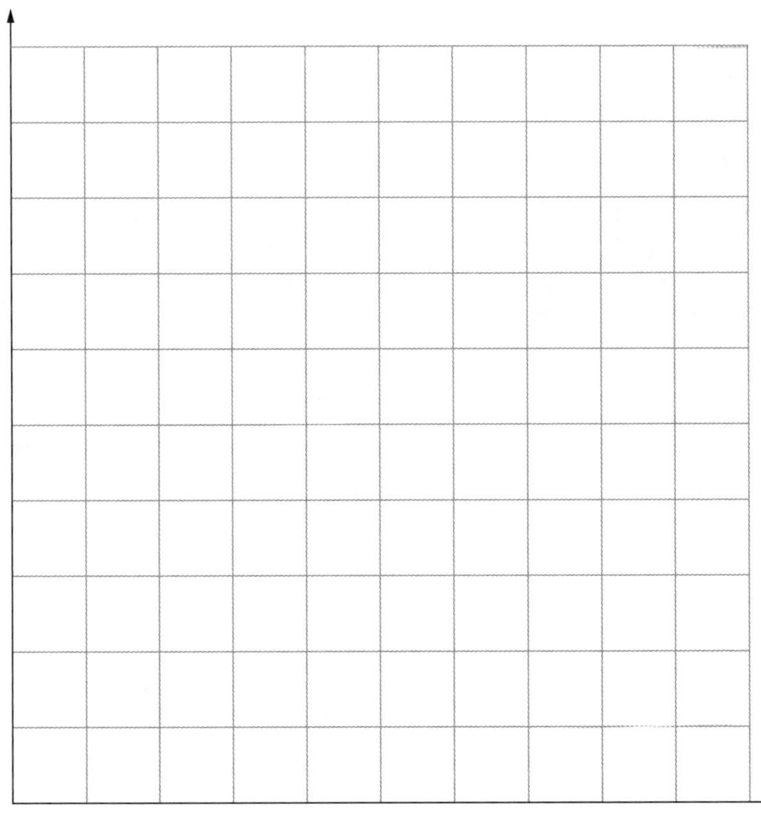

ISBN 978 0 6557 0016 6

DISCUSSION

1 a Comment on your ability to match other people's position–time graphs.

b What were the main clues to establishing how they had originally moved?

2 Describe your motion using the information in one of your graphs.

3 Comment on the data you have obtained from the motion sensor. Describe its strengths in measuring motion and velocity data, and potential weaknesses. Consider its suitability for measuring motion: fast and slow.

CONCLUSION

 ISBN 978 0 6557 0016 6

PRACTICAL ACTIVITY 16

Experiment • Product, process or system development

A reaction timer

SUGGESTED DURATION

- 50 minutes

MATERIALS

- Metre ruler

INTRODUCTION

The acceleration due to gravity provides a simple, reliable and repeatable means of timing a person's reaction time when combined with an understanding of the equations of straight line motion.

If t is the time that it takes a person to react and catch a falling object initially at rest then:

Using $s = ut + \frac{1}{2}at^2$

Where s = distance fallen in metres

u = initial velocity in m s^{-1}

t = time of fall in seconds

a = acceleration in m s^{-2}

AIM

To determine an individual's reaction time using a simple application of the equations of motion.

METHOD

Note: Repeated tests are required in this activity to ensure the object of the test is sufficiently unprepared for the time taken to be a true indication of reaction time.

1. Work in groups of at least two. The tester stands on a desk holding a metre ruler vertically a little out from their body so as to be able to fall freely for the full length of the ruler. The person being tested holds thumb and forefinger around the end of the ruler closest to the ground without touching or impeding the initial fall of the ruler.
2. Once the person being tested is ready, let go of the ruler without alerting the person being tested. You may want to use some mild (but safe!) distraction to ensure the person being tested isn't anticipating the fall. The person being tested grabs the ruler between thumb and forefinger, halting its fall as quickly as possible.
3. Record the distance fallen by the ruler (in metres) in the table below and calculate the reaction time corresponding to this distance using the formula derived in the introduction.
4. Repeat a number of times for both left and right hands and average the results. Repeat for each person in the group.

RESULTS

1 Rearrange the distance equation in the introduction in terms of t.

PRACTICAL ACTIVITY 16

Assume that gravitational acceleration is $9.8 \, m \, s^{-2}$ downwards.

Trial	Distance (m) Right hand	Reaction time (s) Right hand	Distance (m) Left hand	Reaction time (s) Left hand
1				
2				
3				
4				
average				

DISCUSSION

1 Collate results for everyone in the class. Comment on how your reaction time compares with the class average.

2 Based on the whole class's results, state whether there is any correlation between left and right-handedness and the reaction time achieved with each hand.

3 Determine whether there is any correlation between reaction time and the types of sport played by people in the class. For example, fast reaction times are generally one key to success in sprints, while not important for distance running.

ISBN 978 0 6557 0016 6

4 A car is travelling at 60 km h^{-1}. In the event of a situation requiring emergency braking, determine how far the car will travel before the driver can actually start braking if their reaction time is 0.2 seconds.

CONCLUSION

PRACTICAL ACTIVITY 17

Fieldwork • Product, process or system development

Measuring height or distance using kinematics

SUGGESTED DURATION

- Up to 240 minutes. Less with smaller heights or shorter distances.

MATERIALS

- Smartphone with built-in accelerometer or acceleration sensor
- Suitable free software for recording and graphing acceleration. Options include:
  - PASCO SparkVue
  - Physics Accelerometer Lab
  - Phyphox
  - Physics Toolbox and many others
- Suitable location – this can be anywhere from a school lift or multi-storey building (vertical data) to a school oval or private road

INTRODUCTION

The study of kinematics includes the analysis of linear motion graphs including displacement–time, velocity–time and acceleration–time. On an acceleration–time graph, the area under the curve equals the change in velocity.

That is:

$a \times \Delta t = \Delta v$

Knowing the initial velocity and the time taken, the change in displacement can be determined.

The accelerometer of a smartphone or acceleration sensor provides a very portable means of collecting acceleration data while travelling in the lift of a building or horizontally on a bike or cart. Using this data and knowing that acceleration can be used to determine velocity, a good estimate of the height of a tower or horizontal distance travelled can be obtained.

AIM

To determine the height of a building or the length of a track using acceleration–time data.

Do not travel in service lifts – start recording and send your phone or accelerometer up and down alone.

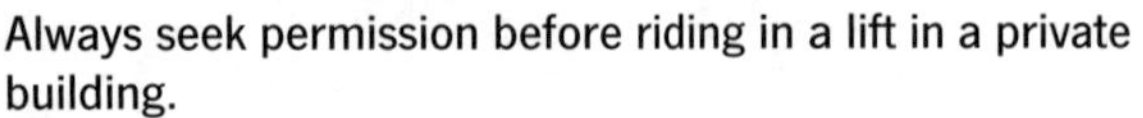
Always seek permission before riding in a lift in a private building.
Always let at least one other person know where you are going.

METHOD

1. Determine a suitable location for the investigation. For vertical heights, higher buildings yield bigger data sets, but a two-storey building will suffice. A long, straight track or school oval provide a great space for measuring horizontal distances. Use a bike or cart so that the accelerometer is moving largely in a horizontal direction.
2. Check that you have suitable software loaded on your device and that you know how it works. Some suggestions are noted in Materials. Ideally, the software will enable measuring acceleration in *x*, *y* and *z* directions independently and allow graphing and/or exporting.
3. Run a quick test to determine the relationship between the orientation of the phone and which axis (*x*, *y*, *z*) of the graphing app will show the vertical acceleration of the lift. Make a note to remind you.
   Vertical acceleration = _____ axis on the app
   Horizontal acceleration = _____ axis on the app
4. Starting at the ground floor, or at the start of the track, start recording as soon as motion commences.
5. Ride the lift or repeat the motion through the length of the vertical or horizontal change. Stop recording as the motion finishes.
6. Repeat at least twice to allow you to calculate an average.

ISBN 978 0 6557 0016 6

PRACTICAL ACTIVITY 17

RESULTS

1 Provide an electronic copy of your results.

2 From the acceleration–time graph of the ride, determine the height of the building or length of the track. Show your working.

DISCUSSION

1 Comment on your result for the height of the building, considering the following points.

- Compare your practical result with the stated height.
- Discuss the factors that you consider gave you a good comparison.
- List other factors that may have affected your result that you hadn't considered.
- State the sampling rate of the phone/device's accelerometer. Estimate the error that would introduce into your results.
- Research whether the phone/device has a maximum acceleration that it is able to measure. Consider and discuss whether this limit would affect your results.

CONCLUSION

 ISBN 978 0 6557 0016 6

PRACTICAL ACTIVITY 18

Experiment

Acceleration down an incline

SUGGESTED DURATION

- 50 minutes

MATERIALS

- dynamics cart or 'smart (sensor) cart' with mass
- stopwatch or motion sensor if sensor cart not available
- dynamics track or board at least 1 m long
- end stop, book or block (to stop the trolley)
- protractor
- metre ruler (if measuring manually)

Avoid rolling carts and other heavy objects off benches.

INTRODUCTION

A cart on an incline will roll down the incline as it is pulled by gravity. The acceleration due to gravity, g, is straight down (see figure below). The component of gravity that is parallel to the inclined surface is $g \sin\theta$, so this is the net acceleration of the cart, if friction is ignored.

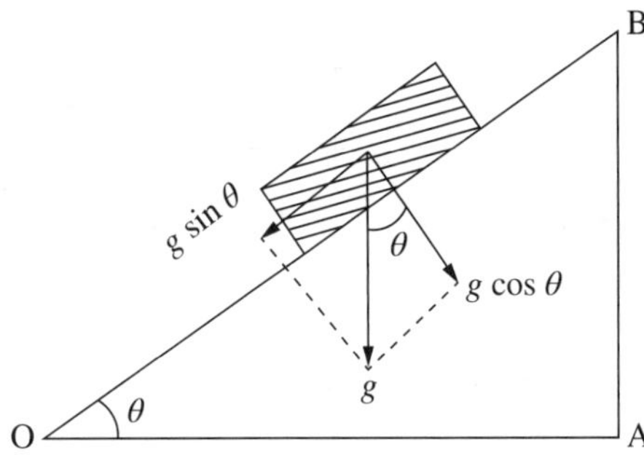

To measure the acceleration, the cart will start from rest and the time (t) it takes for it to travel a certain displacement (s) will be measured.

Since $s = ut + \frac{1}{2}at^2$ and $u = 0$, the acceleration provided by gravity down the plane can be found using: $a = \frac{2s}{t^2}$

A plot of acceleration versus $\sin\theta$ will be a straight line with a slope equal to the acceleration due to gravity (g).

AIM

To study the effect of the angle of an incline on the acceleration of an object.

METHOD

If using a smart cart or motion sensor, use a sample rate of 10–20 Hz. Faster speeds are not required for this activity.

1. Set up the track as shown above, raising the end of the track where the cart is to start about 20 cm. Record the angle the ramp makes with the horizontal.
2. Pull the cart up to the top of the track and record the displacement, s, of this initial position from the end stop where the cart will complete its run. Make sure you record the distance from the front of the cart. Record the uncertainty in the measurement.
3. Release the cart from rest and use a stopwatch to time how long it takes the cart to hit the end stop. Repeat this measurement five times (with different people doing the timing). Record all of the values in the table below, including the uncertainties in the measurements.
4. Lower the end of the track by 2 cm, measure the new angle to the horizontal and the measure the time for five runs.
5. Repeat the experiment for a total of seven angles, lowering the track in increments of 2 cm for each new angle.

PRACTICAL ACTIVITY 18

RESULTS

Uncertainty in individual time measurements: ± _____ s

Uncertainty in height: ± _____m

Uncertainty in length: ± _____m

Height (m)	s (m) ±	θ (°)	t_1 (s)	t_2 (s)	t_3 (s)	t_4 (s)	t_5 (s)	t_{av} (s)	$a = \frac{s}{t}$	$\sin\theta$
								±		
								±		
								±		
								±		
								±		
								±		
								±		

1 Calculate the average time the cart took for its run for each angle, including an estimate of the uncertainty.

2 Calculate the acceleration of the cart using the displacement and the times recorded.

3 Calculate $\sin\theta$ from the angle for each of the heights.

ISBN 978 0 6557 0016 6

4 Plot a graph of acceleration versus $\sin\theta$ in the space provided. Draw a line of best fit for your data and calculate its slope and hence find g.

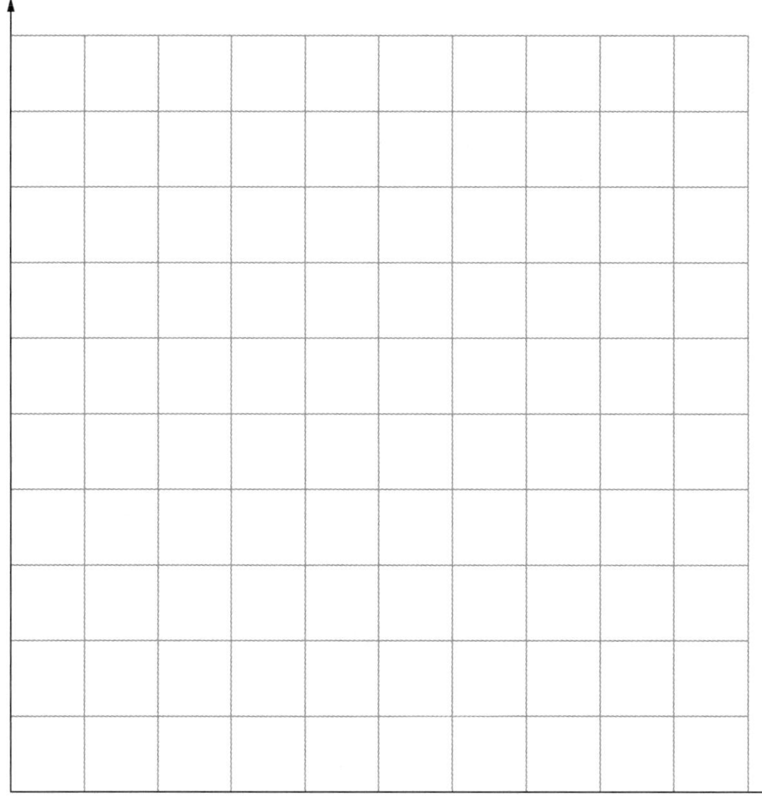

DISCUSSION

1 Explain the importance of carrying out multiple trials with different people doing the timing.

2 Comment on the relationship you found between acceleration and the angle of incline.

3 State the value you obtained for g. Compare your value with the accepted value for your location. Explain any discrepancy.

4 If measuring manually, assess whether your reaction time caused a greater percentage error for greater or smaller angles.

5 If the mass of the cart is doubled, explain any effect on the results. Try it to test your hypothesis.

6 Compare and assess which method provides the most accurate measure of the angle of the track—calculation from length and height, or direct measurement using a small protractor.

CONCLUSION

 ISBN 978 0 6557 0016 6

PRACTICAL ACTIVITY 19

Experiment

Newton's second law

SUGGESTED DURATION

- 50 minutes

MATERIALS

- dynamics cart or 'smart cart'
- pulley with clamp
- string
- stopwatch, motion sensor or photogates (or smart carts)
- electronic balance
- dynamics track (or simple board that can be levelled)
- mass hanger and mass set
- wooden or metal stopping block
- ruler

Avoid dropping masses and carts. The equipment may be damaged and may injure students.

INTRODUCTION

According to Newton's second law, $F = ma$ or $F \propto a$. F is the net force acting on an object of mass m and a is the resulting acceleration of the object.

For a cart of mass m_1 on a horizontal track, attached to a mass m_2 by a string over a pulley (shown below), the net force F on the entire system (the cart and hanging mass) is the force due to gravity on hanging mass, $F = m_2g$, assuming that friction is negligible.

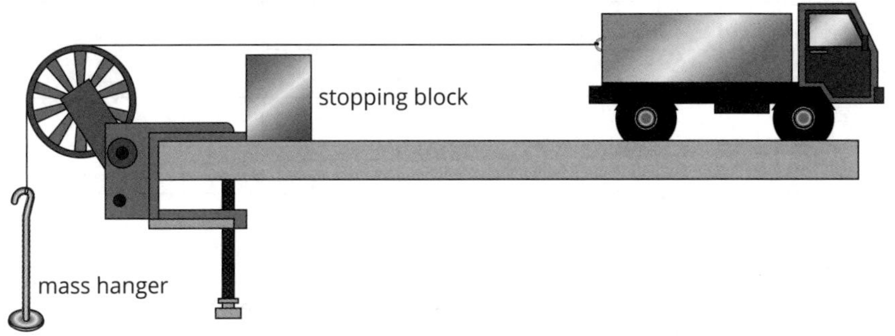

According to Newton's second law, this net force should be equal to ma, where m is the total mass that is being accelerated, which in this case is $m_1 + m_2$. This experiment will verify whether m_1g is equal to $(m_1 + m_2)a$ when friction is ignored.

To find the acceleration, the cart will be started from rest and the time (t) it takes for it to travel a certain distance (s) will be measured. Then, since $s = ut + \frac{1}{2}at^2$ and $u = 0$, the acceleration can be found by rearranging in terms of a, so $a = \frac{2s}{t^2}$

AIM

To verify Newton's second law, $F = ma$.

METHOD

1. Level the track by setting the cart on the track to see which way it rolls. Adjust the levelling feet, or place extra paper or books underneath, to raise or lower the ends until the cart placed at rest on the track doesn't start to move.
2. Use the balance to find the mass of the cart and record the value in the space provided in the Results section, together with an estimate of the uncertainty.
3. Attach the pulley to the end of the track as shown in the diagram. Place the dynamics cart on the track and attach a string to the end of the cart. Tie a mass hanger on the other end of the string. The string must be just long enough so the cart hits the stopping block before the mass hanger reaches the floor.
4. Pull the cart back until the mass hanger reaches the pulley. Record this position and mark it on the track with chalk or similar removable mark. This will be the release position for all trials.
5. Make a test run by simply releasing the cart to determine how much mass is required on the mass hanger so that the cart takes about 2 s to complete the run. Because of your reaction time, too short of a total time will cause a large percentage error. However, if the cart moves too slowly, friction may introduce a significant percentage error. Record the mass of the total hanging mass (the hanger plus masses), including the uncertainty.
6. Place the cart against the end stop on the pulley end of the track, and record the final position of the car.
7. Measure the time it takes for the cart to travel from start to the pulley end position at least four times. Record these values in the table provided in the Results section, together with the uncertainty.
8. Increase the mass of the cart and repeat the procedure.

PRACTICAL ACTIVITY 19

RESULTS

Uncertainty in position: ± _______ m

Uncertainty in mass: ± _______ kg

1 Calculate the total distance travelled by taking the difference between the initial and final positions of the cart: $s =$ _______ m

2 Complete the table for the remaining values calculated from your initial measurements. To determine a measure of the reliability of the comparison, calculate the percentage difference for each trial mass.

Percentage difference, $\%\Delta = \frac{F_{net} - (m_1 + m_2)a}{F_{net}} \times \frac{100}{1}\%$

Trial	Hanging mass m_2 (kg) ±	$m_1 + m_2$ (kg) ±	t_1 (s) ±	t_2 (s) ±	t_3 (s) ±	t_4 (s) ±	t_{av} (s) ±	$a = \frac{2s}{t^2}$ (m s^{-2})	$(m_1 + m_2)a$ (kg m s^{-2})	F_{net} (m_2g) (kg m s^{-2})	%Δ
1							±				
2							±				
3							±				
4							±				
5							±				

DISCUSSION

1 Discuss to what extent your observations, measurements and calculations confirm, or otherwise, Newton's second law. Comment on the reliability of your results with reference to the percentage difference.

2 Explain why the mass in $F = ma$ is not just taken as equal to the mass of the cart.

3 When calculating the force on the cart using mass × gravity, explain why the mass of the cart isn't included.

CONCLUSION

ISBN 978 0 6557 0016 6

PRACTICAL ACTIVITY 20

Experiment • Product, process or system development

Verifying the value of acceleration due to gravity at Earth's surface

SUGGESTED DURATION

- 50 minutes

MATERIALS

- \$2 coin, ball bearing or other small object to drop
- hard surface
- smartphone or tablet with a sound recording application such as Sparkvue, Audacity or similar
- long tape measure
- A metal plate can help amplify the sound of the object hitting the hard surface.

INTRODUCTION

The displacement, *s*, of an object travelling in a straight line can be described by the equation

$$s = ut + \frac{1}{2}at^2$$

where:
u is its initial velocity (m s^{-1})
t is time (s)
a is the acceleration (m s^{-2}).

For an object falling vertically from rest, the acceleration of the object will be the acceleration due to gravity, *g*, near Earth's surface if the effects of air resistance are ignored. By collecting data of the time taken for the object to hit the ground when it falls from a height, *s*, with an initial velocity of zero, the acceleration due to gravity can be found from the gradient of the line. By graphing s versus t^2, the gradient of the line is the acceleration due to gravity.

AIM

To find a value for the acceleration due to gravity on Earth's surface.

Ensure that the area is clear when the object is being dropped, especially if it's dropped from a window, stairwell or other large height. Make sure the object isn't too heavy, to avoid damaging the floor. Complete a risk assessment before starting the activity.

METHOD

1. Decide on five different heights from which to drop the object. The minimum height should be 1 m to provide a reasonable time for the object to fall. Try larger heights (for example, from a stairwell or window) but bear in mind that you need to accurately measure the distance the object falls and also be able to clearly hear the object hit the ground.
2. Nominate one person to operate the recording software, and another to drop the object. Open a new software document and start recording. The student operating the recording software should count down to the drop ('three, two, one, drop'). Make sure that the instruction to drop the object is louder than the countdown, and can be picked up by the microphone (it should register as a peak on the software). Drop the object.
3. The software should then register another peak when the object hits the ground. Make sure the ground is hard (a metal plate is useful in amplifying the sound) so that the object will make a sound when it hits it. It's important to limit background noise so that a clear peak for the original contact can be seen. Stop recording as soon as the object hits the ground.
4. Note the results in the table below for the distance the object has fallen and the time it has taken, with the uncertainty for each measurement.
5. Repeat the same measurements at least twice more to obtain an average.

PRACTICAL ACTIVITY 20

RESULTS

- List the variables in this experiment:

Independent: ______________________________

Dependent: ________________________________

Controlled: _______________________________

Height (m) ±	t_1 (s) ±	t_2 (s) ±	t_3 (s) ±	t_{av} (s) ±	% uncertainty in t	Possible relationship
				±		
				±		
				±		
				±		
				±		

1 Find the average time for each trial and calculate estimates of absolute error in each average. Enter these values in the table.

2 Plot the data from the table in the graph space provided. Label the graph and axes appropriately and include suitable error bars.

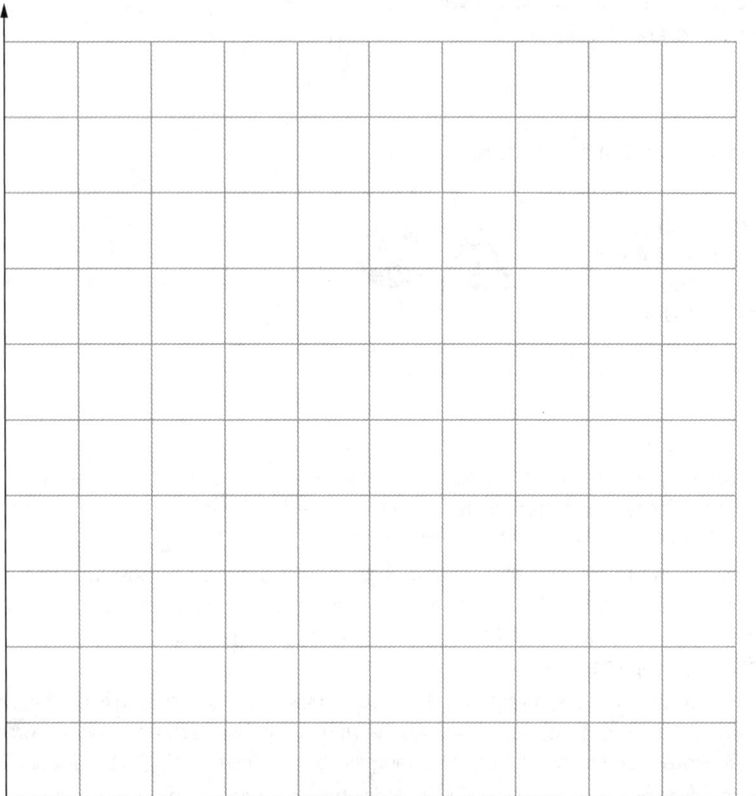

3 Identify the possible relationship between height and time suggested by the shape of the graph.

4 Complete the table with the values based on this relationship.

 ISBN 978 0 6557 0016 6

5 Plot the results on a graph, with your relationship on the vertical axis, and *s* (the independent variable) on the horizontal axis.

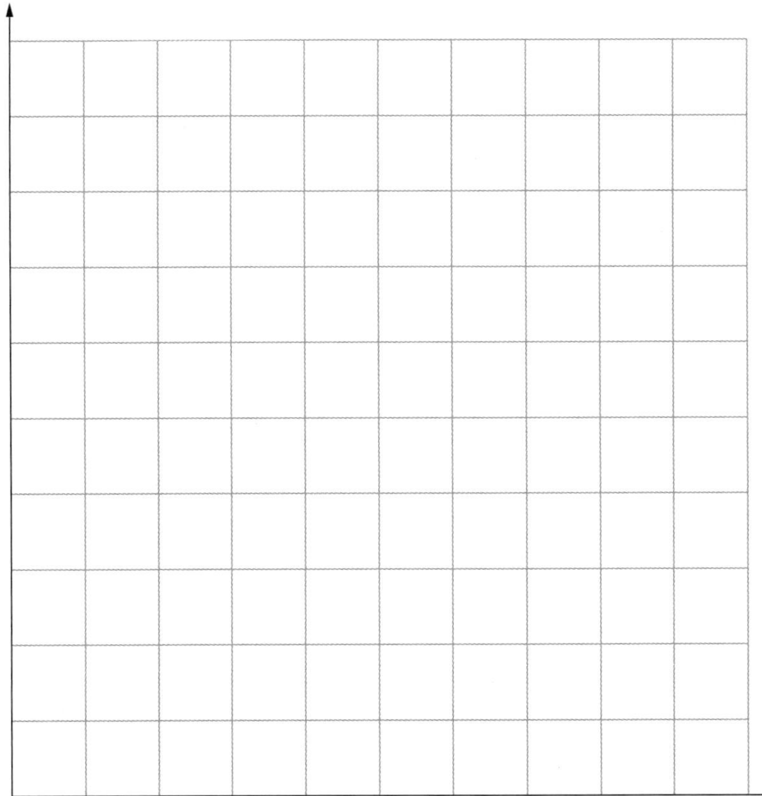

6 Draw a line of best fit and find its gradient. Determine *g* from the gradient.

DISCUSSION

1 Review any points on your graph that do not fit the trend. Explain why this may have been the case.

2 Compare your value for *g* with the values obtained by other groups. Comment on any discrepancies and the possible reasons for these.

3 Compare your graph to the graphs drawn by other groups who dropped different objects. Discuss any variation in the shape of the graphs.

4 The aim of the experiment was to determine the value of the acceleration due to gravity by dropping an object from different heights and measuring the time it took to drop to the ground. Compare your value with the accepted value of *g*.

5 The process of drawing a graph of s versus t^2 to determine g is called linearisation. Explain the value of this approach over calculating g from a graph of s versus t.

6 *Note:* While outside the general scope of this course, an estimate of the uncertainty in t^2 can be found by multiplying the percentage uncertainty in t by 2. Use this to draw error bars on your graph of linearised data, and use your error bars to draw a minimum and maximum line. Then use the minimum and maximum lines to find the uncertainty in your value for the gradient to get the uncertainty in your value of the acceleration due to gravity.

7 Considering your discussion and conclusion, critique the experimental method as an effective means of determining the acceleration due to gravity.

8 Given your critique of the existing method, discuss some potential changes that would provide potentially more reliable results.

CONCLUSION

 ISBN 978 0 6557 0016 6

PRACTICAL ACTIVITY 21

Experiment

Work, energy and power

SUGGESTED DURATION

- 45 minutes

MATERIALS

- data logger
- motion sensor
- force sensor
- dynamics cart and track (or ramp)
- end stop or heavy mass
- pulley and clamp
- mass and hangers
- electronic balance (only one required for the class)
- 1.5 m non-stretch string or braided physics string

INTRODUCTION

Mechanical work is a process in everyday life. It is defined as a net force applied to an object over a distance that causes the object's kinetic energy to change. For example, as a ball falls from rest to the ground, gravity does work, causing a change in the ball's kinetic energy:

$$W = Fs = \frac{1}{2}mv^2 - \frac{1}{2}mu^2$$

In this practical investigation, the motion of a simple cart and track system is observed to better understand this relationship.

AIM

To investigate the relationship between the net force applied to an object over a distance and the resulting change in the object's kinetic energy.

METHOD

1. Place the dynamics track on a lab table with one end hanging slightly over the edge of the table.
2. Place the dynamics cart, stationary, in the middle of the track, and then adjust the track level until the cart does not roll.
3. Mount the pulley and clamp to the end of the track hanging over the edge of the table. Be sure the area below the pulley is clear to allow the mass and hanger to fall cleanly.
4. Mount the end stop to the track (or sit the heavy mass on the track) to prevent the cart from colliding with the pulley.
5. Mount the motion sensor to the other end of the track, with the sensing element pointing towards the pulley. Be sure the motion sensor switch is set on the cart's position (if available) to avoid reflections from objects outside the cart–track system.
6. Mount the force sensor to the top of the cart. You will need to adjust the height of the pulley so that the top of the pulley is even with the force-sensor hook when the cart is on the track.
7. Measure the total mass of the cart and force sensor, and record the value in the table in the results section.
8. Connect the force sensor and motion sensor to the data-collection system.
9. Place the dynamics cart and force sensor on the track, and press the zero button on the force sensor.
10. In the data-collection software, display a force versus position graph. (Refer to your system's manual for instructions.)
11. Set up the cart and mass hanger:
    - Hold the cart on the track at the position you will be releasing it (10 cm away from the motion sensor).
    - Attach a length of string to the force-sensor hook. The string should be slightly longer than the distance from the force sensor to just below the pulley. Attach the mass hanger to the opposite end of the string, hanging over the pulley.
    - Place 50 g on the hanger. Remember to add the mass of the hanger to the 50 g when doing calculations.
12. Start data recording in your data-collection system.
13. Release the cart, and let it run the length of the track.
14. Stop data recording just before the cart collides with the end stop or the mass hits the floor, whichever comes first.
15. If time permits, repeat the experiment using different masses.

ISBN 978 0 6557 0016 6

PRACTICAL ACTIVITY 21

RESULTS

Print out a copy of the force–position graph from the data analysis system and paste it in the space provided, or draw your graph on the grid below.

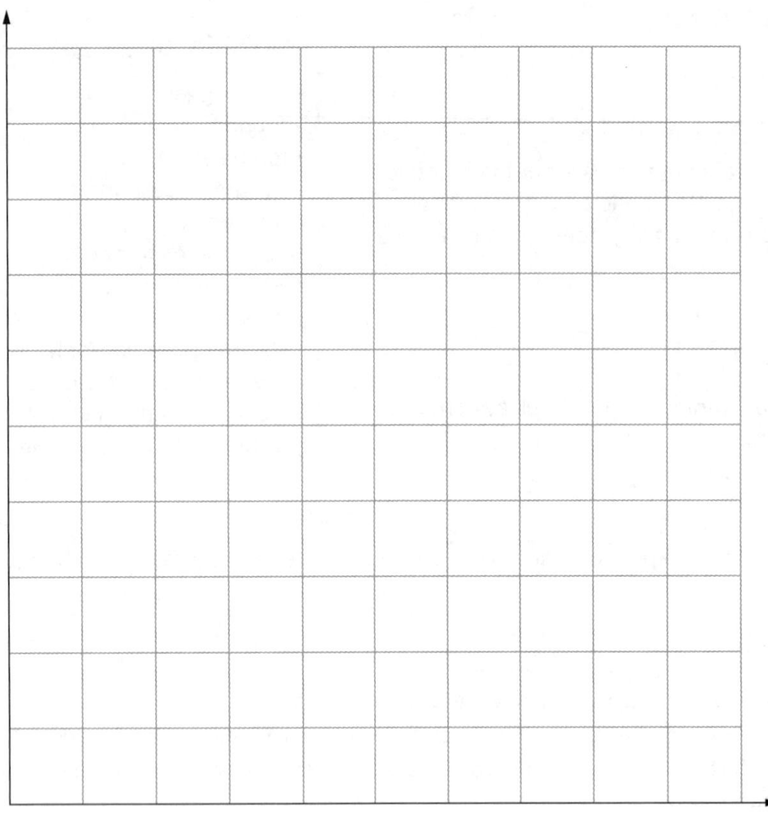

From the graph, find the work done by calculating the area under the force–position graph. Check your answer against the value calculated by the software. Record the value of the work done in the table.

From your data logger, find and record the initial and final velocities of the data run.

Initial velocity: ______________

Final velocity: ______________

ISBN 978 0 6557 0016 6

PRACTICAL ACTIVITY 21

Draw the graph of velocity–time in the space provided below. You can also print and paste in the graph from your data-analysis system if the feature is available.

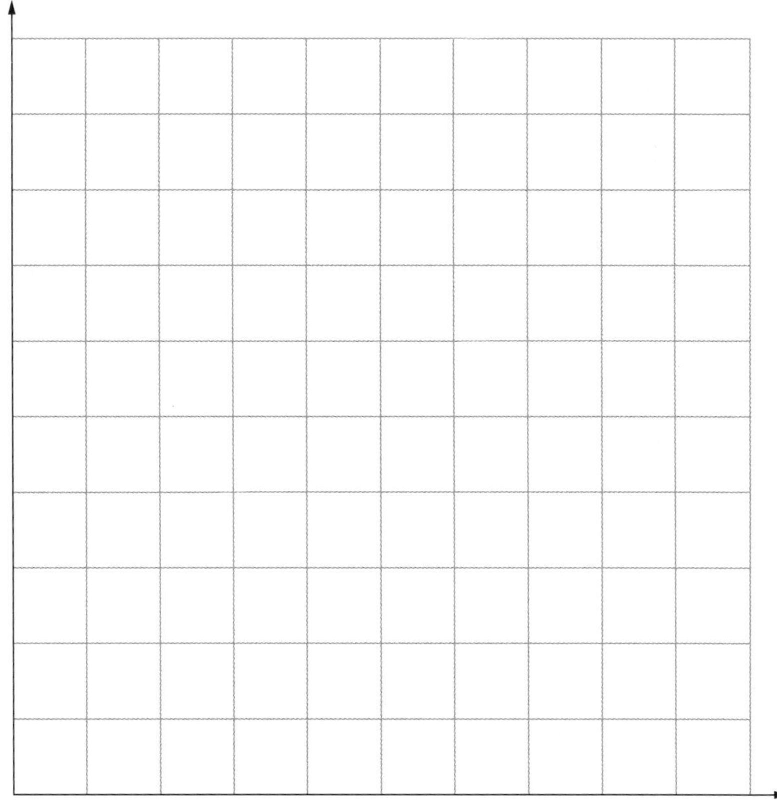

Using the results calculated above, complete the data table below for each mass tested.

	Mass 1	Mass 2	Mass 3
Mass of cart + force sensor + hanging mass (kg)			
Work done (N m)			
$v_{initial}$ (m s^{-1})			
v_{final} (m s^{-1})			
$(E_k)_{initial}$ (J) $= \frac{1}{2}mu^2$			
$(E_k)_{final}$ (J) $= \frac{1}{2}mv^2$			
$E_k = (E_k)_{final} - (E_k)_{initial}$ (J)			

PRACTICAL ACTIVITY 21

DISCUSSION

1 Why is it important that the force-sensor hook be at the same height as the top of the pulley?

2 Why is a force–position graph used for this investigation?

3 What method did you use to find the area under the force–position graph?

4 What is the significance of the initial and final velocities to work done?

5 Using the definition of power, how could you find the average power of this system from the collected data?

6 Calculate the percentage difference between the change in work done and the change in kinetic energy. Using this value to compare the two measures, comment on how well, or otherwise, your experiment confirmed that $W = E_{k.}$

7 What are some possible reasons for any difference?

8 What are some other forms of mechanical energy?

9 Why do you think we can ignore these other forms of mechanical energy in this experiment?

 ISBN 978 0 6557 0016 6

PRACTICAL ACTIVITY 21

10 A light has been designed that uses a falling mass to power it. As the potential energy is transformed into kinetic energy, the light turns on. The light itself needs 0.1 W to turn on. How does this compare to the average power of the system for each of the masses?

CONCLUSION

PRACTICAL ACTIVITY 22

Experiment

Conservation of momentum

SUGGESTED DURATION

- 50 minutes

MATERIALS

- 2 dynamics trolleys
- masses
- dynamics track, or board at least 1.5 m long
- metre ruler
- mass balance
- chalk

Note: This activity can also use an airtrack and gliders.

INTRODUCTION

When two trolleys push away from each other and no net force exists, the total momentum of both trolleys is conserved:

$p = m_1v_1 - m_2v_2 = 0$

Because the system is initially at rest, the final momentum of the two trolleys must be equal in magnitude and opposite in direction, so the resulting total momentum of the system is zero.

The ratio of the final speeds of the trolleys is therefore equal to the ratio of the masses of the trolleys:

$$m_1v_1 - m_2v_2 = 0$$
$$m_1v_1 = m_2v_2$$
$$\frac{v_1}{v_2} = \frac{m_1}{m_2}$$

In this investigation, the starting point for both trolleys is their position at rest, so that the two trolleys reach the end of the track simultaneously. To determine the speed, the distance travelled can be measured, since the time travelled by each trolley is the same. This eliminates one potential source of error from the experiment, and the ratio of the distances is equal to the ratio of the masses:

$$\frac{\Delta s_1}{\Delta s_2} = \frac{m_1}{m_2}$$

AIM

To demonstrate conservation of momentum for two trolleys pushing away from each other.

METHOD

1 ▪ Level the track by adjusting the levelling feet until a trolley placed on the track does not move. (If there are no levelling feet, use cardboard or books for levelling.)

For each of the following cases, place the two trolleys against each other with the plunger of one trolley pushed completely in and latched in its maximum position.

2 ▪ Use a pencil to push the plunger release button of one trolley, and watch the two trolleys move in opposite directions to the ends of the track. Experiment with different starting positions until the two trolleys reach their end of the track at the same time. Mark this starting position with chalk to ensure it is exactly the same for each trial.

3 ▪ Weigh the two trolleys and record the masses and the starting position. Carry out the following trials. Each trial should be run at least three times, and the distance travelled by each trolley recorded for each run in the Results table.

Trial 1: Trolleys of equal mass—use two trolleys without mass bars.

Trial 2: Trolleys of unequal mass—put one mass bar in one trolley, and none in the other.

Trial 3: Trolleys of unequal mass—put two mass bars in one trolley, and none in the other.

Trial 4: Trolleys of unequal mass—put two mass bars in one trolley, and one mass bar in the other.

 ISBN 978 0 6557 0016 6

PRACTICAL ACTIVITY 22

RESULTS

1 For each of the trials, measure the distances travelled from the starting position to the respective ends of the track for each trolley and record them in the table below.

2 Calculate the ratio of the distances travelled and record your results in the table.

3 Calculate the ratio of the masses and record this in the table.

Trial	$s_{\text{trolley 1}}$ (m)	$s_{\text{trolley 2}}$ (m)	$\frac{s_1}{s_2}$	$\frac{m_1}{m_2}$
Trial 1, Run 1				
Trial 1, Run 2				
Trial 1, Run 3				
Trial 2, Run 1				
Trial 2, Run 2				
Trial 2, Run 3				
Trial 3, Run 1				
Trial 3, Run 2				
Trial 3, Run 3				
Trial 4, Run 1				
Trial 4, Run 2				
Trial 4, Run 3				

DISCUSSION

1 Does the ratio of the displacements equal the ratio of the masses in each of the cases? In other words, is momentum conserved? Comment on your results.

2 When trolleys with unequal masses push away from each other, which trolley has more momentum?

3 When trolleys with unequal masses push away from each other, which trolley has more kinetic energy?

4 Does the starting position depend on which trolley has its plunger set? Why?

5 No units are shown in the table for the ratios of distance and of mass. What should the units be for each ratio?

CONCLUSION

 ISBN 978 0 6557 0016 6

PRACTICAL ACTIVITY 23

Experiment

Conservation of energy

SUGGESTED DURATION

- 50 minutes

MATERIALS

- dynamics trolley with plunger
- masses
- pulley with clamp
- string
- mass balance
- dynamics track or board at least 1.5 m long
- metre ruler
- mass hanger and mass set (several kilograms)

INTRODUCTION

The gravitational potential energy gained by a trolley as it climbs an incline is given by:

$E_g = mgh$

where:

m is the mass of the trolley (in kg)

g is the gravitational acceleration ($9.8\,m\,s^{-2}$ downwards on Earth)

h is the vertical height the trolley is raised (in m).

The height is given by:

$h = s\sin\theta$

where:

s is the displacement along the incline (in m)

θ is the angle between the incline and the horizontal.

The potential energy of a spring compressed a distance x is given by:

$E_s = \frac{1}{2}kx^2$

where k is the spring constant.

The force exerted by a spring is proportional to the distance the spring is compressed or stretched. That is:

$F = -kx$

So, the spring constant can be determined by applying different forces to stretch or compress the spring by different amounts. A graph of force versus distance is then a straight line with gradient equal to k.

If energy is conserved, the potential energy in the compressed spring is converted completely into gravitational potential energy.

AIM

To examine gravitational potential energy and spring potential energy to show how energy is conserved.

METHOD

Determining the spring constant

1. Level the track by adjusting the levelling feet until a trolley placed on the track does not move. (If there are no levelling feet, use cardboard or books for levelling.)
2. Use the balance to find the mass of the trolley. Record this value.
3. Set the trolley on the track with the spring plunger extended fully and directly against a stopping block. Attach a string to the trolley and attach the other end to a mass hanger, passing the string over the pulley. Record the trolley's position.
4. Add a mass to the mass hanger so that the mass is compressing the trolley's plunger and record the new position. Repeat this for a total of five different masses. Record each trial in Table 1.

PRACTICAL ACTIVITY 23

Gravitational potential energy

1. Remove the string from the trolley and set the spring plunger to its maximum compression position. Place the trolley against the end stop. Measure the distance the spring plunger is compressed and record this value.
2. Incline the track and measure its height and the length of the track to determine the angle of the track. Record the distances measured for checking later and calculate the angle of incline. Record the initial position of the trolley.
3. Release the plunger by tapping it with a stick and record the distance the trolley goes up the track. Repeat this five times. Record the maximum distance the trolley travelled.
4. Change the angle of inclination and repeat the measurements.
5. Add mass to the trolley and repeat the measurements.

RESULTS

Mass of trolley: __________ kg

Initial distance plunger is compressed __________ m

Percentage difference = $\%\Delta = \frac{E_g - E_s}{E_g} \times \frac{100}{1}\%$

1 Using your initial data, plot a graph of force versus displacement. Draw a line of best fit through the data points and determine the slope of the line. The slope is equal to the effective spring constant, *k*.

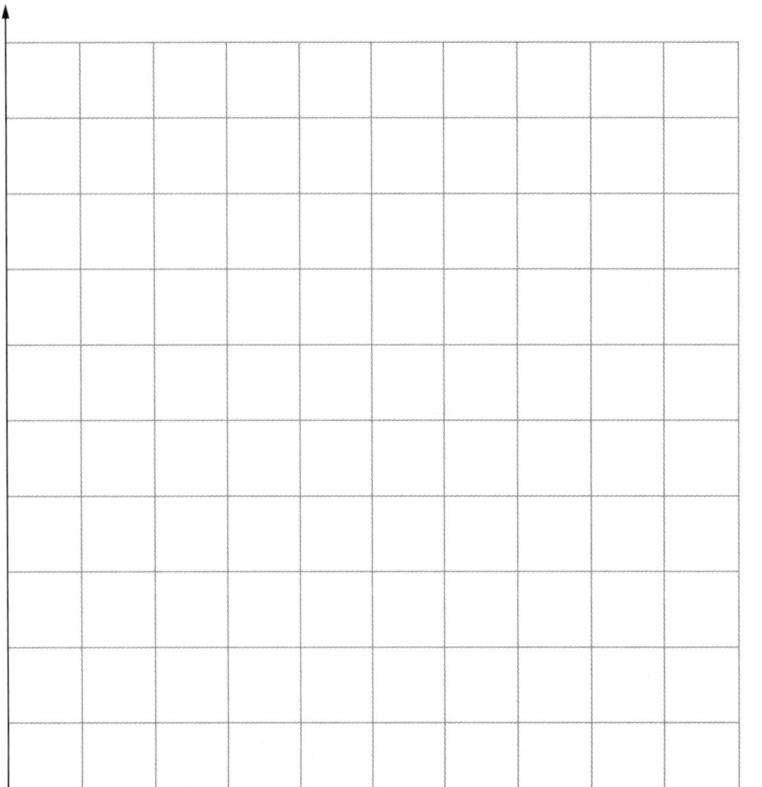

2 Calculate the spring potential energy and record this in Table 1.

ISBN 978 0 6557 0016 6

TABLE 1 Spring potential energy

Mass on hanger (kg)	Position (m)	$E_s = \frac{1}{2}kx^2$ (J)
0		

3 Calculate the gravitational potential energy for each trial and record this in Table 2.

4 Calculate the percentage difference between the spring potential energy and the gravitational potential energy and record it in Table 2.

TABLE 2 Gravitational potential energy

Height of track (m)	Track length (m)	θ (°)	Distance travelled (m)	Height travelled $h = s\sin\theta$ (m)	Mass of trolley (kg)	$E_g = mgh$ (J)	% difference

DISCUSSION

1 Comment on your results. Can you state that energy was conserved?

2 Assuming that there was a discrepancy, which of the potential energies was larger? Where did this 'lost' energy go?

3 When the mass of the trolley was doubled, why did the gravitational potential energy remain about the same?

CONCLUSION

 ISBN 978 0 6557 0016 6

EXAM-STYLE QUESTIONS

Multiple-choice questions

Consider the following quantities when answering questions 1 and 2:

A. 4 m s^{-1}

B. 5 N downwards

C. 45 kg

D. 12 m s^{-2} east

E. 76 units to the right

F. 64 km

G. 45 km h^{-1} at 337°T

Question 1

List the quantities that are correctly expressed as vectors.

Question 2

List the quantities are correctly expressed as scalars.

Question 3

In a 100 m race at the school swimming sports, Jeni completes four laps of the 25 m pool in 72 s. Identify which of the following statements about the magnitudes of her speed and velocity is true.

A. Her average speed and average velocity were both 0 m s^{-1}.

B. Her average speed was 0 m s^{-1}, and her average velocity was about 1.4 m s^{-1}

C. Her average speed was about 1.4 m s^{-1}, and her average velocity was 0 m s^{-1}.

D. Her average speed and average velocity were both 1.4 m s^{-1}.

Question 4

Starting from rest, a cyclist accelerates to 12 m s^{-1} in a time of 4.0 s. Identify the option that correctly states the magnitude of her average acceleration during this time.

A. 0 m s^{-2}

B. 0.33 m s^{-2}

C. 3.0 m s^{-2}

D. 48 m s^{-2}

Question 5

A 1200 kg car travelling at 60 km h^{-1} needs to exert a force of 900 N to maintain a constant speed on a straight road.

Identify the option that represents the sum of all the resistance forces acting on the car.

A. 0 N

B. 900 N forwards

C. 900 N backwards

D. 3300 N forwards

E. 3300 N backwards

EXAM-STYLE QUESTIONS

Question 6

If the driver wants to accelerate at $2.0\,m\,s^{-2}$, identify the force that must now be applied to overcome resistance.

A. 0 N

B. 900 N forwards

C. 900 N backwards

D. 3300 N forwards

E. 3300 N backwards

Question 7

Identify which of the following descriptions for calculating torque is correct.

A. Torque can be calculated using either the perpendicular force or the perpendicular lever arm.

B. Torque can only be calculated using the perpendicular force.

C. Torque can only be calculated using the perpendicular lever arm.

D. Torque can only be calculated using both the perpendicular force and the perpendicular lever arm together.

Short-answer questions

Question 1 (3 marks)

A car is observed moving along a road at a steady speed of $60\,km\,h^{-1}$.

a. Calculate how far, in kilometres, it will move in 1 min. — 1 mark

b. Determine how long it would take to travel 20 km. — 1 mark

c. Calculate the distance, in metres, that it would travel in 30 s. — 1 mark

Question 2 (10 marks)

A sports car takes 6 s to accelerate uniformly from rest to a speed of $30\,m\,s^{-1}$. It then maintains this velocity for 14 s before decelerating uniformly to a stop in a distance of 30 m.

a. Draw a velocity–time graph illustrating this motion. — 4 marks

ISBN 978 0 6557 0016 6

EXAM-STYLE QUESTIONS

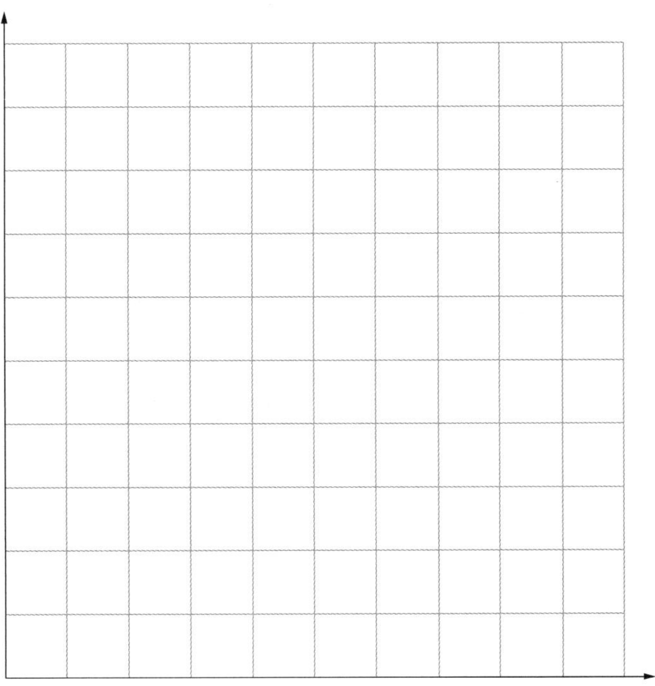

b. Determine the distance the car travels through its journey. 4 marks

c. Calculate the time taken for the journey. 2 marks

Question 3 (2 marks)

Describe, in terms of its velocity, the acceleration of a ball when bouncing off a wall. Using the wall as the frame of reference, state the direction that the acceleration will have.

EXAM-STYLE QUESTIONS

Question 4 (6 marks)

A girl pulls a trolley 2.6 m from rest along a path, using a cord inclined at an angle of 24° to the horizontal. She applies a constant force of 15.0 N. The trolley has a mass of 3.0 kg and the frictional force resisting the motion of the trolley is a constant 9.6 N.

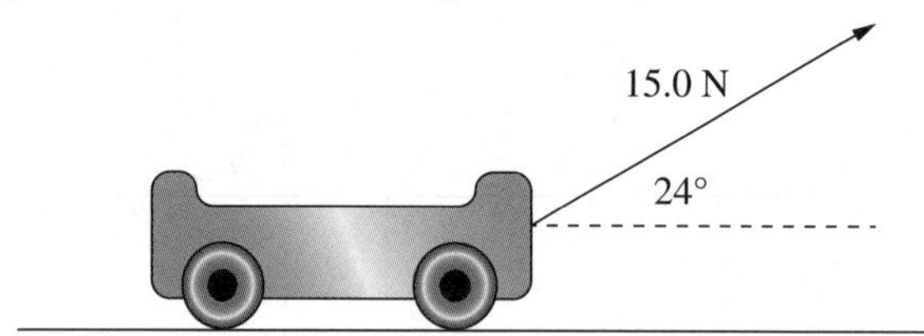

a. Calculate the work done on the trolley by the girl in moving it 2.6 m. 2 marks

b. Calculate the work done on the trolley by friction. 1 mark

c. Determine the kinetic energy of the trolley after it has moved 2.6 m. 1 mark

d. Determine the work done on the trolley by the normal contact force. Explain your answer. 2 marks

Question 5 (5 marks)

A boy swings off a platform 2.0 m above a river by hanging onto the very end of a rope that is 4.0 m long. The rope is attached to a tree growing on the edge of the river, 5.0 m above the water.

a. Determine how fast the boy is going at the lowest point of the swing. You may want to draw a diagram of the situation to help visualise what is happening. 3 marks

 ISBN 978 0 6557 0016 6

b. Several other children now do the same thing, with each child being recorded on video. The recordings are later analysed carefully and it is found that every child, regardless of their mass and when they let go of the rope, hit the water at the same speed. Using your understanding of the conservation of mechanical energy, explain why this occurred. 2 marks

Question 6 (7 marks)

A train wagon of mass 23 tonnes is rolling along a horizontal track at 8.3 m s^{-1} when it collides with a stationary loaded wagon that has a mass of 34 tonnes. The two wagons become locked together.

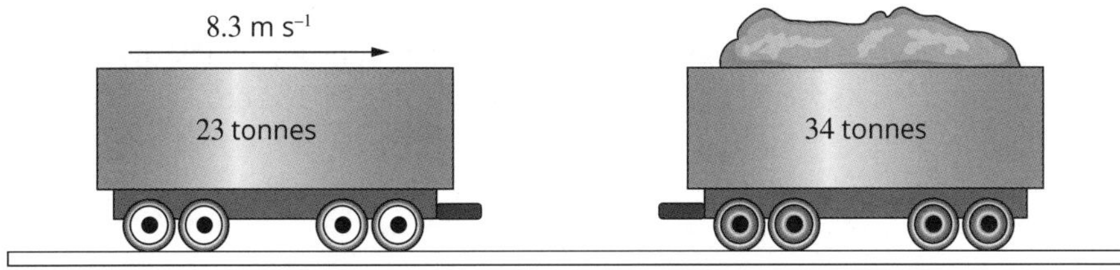

a. Calculate the speed at which the two wagons move off together. 2 marks

b. Calculate the kinetic energy lost in the collision. 3 marks

c. State whether this is an elastic or inelastic collision. Justify your statement. 2 marks

Question 7 (3 marks)

A rope is attached at 30.0° to a freshly planted tree. The line of action of the force is along the same line as the rope, and the rope is attached 1.50 m up from the bottom of the tree. Assume the base of the tree is the pivot point.

a. Calculate the length of the perpendicular force arm of the rope. 1 mark

b. Calculate the torque on the tree if the force applied to the tree by the rope is 12.5 N. 2 marks

UNIT 2

How does physics help us to understand the world?

AREA OF STUDY 2

Options: How does physics inform contemporary issues and applications in society?

Outcome

Investigate and apply physics knowledge to develop and communicate an informed response to a contemporary societal issue or application related to a selected option.

Options

One option is to be selected by the student from the following:

- How does physics explain climate change?
- How do fusion and fission compare as viable nuclear energy power sources?
- How do heavy things fly?
- How do forces act on structures and materials?
- How do forces act on the human body?
- How is radiation used to maintain human health?
- How does the human body use electricity?
- How can human vision be enhanced?
- How is physics used in photography?
- How do instruments make music?
- How can performance in ball sports be improved?
- How can AC electricity charge a DC device?
- How do astrophysicists investigate stars and black holes?
- How can we detect possible life beyond Earth's Solar System?
- How can physics explain traditional artefacts, knowledge and techniques?
- How do particle accelerators work?
- How does physics explain the origins of matter?
- How is contemporary physics research being conducted in our region?

Students must address the key knowledge specified by the VCE Physics Study Design for their selected option. In addition, all options must address the following key science skills.

Key knowledge

Communicating physics

- evaluate validity of sources of information
- apply physics concepts specific to the investigation: definitions of key terms, and use of appropriate scientific terminology, conventions and representations
- apply the use of data representations, models and theories in organising and explaining observed phenomena and physics concepts, and discuss the limitations of the explanations
- discuss the influence of sociocultural, economic, legal and political factors relevant to the selected issue or application
- apply physics understanding to justify a stance, opinion or solution to the selected issue or application.

SCIENTIFIC INVESTIGATION TEMPLATE

The following template can be used as a guide when conducting your investigation for Unit 2 Area of Study 2. Further support materials addressing the following options are available for download via your Pearson Places bookshelf.

- Option 2.1: How does physics explain climate change?
- Option 2.2: How do fusion and fission compare as viable nuclear energy power sources?
- Option 2.10: How do instruments make music?
- Option 2.11: How can performance in ball sports be improved?
- Option 2.12: How can AC electricity charge a DC device?
- Option 2.15: How can physics explain traditional artefacts, knowledge and techniques?

Space has been provided in the template but you must keep a logbook that includes every detail of your research. The logbook will form part of your assessment.

AIM

To select from the 18 options provided in the VCE Physics Study Design and carry out a scientific investigation.

CHOOSING AN OPTION

When choosing a topic for investigation, consider the following:

- Choose a research question you find interesting.
- Start with a topic for which you already have some background information, or some ideas about how to perform the experiment.
- Check that your school laboratory has the resources for you to perform the experiment or investigate the topic.
- Choose a topic for which you can generate clear, measurable data.

Which of the 18 options have you selected for your investigation? Explain your choice.

PLANNING YOUR INVESTIGATION

Read through the Scientific investigation template statements in the VCE Physics Study Design relevant to your chosen option. Start building a list of key terms and their definitions. You can add to this list throughout your investigation as you discover new key terms relevant to your research.

Key term	Definition

SCIENTIFIC INVESTIGATION TEMPLATE

From your chosen option, what would you like to find out? Write this down as a question. This will become the research question for your investigation.

List three or four questions that would help answer your main question.

Do some initial research into answering these questions. You might need to rephrase your questions to make them as clear and specific as possible. Use this space to make notes. Be sure to list references so that you can return to the information later.

What type of investigation methodology is best used to answer your research question? See page 13 of the VCE Physics Study Design for a list of possible methodologies.

You can choose more than one methodology for your investigation. For example, you might create a model and conduct an experiment to test the relationship between variables that your model represents. List your chosen methodology or methodologies and why you chose it/them.

ISBN 978 0 6557 0016 6

SCIENTIFIC INVESTIGATION TEMPLATE

Look back at your main question. Construct a hypothesis that can be applied to answer your question and write it below. (You can find more on hypotheses in the Toolkit at the beginning of this book.) This becomes your working hypothesis and should summarise the answer to your main question. It may change after further research.

Work in small groups to share and evaluate the selected topics. What are the strengths of other students' investigations? Write below how you could improve your own investigation or research question.

Research your option. Use the Scientific investigation template statements in the VCE Physics Study Design to guide you in this process. Remember to include every detail of your research in your logbook and to date each entry.

Summarise key points as you proceed so that your topic has a clear focus and development. You may want to create a tree diagram such as the one below to link your development back to your original hypothesis.

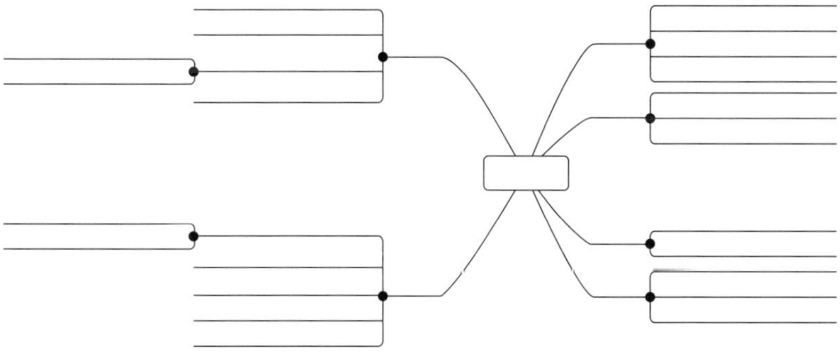

CONDUCTING YOUR INVESTIGATION

Carry out your investigation.

You could use the following space to:

- write out your experimental methods
- describe the model/simulation you are developing
- plan the structure of your research report or literature review.

SCIENTIFIC INVESTIGATION TEMPLATE

Keep a list of any secondary sources used throughout your investigation. Evaluate whether each is a valid source.

Source	Validity

 ISBN 978 0 6557 0016 6

SCIENTIFIC INVESTIGATION TEMPLATE

PROCESSING YOUR DATA

How best to process your data is dependent on the type of data collected. Tables and graphs are common tools to communicate both qualitative and quantitative data. Summarise key pieces of processed data from your investigation.

ANALYSING YOUR DATA

Were you successful in answering your original research question? Did you need to rephrase it? Was your hypothesis supported or refuted?

Do your research and secondary data sources support your conclusions? How reliable is the data?

Have you used a model or theory to explain the physics concept researched? In what ways might the model or theory limit your conclusions?

SCIENTIFIC INVESTIGATION TEMPLATE

COMMUNICATING YOUR FINDINGS

How are you communicating your investigation? Examples include a report, poster or media analysis. Explain your choice.

Review other students' research. Are they presenting evidence-based arguments in a form readily understood by the intended audience?

How does your research affect the real world? Use the following table to make notes on any sociocultural, economic, legal or political factors that may be relevant to your investigation.

Sociocultural	Economic	Legal	Political

Summarise the solution to your research question. Your summary can be adapted to use as a conclusion in your chosen presentation format.

 ISBN 978 0 6557 0016 6

UNIT 2

How does physics help us to understand the world?

AREA OF STUDY 3

How do physicists investigate questions?

Outcome

Draw an evidence-based conclusion from primary data generated from a student-adapted or student-designed scientific investigation related to a selected physics question.

Key knowledge

Investigation design

- apply the physics concepts specific to the selected investigation and explain their significance, including definitions of key terms, and physics representations
- evaluate the characteristics of the scientific methodology relevant to the investigation, selected from: experiment, fieldwork, classification and identification, modelling, simulation, and the development of a product, process or system
- apply techniques of primary qualitative and quantitative data generation relevant to the investigation
- identify and apply concepts of accuracy, precision, repeatability, reproducibility, resolution, and validity of data in relation to the investigation
- identify and apply health, safety and ethical guidelines relevant to the selected scientific investigation

Scientific evidence

- distinguish between an aim, a hypothesis, a model, a theory and a law
- identify and explain observations and experiments that are consistent with, or challenge, current models or theories
- describe the characteristics of primary data
- evaluate methods of organising, analysing and evaluating primary data to identify patterns and relationships including scientific error, causes of uncertainty, and limitations of data, methodologies and methods
- model the scientific practice of using a logbook to authenticate generated primary data

Science communication

- apply the conventions of scientific report writing including scientific terminology and representations, standard abbreviations, units of measurement, significant figures and acknowledgement of references
- apply the key findings of the selected investigation and their relationship to key physics concepts.

Crumple zones and collisions—How can impulse be used to improve the safety of vehicles?

SCIENTIFIC INVESTIGATION

Students adapt or design and then conduct a scientific investigation to generate appropriate primary qualitative and/or quantitative data, organise and interpret the data, and reach and evaluate a conclusion in response to the research question. The scientific investigation relates to knowledge and skills developed in Area of Study 1 and/or 2.

ASSESSMENT FOR OUTCOME 3

A report of a practical investigation (student-designed or adapted) using an appropriate format: for example, a scientific poster, practical report, oral communication or digital presentation.

SUGGESTED DURATION

A minimum of seven hours of class time should be devoted to undertaking and communicating findings related to Area of Study 3. As per Areas of Study 1 and 2, your teacher will be your primary guide. To help you, the key steps to follow, relevant poster section and suggested time allocation are set out below.

The following sample investigation steps you through a controlled experiment, conducted following the designing and planning phase of the investigation. The sample investigation also provides a guide for writing your scientific report in the format of a scientific poster.

Refer to the Toolkit at the beginning of this book for more detailed information on designing and conducting scientific investigations, and presenting a scientific report.

USING THIS GUIDE

There is scope for developing an investigation on a range of topics relevant to Unit 2. This sample investigation is drawn from the key knowledge related to net force, momentum and impulse as addressed in Unit 2 Area of Study 2. In particular, it further explores the application of motion concepts in vehicle safety.

INTRODUCTION

Background

Road accidents are an unfortunate but inevitable part of highway and city driving. Most modern vehicle designs include sophisticated crumple zones and strategically placed impact absorbers, airbags and more.

The impulse, or change in momentum, experienced by a vehicle during a crash is given by the equation:

$$\Delta p = F\Delta t$$

This means that by increasing the time taken during the collision, the force imparted will be reduced. In this investigation, you will design and construct a crumple zone for a model vehicle that minimises the impact forces experienced in a collision, while also minimising size and weight. Your design will be tested in up to three separate trials, not including initial trials to determine the initial force in your design.

The question under investigation is, 'How can impulse be used to improve the safety of vehicles?'

Aim

The aim should directly mention the variables involved in the investigation.

Hypothesis

When constructing your hypothesis, remember that it should propose a relationship between two or more variables. It should predict that a relationship exists or does not exist.

METHODOLOGY AND METHODS

Remember, the methodology is a brief description of the general approach taken to investigate the research question or hypothesis and the reasons why this approach is taken. The methods are the specific steps that are to be taken to collect data during the investigation.

Scientific investigation section	Key step	Suggested time allocation
Planning your investigation	Step 1: Developing aims, hypotheses and predictions	60–120 minutes
	Step 2: Determining appropriate Methodology and methods	60–90 minutes
Conducting your investigation and recording and presenting data	Step 3: Conducting your investigation to generate primary data	90–120 minutes
	Step 4: Recording, organising and presenting your data	90–120 minutes
Discussing your investigation and drawing evidence-based conclusions	Step 5: Analysing and evaluating your data	60–120 minutes
	Step 6: Referencing	30 minutes
Reporting on your investigation	Step 7: Preparing your scientific report	120–180 minutes

ISBN 978 0 6557 0016 6

MATERIALS

Include a list of the materials used in your investigation. The following are examples of materials you might use.

- 1 m^2 cardboard
- 6 sheets of A4 paper
- 6 rubber balloons
- 0.3 m^2 aluminium foil
- 120 g soft clay
- 10 rubber bands
- 20 toothpicks
- 10 cm length of Velcro
- ramp
- force sensor

DISCUSSION

Discuss and analyse your results. Here are some key questions to guide your discussion:

1 Evaluate other students' designs and agree collaboratively on the most effective design. Record the important design points and your reasons for assessing them as important.

2 What was the biggest reduction in peak force recorded by the class? How did this value compare with your lowest peak force value?

3 What would you change in your design to make it more effective? Why do you think these changes would make the design more effective?

METHODS

Prepare your methods, outlining each step. Always consider any potential hazards and make sure your methods allow for a valid and reliable investigation. You may want to talk to your teacher before proceeding.

Design requirements:

- The design must not impede the trolley's ability to move.
- The design cannot extend more than 5.0 cm in length.
- The design must not add more than 200 g to the mass of the trolley.
- The design must be constructed so that it attaches firmly to the front of the trolley but can be attached and removed without modifying the trolley itself.

RESULTS

The table and graph below may be helpful in collating your results.

CONCLUSION

The conclusion to a scientific report or paper links the collected evidence to the aim and hypothesis and provides a justified response to the research question. Include recommendations for future research.

REFERENCES AND ACKNOWLEDGEMENTS

Remember to acknowledge any sources used in the course of the investigation. This might include:

- scientific journals
- articles and texts
- internet sources
- newspaper articles.

When referencing published sources, follow accepted protocols for presenting bibliographical data, such as APA citation style. For example:

Black, L., Dommel, A., Dommel, N., Fischer, T., Jobson, K., Lewis, G., Madden, D., Moran, G., Trafford, S., White, G. (2023). *Heinemann Physics 11* (5th ed.) Pearson Australia.

Table 1 Include an appropriate title for your table

	Force (N) Trial 1	Force (N) Trial 2	Force (N) Trial 3	Average force (N)	Time (s) Trial 1	Time (s) Trial 2	Time (s) Trial 3	Average time (s)	Impulse ($N s^{-1}$)
Control									
Design 1									
Design 2									
Design 3									

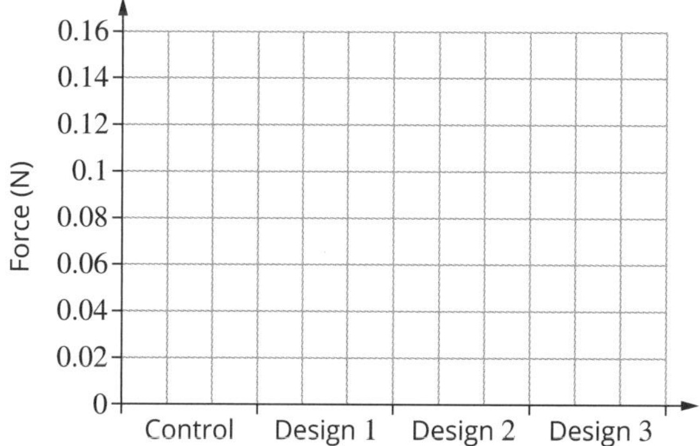

Graph 1 Include an appropriate title for your graph